THE SPIRIT OF DEVELOPMENT

The Spirit of Development

*Protestant NGOs, Morality,
and Economics in Zimbabwe*

Erica Bornstein

*Stanford University Press
Stanford, California
2005*

Stanford University Press
Stanford, California

Originating publisher: Routledge, New York, ©2003.

Chapter 2 (Theologies of Development: Faith, Holism, and Lifestyle Evangelism) was previously published as "Developing Faith: Theologies of Economic Development in Zimbabwe," *The Journal of Religion in Africa* 32 (1), 2002.

Chapter 3 (Child Sponsorship, Evangelism, and Belonging) was previously published as "Child Sponsorship, Evangelism, and Belonging in the Work of World Vision Zimbabwe," *American Ethnologist* 28 (3), August 2001.

Chapter 6 (Good, Evil, and the Legitimation of Success) was previously published as "The Verge of Good and Evil: Christian NGOs and Economic Development in Zimbabwe," *Political and Legal Anthropology Review* 24 (1), May 2001.

Printed in the United States of America on acid-free, archival-quality paper

Library of Congress Cataloging-in-Publication Data

Bornstein, Erica, 1963–
    The spirit of development : Protestant NGOs, morality, and economics in Zimbabwe / Erica Bornstein.
        p.   cm.
    Originally published: New York : Routledge, 2003.
    Includes bibliographical references and index.
    ISBN 0-8047-5336-9 (pbk. : alk. paper)
        1. Non-governmental organizations—Zimbabwe.   2. Zimbabwe—Economic policy—Moral and ethical aspects.   3. Christianity—Zimbabwe.   I. Title.
HC910.B67 2005
261.8'5'096891—dc22   2005012302

Original Printing 2005
Last figure below indicates year of this printing:
14   13   12   11   10   09   08

For Elijah

Contents

Acknowledgments ix

Abbreviations xi

Introduction: An Ethnography of Faith-based Development 1

1. Background: Three Perspectives on Missions in Zimbabwe 9

2. Theologies of Development: Faith, Holism, and
   Lifestyle Evangelism 45

3. Child Sponsorship, Evangelism, and Belonging 67

4. The Politics of Transcendence 97

5. Participation as a Religious Act 119

6. Good, Evil, and the Legitimation of Success 141

Conclusion 169

Appendices
1. Interviews, Group Discussions, and Events 173

2. Zimbabwe Council of Churches 179

Notes 181

Bibliography 193

Index 209

Acknowledgments

The debts incurred in the making of this book are greater than I can acknowledge in print. I suspect the years spent on this project have generated a lifetime of reciprocal obligation. Many people have helped me along the way, with friendship, financial assistance, and advice. To everyone in Zimbabwe who offered their time, their opinions, and a glimpse of their worlds, I offer my respect and gratitude. Special thanks are due to A. Aneesh, whose ongoing collaboration in my life and my work entails reading multiple drafts, which he manages to accomplish with a patience and willingness for intellectual dialogue that continues to surpass my wildest expectations. Our partnership began alongside this project and lives beyond it.

The first incarnation of this writing was a doctoral dissertation. Immense appreciation goes to Liisa Malkki, who saw me as an anthropologist long before I did. Her encouragement and unending enthusiasm for this project kept it alive, while her intellectual generosity and creativity are models to which I can only hope to aspire. Jim Ferguson and Bill Maurer were also tireless in their support. I am grateful to Jim for his valuable comments as he gently encouraged me toward greater logical rigor, and to Bill, whose efficiency and pragmatism made writing the dissertation possible. I revised this book while a postdoctoral visiting scholar at the Center for African Studies at University of California, Berkeley; thanks to Gillian Hart for making this possible. Thanks are also due to Frank Reynolds, who offered sound advice and inspiration for rethinking crucial aspects of the text as a book.

In Zimbabwe, Fatuma Hashi was the first to open her home and offer friendship. Paul Gundani brought me into his family in the early months of research. The Department of Religious Studies, Classics, and Philosophy at the University of Zimbabwe was kind enough to host me during my stay in Zimbabwe. Bella Mukonyora was a great help when I needed a friend most. John Hanson's humor and kindness led to a lasting friendship. Lazarus

Chidaushe was my very patient research assistant and Shona tutor. I would also like to thank Di and Mike Auret, Bruce Bradshaw, Max Chigwida, Kudzai Chingwe, Shephard Dhlamini, Gordon Gandiya, Mr. Gwazo, Elizabeth Maneya, Toniel Marimba, Edith Mtetwa, Kenny Musanje, Netsai, and Funganyi Nhamo. Sadly, Frank Mandhlokuwa did not live to read the results of this research. His spirit lives on in these pages.

Family, friends, and colleagues offered ongoing emotional and intellectual support during the writing of this book and the dissertation that preceded it. Thanks to: A. Aneesh, Alex Balasescu, Eren Berkenkotter, Gloria Bornstein, Jenny Bornstein, Karin Bornstein Swope, Mina Bornstein, Paul Bornstein, Allaine Cerwonka, Marie Cieri, Sharon Cooper, Angela Davies, Sara Rich Dorman, Matthew Engelke, Harri Englund, David Hughes, Eric Kaldor, David Maxwell, Dona Ann McAdams, Hiro Miyazaki, Yasuo Mori, Chrisy Moutsatsos, and Viviane and Jonas Schultz.

The research for this book was made possible through a generous grant from the Pew Charitable Trusts Dissertation Research Fellowship 1996-1997, administered through the Research Enablement Program of the Overseas Ministries Study Center. A Charlotte W. Newcombe Foundation Doctoral Dissertation Fellowship and a University of California Regents Dissertation Writing Fellowship provided support for dissertation writing in 1998-1999. A University of California Regents Research Grant and a Social Relations Program Travel Grant facilitated preliminary research in Zimbabwe in 1995. A Foreign Language and Area Studies Fellowship (FLAS) supported my attending an intensive Shona language course in 1995 at the African Studies Center of Michigan State University.

List of Abbreviations

Agritex	Department of Agricultural, Technical and Extension Services, Ministry of Agricultural Extension and Rural Resettlement, Government of Zimbabwe
ADP	Area Development Project
ANC	African National Congress
CCJP	Catholic Commission for Justice and Peace
CCR	Christian Council of Rhodesia
CDP	Community Development Project
ESAP	Economic Structural Adjustment Program
LMC	Local Management Committee
MP	Member of Parliament
NGO	Non-governmental Organization
PRA	Participatory Rural Appraisal
PVO	Private Voluntary Organization
UDI	Unilateral Declaration of Independence
VIDCO	Village Development Committee
WCC	World Council of Churches
WV	World Vision
WV International	World Vision International
WV USA	World Vision USA
WV Zimbabwe	World Vision Zimbabwe
ZAOGA	Zimbabwe Assembly of God in Africa

| ZANU-PF | Zimbabwe African National Union Patriotic Front |
| ZCC | Zimbabwe Council of Churches |

THE SPIRIT OF DEVELOPMENT

An Ethnography of
Faith-based Development

THE PHRASE "FAITH-BASED DEVELOPMENT" CONJURES A LINGUISTIC contradiction. How can economic development, a symbol of this-worldly, material improvement, of science, and of progress, be based on faith? Is economic development not a move away from the logical ambiguities of mysticism toward the scientific promise of technological advancement? Scholarly studies of economic development seem to rely on these logical assumptions. For the most part, they have excluded the topic of religion. The separation of religion and economic development reinforces modernization theories that declare a progressive differentiation between religious and economic domains of social life, reflected, for instance, in the historical separation of church and state in the West. Language that places the spiritual and the practical in two distinct realms also bears the mark of such thinking. However, the newly gained political support for faith-based charitable work in the United States complicates such a linear and historical trajectory toward a progressive religious/economic divide. The transnational reach of faith-based humanitarian aid through the work of non-governmental organizations (NGOs), and the increasing political and economic importance of religious NGOs in Africa, further complicate the matter.

Examining how religious ideas inform and intersect with the moral dynamics of economic development in Zimbabwe, Africa, I attempt to bring the two realms of study together with the hope of opening a space for meaningful dialogue. This book addresses issues crucial for those interested in Protestant Christianity as a transnational religion, and those interested in the strengths and weaknesses of development theory and practice. It is an ethnography of a particular intersection—historical, spiritual, and material—that

1

shaped a unique social form: the Protestant NGO. The ethnography focuses on the work of two Protestant NGOs in Zimbabwe, in the late 1990s: World Vision International and Christian Care. However, the scope of my analysis criss-crosses the globe. It highlights the moral struggles of development workers and donors in Zimbabwe and in the United States, and of rural beneficiaries in Zimbabwe. A broad aim of this book is to initiate a critical discussion on the politics of faith in international development. A more modest goal is to empha-size the significant influence of Christianity in the economic development of southern Africa.

I use the concept of religion in the spirit of Clifford Geertz, who defines it as both a model for, and a model of, lived reality (Geertz 1973:93).[1] Geertz's approach affirms that through the systematic use of religious belief, meaning is made in and of the world. He explicitly argues that religion, as a "cultural sys-tem," is visible in the everyday world in cultural acts and social events as "pub-lic as marriage and as observable as agriculture" (1973:91). I hasten to add the practices of economic development. Religious beliefs inform the ways that economic development projects are received, interpreted, and accepted in specific social and historical contexts. Religious beliefs also inform the ways in which development projects are constructed by development organizations. They inform the way development is planned, conceptualized, motivated and instituted. These systems of belief, or cosmologies, which link experiences of the material world with conceptions of a spiritual realm (or lack of it) are inte-gral to the processes through which individuals order their worlds and make sense of experience. This is especially important in contexts of change, such as economic development, in which cosmological assumptions provide the "moods and motivations" (Geertz 1973) that propel the enterprise of develop-ment and inspire its practice by NGO workers.

More broadly, ideas of economic rationality and perpetual growth, the bedrock of classical and neoclassical economics as well as contemporary pro-grams of economic development, can also be seen to function as a religious sys-tem. Economic rationality offers "a world view or cosmology; a system of legit-imizing values, orderliness, and coherence as a belief system; more or less derivable moral implications; and factual claims about the empirical world" (Smelser 1995:91). Economic rationality and religious thought both depend on an implicit utopian realm in which the greater good is manifest. Socially, eco-nomic models describe Edenic situations in which tastes are orderly, the world is free of error, and the environment is predictable (ibid: 79). For example, Bentham's utilitarianism presents the free market as "realizing the greatest good for the greatest number" and Adam Smith's "invisible hand of the mar-ket" purports to maximize social welfare via the individual pursuit of self-inter-est.

In Judeo-Christian history, economics was a theological concern. Governance of the ownership and sale of land is clearly delineated in the Old and New Testaments, and the origin, use, and allocation of wealth are all central concerns of Judeo-Christian discourse and law. Hebrew law identified the ultimate owner of land as God, and Christian theologians such as Augustine took on the task of defining proper uses and abuses of private property. Almsgiving, as a way of atoning for sin, was a means of "transferring one's wealth to heaven" (Gonzalez 1990:27). Religion regulated attitudes toward accumulation, and provided economic rationality. The Bible offered basic governing principles of social and economic justice, as well as proscriptive attitudes toward charity, humanitarian activity, the equity of land tenure, and the distribution of wealth.[2]

Perhaps the omission of religion from critiques of development in Africa is due to Enlightenment thought and its rejection of the historical link between theology and economics. Curiously, most approaches—liberal and Marxist—relegate religion to an illusionary realm. Many Marxist works that employ a political-economic frame emphasize the exploitative historical effects of colonial markets on nation states and local economies (Amin 1976; Bates 1981; Davidson 1974; Dumont 1969; Hyden 1980; Palmer and Parson 1977; Rodney 1974). Even scholars who have moved beyond such a strict economic focus tend to ignore the importance of religion (Auret 1990; Chambers 1983; Crewe and Harrison 1998; Hill 1986; Verhelst 1990). While there are a few ethnographic exceptions to this omission (Donham 1999; Long 1968; Poewe 1989), and there has been recent, influential research on the discursive culture of development itself (Cowen and Shenton 1996; Escobar 1995; Ferguson 1994; Moore 1995; Moore and Schmitz 1995; Rahnema and Bawtree 1997; Riles 2000; Sachs 1992), there have unfortunately been few studies on how religious ideas factor into the discourse of development. I believe this is a grave oversight. The degree to which one can assert that an economic context is "secular" in southern Africa (or anywhere) may be governed largely by Western assumptions of divisions between the secular and the religious.

PROTESTANT IDEAS IN ECONOMIC DEVELOPMENT

Development workers employed by Protestant NGOs in Zimbabwe, like Calvinists in Max Weber's famous example of *The Protestant Ethic and the Spirit of Capitalism* (1958 [1920]), draw upon ideas of salvation, rationality, progress, and the role of the individual in relation to God in their economic development work. These ideas are central to the work of NGOs like World Vision and Christian Care. One question that concerns us here is how religious NGOs combine and merge ideals of religious and material progress. In development practice, the emphasis of Protestant NGOs on improvements in material and spiritual life seems a theoretical inversion of what Weber called ascetic religiosity (Weber 1946 [1915]).[3] Weber's Protestant ethic (1958 [1920]) sits within his typology of religious life that abnegate the material world in favor of salvation at the ascetic end—advocating proof of one's devotion to God through work in this world, and adopting the world as a religious responsibility. The discourse of Protestant NGOs echoes these objectives: the divine imperative to transform the world has this-worldly consequences. A primary concern of Weber's thesis on Protestant religion and rationality is how the ascetic ideal of methodical, rational and careful action leads to the generation of wealth in this world, and how this rational logic gets unhinged from its religious origins, leading to the rise of instrumental rationality and the supposed disenchantment of the world.[4] Protestant NGOs involved in development projects are particularly suited to address this tension, between enchantment and the material improvement of lives.

For Weber, while the methodological approach to salvation is the result of life's systematic rationalization, the idea of salvation itself creates a series of tensions that exist between religion and this-worldly life forces. This process—of inspiring and contending with problems of its own invention—is one we will see in the economic development work of World Vision and Christian Care. Weber (1993 [1922]) articulates how in economics rational asceticism creates, and must contend with, the very wealth it rejects. In the sphere of politics, the democratic ideal of brotherly love (fraternity) competes with the dispassionate bureaucratic state apparatus with its monopoly on the legitimate use of violence. In the realm of intellectual life, theological thought encourages, and must compete against, rational empirical knowledge and science, which lead to disenchantment through the world's translation into a causal mechanism. In the spheres of aesthetics and sexuality, religion's promise of an otherworldly salvation is in competition with artistic and erotic threats of a this-worldly, irrational salvation. In Weber's analysis of Calvinism, the need for salvation is a consciously cultivated aspect of religiosity that results from the systematic rationalization of life. Because this type of religion declares the imperfection of this world as an ethical postulate (original sin), it competes with sectors of social life that threaten its monopoly on enchantment. While Calvinists accumulated wealth but rejected consumption, the world-changing discourse of Christian NGOs promotes lifestyles that encourage accumulation and consumption—under the guise of Christian works. The Christian "lifestyle" advocated by Christian NGOs is closely tied to a capitalist lifestyle that echoes earlier missionary discourses in southern Africa about correct ways of living, about being "civilized," and about progress (Comaroff 1991; Comaroff and Comaroff 1991, 1997).

The idea of progress is important to Christianity and economic development, and to the work of Protestant NGOs. Animating neoliberal and neo-classical discourses of ceaseless economic and social growth, the idea of progress echoes the civilizing mission of colonial missionaries and is historical-ly related to the development of Christian thought (Nisbet 1980). Early Christian philosophers gave ideas of progress a spiritual force, emphasizing the unity of humankind and historical necessity. In contemporary definitions as well, progress involves faith—in science and technology, or in religious ideas. Progress is an ideal, a destiny, and a theodicy. The entry for "Progress" in the *Development Dictionary* describes this logic: "Progress possesses the bright-ness derived from its close link with the sacred. . . . It has the luster of tran-scendence" (Sbert 1992:195). Progress explains current phenomena in terms of possible future perfection: it is comparable with religious messianism, mil-lenarianism, and eschatology. Sbert continues. "Trust in progress may in truth pertain to the realm of faith in a sense similar to the Christian assurance of things hoped for in the beyond." Elsewhere, Asad (1993) has noted how eigh-teenth-century European Christian attitudes toward historical time that included salvational expectations combined with secular practices of rational prediction to form the modern idea of progress and its correlative philosophy of individual agency.

The idea of the individual in relation to a Christian God is another foun-dational idea employed by Protestant NGOs. The construction of individuals in relation to the divine, as conceived of by the Christian discourse of faith-based NGOs, parallels neoliberal assumptions of individual "choice" that underlie the discourse of a "free-market." Historically, the Protestant Reformation in Europe laid the foundations for this conceptual approach to the world by producing a new kind of state, a new science, and a new legal and moral subject (Asad 1993). Anthropological concepts of religion (such as Geertz's moods and motivations, ritual, and belief) are also embedded in this specific European, Christian history, marked by a shift in religious practice from public life to the private or individual space of believers. The work of Asad suggests that distinctions between the secular and religious in economic development may be inappropriate, uniquely Western assumptions.[3] This book is an attempt to re-investigate a space where religious and economic ideals merge.

THE STRUCTURE OF THE BOOK

The book moves between four analytical frames, each of which is integral to the constitution of the text as a whole. The first frame maps the historical and philosophical background of religious NGO-work in southern Africa. The sub-sequent three frames explore the moral politics of development from transnational, national and local perspectives. By structuring the book in this way, I aim to mirror the experiences of NGO workers as they engage with what are at times opposing forces: the directives of international donors, the politics of the Zimbabwean state, and the desires of rural beneficiaries in Zimbabwe. I urge readers to keep in mind that development in its "local" form, particularly the moral tangles that development seems to inspire in local contexts, would not exist without the transnational and national scope of economic development described in the early part of this book. All of the chapters speak, in slightly different ways, to the main themes of how religion and economic development are bound together, and how ideas of salvation, progress, the individual, and neoliberal economics factor into the work of World Vision and Christian Care.

Chapters 1 and 2 provide the background for the book. They orient readers to the subject with detailed historical information on economic and religious "missions" in Zimbabwe. They define the theological approach of World Vision and Christian Care, and offer a reflexive analysis of my own ethnographic approach. Chapter 1 traces the foundational missionary histories that make religion and economic development inseparable in southern Africa. It also illustrates how the idea of salvation and the drive to change the world, materially and spiritually, are linked to the global missionary movements of evangelicalism and ecumenicism, which spawned World Vision and Christian Care respectively. Chapter 2 is about faith in action: how the concept of salvation, when combined with the idea of material progress and the beliefs of individuals, is transformed into a particular, Protestant approach to development called "lifestyle evangelism." In the work of World Vision and Christian Care, it is an NGO theology. The urgency with which spiritual and material approaches to development are combined is explained by another theological practice called "holism."

Chapters 3 and 4 focus on transnational and national issues: on giving and receiving across borders, and on the confluence of neoliberal economic discourse with the Protestant discourse of World Vision and Christian Care. Chapter 3 looks exclusively at the "child sponsorship" program of World Vision Zimbabwe. It demonstrates how transnational processes of giving and membership in a global Christian family contrast with Zimbabwean interpretations of humanitarian assistance and efforts to initiate a local child sponsorship program amidst growing inequalities. In effect, new perceptions of economic disparity were produced by the very humanitarian efforts that strove to overcome them. The personal relationships fostered by child sponsorship—founded upon an evangelistic understanding of individuals and built through correspondence—stirred up jealousies, desires, and altered senses of belonging for rural beneficiaries and donors in Zimbabwe. Chapter 4 is about how the efforts of NGOs intersected with national Zimbabwean politics. In the late 1990s, many Zimbabweans experienced the brunt of IMF/World Bank structural-adjustment programs in the form of price increases and rising unemployment. NGOs such as Christian Care and World Vision rose to the occasion, providing micro-enterprise and agricultural development programs to alleviate poverty. The chapter looks at NGO/state interdependence to question how the development efforts of World Vision and Christian Care mollified the threat of political and economic discontent from an increasingly frustrated populace. Through two discourses of transcendence, the Kingdom of God and neoliberal economics, the work of religious NGOs masked and assuaged emerging political tensions.

Chapters 5 and 6 investigate the moral contradictions of faith-based development in specific NGO practices. Chapter 5 explores the Protestant aspects of "participation" in development, namely, the sacralizing discourses of community participation and individual potential that are part of a development practice called "participatory rural appraisal." It describes how development becomes a religious act for some of the key actors involved. Chapter 6 interrogates how specifically Christian categories of good and evil intertwined with definitions of success and expressions of jealousy at rural development sites; how Protestant morality made individual wealth accumulation an acceptable antidote to the jealousy and witchcraft that defined the accumulation of wealth by individuals as evil in the Zimbabwean context. The ambiguities of this intersection, fraught with the spiritual dangers of witchcraft and envy, constituted a terrain where a "Christian" approach to business was offered as a practical solution to moral and economic ills.

This ethnography is intended to be a beginning of what I hope will be more work on this subject. It offers testament to the contemporary importance of faith in people's lives and to its integral role in economic development. In an African religious context, faith is a form of power: not to be taken lightly, often to be feared, and sometimes to be called upon for assistance. Whether in the form of Christianity or ancestors, God or witchcraft, religious faith is a factor in perceptions of economic development. Protestant NGOs like World Vision and Christian Care are uniquely equipped to deal with these material and spiritual challenges of faith. Economic development is an intensely moral endeavor, and religious NGOs offer a discursive space where issues of good, of evil, of the injustices of poverty and the moral dangers of individual success, can be discussed alongside fears of demons and hopes of salvation.

For the "secular" academic who dares to see the world through the eyes of NGO workers, faith no longer becomes antithetical to development. Faith-based development is no longer a contradiction. Instead, faith becomes the conceptual fuel for the prospect of change. It inspires a particular form of charitable giving between individuals with the promise of generating lasting mate-rial improvements in people's lives. It gives language to the political tangles of development and offers solutions to theological problems. It gives meaning to development—to the *why* along with the *how* of economic change. Whether or not one is a believer in Protestant faith, its significance in international development can no longer be denied.

CHAPTER 1

Background: Three Perspectives on Missions in Zimbabwe

To set the stage for my ethnography of World Vision and Christian Care, I introduce three lenses, through which I look at Christian development: *historical, productive,* and *reflexive.* Through a historical lens, I present an overview of how Christian mission work in southern Rhodesia (later, Zimbabwe) was a precursor to NGO-supported programs of economic development. In the historical landscape of faith-based development in Zimbabwe, NGOs are recent phenomena. The history traces how, over time, shifts in the interdependence of church and state in Zimbabwe have determined the politics of faith-based development. The chapter continues by documenting the religious philosophies behind World Vision and Christian Care, and the global missionary movements of evangelicalism and ecumenicism out of which the two NGOs emerged. The productive lens focuses on the types of development projects that Christian Care and World Vision are involved in, and the economic context that made development a "necessary" and a sought-after endeavor in Zimbabwe in the late 1990s. Finally, the reflexive lens focuses on the process of research itself. This last part is a methodological reflection on conversion and what it means, spiritually and economically, to conduct institutional ethnographies with faith-based NGOs.

PART I: HISTORICAL LENS

NGOS AS MISSIONARIES

In Zimbabwe and much of southern Africa, faith-based institutions such as churches and religious NGOs have historically been leaders of what is today considered economic development. However, the way churches and religious NGOs have worked with and contested state governance has changed alongside development. Development, once the charitable act of colonial missionaries in late nineteenth-century southern Rhodesia, shifted during the first decade of Zimbabwean independence to become a hopeful entitlement for citizens of the newly liberated nation. In late twentieth-century Zimbabwe, however, development once again became a charitable act—this time of transnational Christian NGOs driven by neoliberal market initiatives. Roughly four eras are distinguishable by the ways churches and NGOs have worked in collaboration with and in opposition to the state regarding "development." They are: (1) British colonialism, 1890–1965,[1] (2) The isolationist settler state, including the liberation struggle and the Rhodesian Front's Unilateral Declaration of Independence, 1965–1980, (3) Independent and socialist Zimbabwe: the first decade, 1980–1990, and (4) Zimbabwe's encounter with structural adjustment and the prevalence of NGO-supported welfare programs, 1990–2000.

Land, and contestation over its use and development in Zimbabwe, has been a historic site of struggle that continues into the present. At the time of this writing, for example, struggles over land dominated both the ruling party's (ZANU-PF)[2] discourses of sovereignty and international discourses of human rights. Such struggles are forged, and expressed, on the turf of NGO-sponsored development projects. Such struggles are also silenced through development (a topic dealt with at greater length in Chapter 4). The sovereignty of the state in Zimbabwe has been predominantly an issue of hegemonic control over the peasantry (Munro 1998), and conflicts over the legitimacy of the state in its interactions with rural peasant social life have been waged as conflicts over "development" and "community." The Rhodesian and Zimbabwean states historically were driven by dual and at times contradictory imperatives of domination and incorporation, control and consent over the peasantry; development policies played a central role in state strategies to "stabilize" and control rural populations. The colonial and postcolonial state set out, through rural development, to manage the technical and social arrangements of production in agrarian communities. Development, through its interaction with the rural peasantry on behalf of the state, is a political process through which the state provides a normative, managerial, and disciplinary framework for linking public goods and their social provision to community membership (Robins 1994; Worby 1998). Development is a form of governmentality that constitutes rural populations as fields of intervention and planning. As such, the aims of neoliberal programs of development are not too remote from the aims of colonial Christian missionaries.

Colonialism, 1890s–1965

During the colonial era, the state advocated national development through resource management in order to control rural communities and regulate their incorporation into emerging colonial capitalism. During this era, which was quite long and contained more variation than I address, the state implemented policies in the name of conservation, such as the centralization of villages and adjustment of land rights that extended state control over peasants. These policies provoked widespread peasant resistance (Ranger 1967, 1985). The welfare of Africans during colonialism was also shaped by missionary efforts that complemented the colonial state, characterized by a paternalistic concern for the natives through the civilizing mission. Borrowing Livingston's phrase "Christianity and commerce," missionaries assisted state building by providing structures of moral governance that bolstered colonial administration. Preceding the British South Africa Company (BSAC), mission churches helped build the initial infrastructure of colonial Rhodesia. As a philosophical ancestor to contemporary NGO development programs, colonial missionaries preached the gospels of the plough and of work, and with the help of native catechists sunk "roots" for what today has become African Christianity (Sundkler 1960, 1961).

In terms of development in the colonial era, the church provided education and what would today be termed "development" for Africans on the model of charitable church acts (Brand 1977; Ranger 1962; Weller and Linden 1984; Zvobgo 1996). These historical ties laid the foundations for contemporary development efforts: Christian missions worked arm-in-arm with the state to provide education and agricultural training in attempts to "civilize" Africans, and at the same time, to create a docile, productive rural labor force for colonial capitalism. There has been extensive scholarship on colonial missions in Africa (Brand 1977; Comaroff 1985; Comaroff and Comaroff 1991, 1997; Ranger 1962, 1989; Weller and Linden 1984; Zvobgo 1996). Many of these works describe a historic encounter between two disparate cultures as they clash and dialectically converge. This approach makes sense in colonial contexts where there were two recognizable ideological spheres, or where missionaries were not natives (Comaroff 1985; Comaroff and Comaroff 1991, 1997). However, in the context of Christian NGOs, with Africans converting Africans to Christian development, the clear lines of encounter are more difficult to determine.[3]

The colonial era was marked by the attempts of the state to control the work of missionaries (Ranger 1962), and by tensions of complicity between missionaries and colonial administrations (also Cooper and Stoler 1989; 1985).

These dynamics are significant not only in terms of historical context, but as points of reference, as they are visible in the contemporary work of Christian NGOs. In southern Rhodesia, missionaries worked in collaboration with colonial administrators, bargaining with Cecil Rhodes, the head of the British South Africa Company, for land to build schools, chapels, and hospitals. The system of indirect rule positioned local rulers against missionaries. Although missions served the colonial regime by mediating the spread of Western culture and morally legitimizing colonial rule, they also undermined the regime's dependence on customary authority and "heathen" practices. In northern Rhodesia, this turned explosive, when native catechists worked against the customs of the customary rulers supported by British indirect rule (Fields 1985). As much as the command of African chiefs depended on the culture and customary infrastructure of social life, missionaries produced a new type of "disorder" from the perspective of the colonial administration in the form of millennial movements. Comaroff (1989) documents how in South Africa, as missionaries advocated nonconformist native relations and abolitionist movements, they were placed in competing and collaborative relationships with the colonial and settler states.

The Isolationist Settler State and the Liberation Struggle, 1965-1980

In Rhodesia, the isolationist settler state of 1965-1980 and the rural peasant resistance it incited transformed church-state relations. Religion, particularly "traditional" religion, became a vehicle of social activism in resistance to the state (Lan 1985). The Rhodesian Front government formulated a community development policy in the late 1950s and implemented it in the early 1960s, in an effort to shift the responsibility of social welfare and development away from the state toward rural communities through self-help. Those fighting for the liberation of southern Rhodesia (African nationalists) denounced these policies as forms of apartheid and used them to organize rural resistance against the settler state (Munro 1998). During the liberation struggle, church leaders became activists in an environment where advocacy on behalf of Africans was seen by the state as a politically subversive act. This era was characterized by increased state efforts to control religious organizations, as mainline mission churches shifted alliance from white and Rhodesian to black and African (or pro-African) leadership. Under this new leadership, churches started humanitarian programs to assist people who were displaced and disenfranchised in the liberation struggle. Development took a back seat to emergency aid and relief efforts, and international NGOs, both religious and secular, arrived in Zimbabwe to assist those directly affected by the war, including political detainees and refugees. Although many NGOs boycotted Rhodesia during the UDI period, a flood of NGOs came after the fall of Ian Smith's isolationist government. One of the NGOs addressed in this book, World Vision

International, entered Zimbabwe in 1973 during the liberation struggle to assist with relief efforts for victims of the war, specifically by supporting orphanages for children.

The war brought a crisis of consciousness to the mission churches, which for years had seen themselves as advocates of Africans. The global ecumenical body, the World Council of Churches (WCC), financed the Christian Council of Rhodesia (CCR, later to become ZCC, the Zimbabwe Council of Churches), which protested the minority rule that was at odds with other colonial powers pulling out of Africa during the 1960s. There was a growing cleavage between churches and the white minority state during this time, as churches became increasingly vocal in their criticism of the political regime (Gifford 1995; Hallencreutz 1988a; Maxwell 1995). The Christian Council of Rhodesia was an early forum for interracial dialogue. It represented an African-inspired movement to "create a forum where Church leaders from different denominations could tackle matters of mutual concern in an increasingly tense political situation," and to rectify injustices meted out to Africans by the settler state (Hallencreutz 1988a:52).

While the Christian Council was not formed to handle overtly political issues, it became intensely involved in politics in the mid-1960s, during the early years of the liberation struggle. Although its objectives were defined in religious and ecumenical terms, these quickly became the highly politicized issues of racial unity. First, CCR rejected Ian Smith's UDI (Unilateral Declaration of Independence) of minority rule. It launched an extensive critique of UDI and proposed a policy of non-cooperation with Smith's regime (Hallencreutz 1988a:65). The Church Council, viewing itself as nonracialist in contrast to racialized government, also opposed legislation that restricted Africans to Tribal Trust Lands (or "Native Reserves") based on human rights and social justice.[4] There were close contacts between CCR and South Africa's ANC during the liberation struggle, and by the end of the war, in 1979, it acted as a "council in the middle" between the moderate nationalism of ANC (later UANC) and the more militant nationalism of the liberation movements operating from bases outside Zimbabwe (Hallencreutz 1988a:100). During the liberation war, the Council was actively involved in drought-relief, and supported humanitarian programs for the political prisoners of Smith's regime through its development arm, Christian Care. In 1968, Christian Care was formed as a separate non-governmental organization to serve as the development arm of the Council of Churches. It was created in an effort by the Council to ease political tensions that had developed between CCR and the government, and to facilitate its humanitarian programs without the danger of political attacks on specific churches. At the end of this period, in 1979, CCR initiated the Ministry of Reconciliation.

The Rhodesian state during Smith's regime sought to control the acts of protesting humanitarian organizations by passing The Welfare Act of 1966, an early legislative attempt by the state to control organizations that are today called NGOs. The legislation required welfare organizations to register with the government. What is interesting for the purposes of this study is how the state defined a welfare organization. At the time, it included organizations working for social welfare, charity, and the prevention of cruelty to animals. It excluded "any religious body in respect of activities confined to religious work."[5] Thus, churches were not considered welfare organizations. The Act prohibited a welfare organization from "carrying on its activities, seeking financial assistance from any source, or collecting contributions from the public" without first registering with the government. Upon approval, welfare organizations were given certificates. The Act was intended "to provide for the registration of welfare organizations, for the control of the collection of contributions for the objects of such organizations and of certain institutions, and for matters incidental thereto."[6] The Welfare Act was articulated as an effort to control the flow of financial resources to NGOs during the period when international NGOs with human rights agendas entered Zimbabwe to assist Africans and refugees from the liberation war. The NGOs that began their work in Zimbabwe as relief organizations in the 1960s and 1970s are today's rural development organizations. They are World Vision and Christian Care.[7]

Independent and Socialist Zimbabwe: The First Decade, 1980–1990

After independence and through the newly formed socialist state, ZANU-PF renewed and transformed discourses of community development from development-as-charity in the colonial era to development as the entitlement of Zimbabwean citizens. In so doing, the state faced a challenge of legitimacy as it sought to gain authority over a rural population that had been politicized against the Rhodesian state during the war. As the mission-educated African elite came to power in newly independent socialist Zimbabwe, the church once again (as in the colonial era) was politically aligned with the state. In the early years of independence, doctrines of Christian socialism enforced a welfare state that promised to ease economic inequalities created by colonialism and to bring justice to all Africans. This period saw a large proliferation of NGO activity in Zimbabwe as the international effort to build the nation coincided with Cold-War ideological struggles over democracy, capitalism, socialism, and development on the international stage. The significant factor during this transition period was that southern Rhodesia had been isolated from the global economy due to international sanctions during the Unilateral Declaration of Independence. Churches, sometimes as NGOs and registered as welfare organizations, were at the forefront of the process of leading development efforts and rebuilding the nation. At independence in 1980, the political detainees of Ian Smith's regime who fought for the liberation of Zimbabwe, and who were educated and given legal support by the Zimbabwe Council of

Churches (ZCC) through Christian Care, became the new political leaders of independent Zimbabwe. The early postcolonial years of independence were characterized by church-state socialism. Prime Minister Robert Gabriel Mugabe called on the church to assist in national development, and the State President, Canaan Banana, a Methodist minister, strongly influenced ZCC's programs and priorities. He "deliberately pressed for immediate interaction between the Church of the People and the People's Government" (Hallencreutz 1988b). Meanwhile, Prime Minister Mugabe challenged leads of church denominations and the ZCC during the first International Development Consultation to "define the churches' priorities in development with reference to the national planning of the Government" (Hallencreutz 1988b:301). As Christianity intersected with socialism in Zimbabwe, the church allied with the state in national development. During this time, the interests of the church were difficult to separate from national interests. President Banana espoused a "theology of development," and advocated "religious socialism" (Banana 1982; Gifford 1998; Maxwell 1995; Moyo 1987). In partnership with the state, the church set up rural development programs in educational, medical, and agricultural arenas (Gundani 1988; McLaughlin 1996).

Internationally, during the 1980s, Western governments and foundations were reluctant to give funds to what they suspected were "unreliable" (and socialist) African governments, and opted instead to channel their assistance through NGOs and church bodies. Scholars described the period as the "NGO-ization of the mainline churches" (Gifford 1994:521), because churches in effect became NGOs involved in development programs. In the late 1980s churches also played a crucial role in efforts to "democratize" Africa. Local church bodies worked collaboratively with, and were funded by, international religious NGOs. These NGOs, such as Christian Care and World Vision International, acted as umbrella organizations, hiring local field staff and working through national churches and religious groups. Ecumenical in the field, they collaborated with agencies of different denominations and with non-religious NGOs. Christianity affected and colored their humanitarian work. Towards the end of this period, the growth of churches and Christianity in Africa reflected a "disenchantment with governments that are less and less capable of meeting social needs and of providing economic incentives" (Jenkins 1994:84).

Structural Adjustment, 1990-2000

With the end of the Cold War came the beginning of IMF and World Bank structural adjustment programs (SAPs) and an even greater proliferation of NGO activity in Zimbabwe. Religious and secular NGOs collaborated with the Zimbabwean state in programs of economic development as the state was streamlined and civil services were trimmed. NGOs, espousing democracy, good governance, and capitalism in their programs, vowed to assist the liberalizing state. During this period, there was a fresh influx of NGOs in Zimbabwe, both local and international. Due to neoliberal trends in foreign aid to bypass the state and to fund NGOs and community based organizations (CBOs) directly, the Zimbabwean state became increasingly weak and unstable. This was not without ethical consequences. Hanlon (2000) has described this process as one in which governments are "decapacitated" (cf. Kilby 2000). Such neo-liberal projects to democratize Zimbabwe were similar to the efforts of churches and NGOs in other parts of Africa (Chepkwony Ongaro 1991; Gifford 1995; Jenkins 1994; Maxwell 1995).

During the 1990s, Zimbabwe witnessed two phases of "structural adjustment" programs initiated by the World Bank and the IMF: ESAP I and ZIMPREST. These external controls on the Zimbabwean state generated yet another transformation of church-state-NGO relations. After eras of collaboration, resistance, and more collaboration between religious NGOs and the Zimbabwean state, friction between NGOs and the state grew during programs of economic liberalization. As the state was given orders to shrink, tensions between morality and governance, fueled by questions of socio-economic justice, were taken up by NGOs. While churches solidified their position as the moral conscience of Zimbabwe, they debated the economic well-being of Zimbabweans. The relation between church and state, and the role of religious NGOs within it, continued a long historic relationship. In the late 1990s, the Catholic Commission for Justice and Peace (CCJP) worked to rewrite the Zimbabwean constitution, and ZCC held annual nation-wide meetings on the national budget to provoke questions on processes of unequal development and issues of social justice. As such, NGOs as non-state actors were actively involved in supplementing the receding role of the state in development (MWENGO 1993).

Since the late 1980s, churches in Zimbabwe have occupied an increasingly overt political role. More generally, in Africa, Christianity is no longer merely a component of colonialism but an inextricable presence in postcolonial African identity. Paul Gifford (1994) has compared the mushrooming of new African churches to social transformations in Latin America, where some independent churches have become mega-churches. Ezekiel Guti's Zimbabwe Assemblies of God Africa, founded in the 1950s, is an example of a church that has more followers in Zimbabwe than either the Catholic, Methodist or Anglican churches (Gifford 1994; Maxwell 2000). These new churches preach "the faith gospel of health and wealth," a theology that springs from American media evangelists in the 1950s and 60s. Indeed, as Gifford notes, there has been a missionary explosion since the 1980s in Africa. As African governments collapsed and receded, international NGOs flooded in to take their place. Other authors, as in Pieterse's edited collection (1992; Gifford same volume

1992), contend that evangelical activity in southern Africa is part of a wider hegemonic process of the American right wing. Global evangelism, as the religion of a transnational neoliberal market society, is associated with a neocolonial, religious "Coca-Colonization" or Christian "McDonaldization." Historically, colonial churches in Zimbabwe were funded by international mission societies, and NGOs like World Vision and Christian Care tread these well-worn transnational paths. International church bodies and global, secular bodies such as the World Bank and USAID provide support for religious NGOs today. These global networks are an important part of NGOs, offering fiscal directives and structuring the types of programs supported.

WORLD VISION AND AMERICAN EVANGELICALISM: GOD AND THE INDIVIDUAL

The global networks that fund and influence World Vision and Christian Care have specific philosophical histories, which can be traced to the religious movements of American evangelism and European ecumenism. The philosophy of World Vision International grew out of the movement in American evangelicalism of the 1940s called "new evangelicalism" (Marsden 1975; Marty 1975; Noll, Bebbington, and Rawlyk 1994; Wells and Woodbridge 1975). The key to evangelical theology is a belief in the inerrancy of biblical scripture, which is considered the word of God. Because evangelicals believe in an individual orientation toward spiritual salvation, involving a personal trust in Christ and his atoning work, eternal salvation is possible only by being born again. Within the American evangelical movement, evangelicals are characterized by the use of proselytizing in order to convert non-believers to an evangelical belief system. This practice includes leading a spiritually transformed life marked by moral conduct, personal devotion through Bible reading and prayer, and a zeal for evangelism and missions (Marsden 1987a). Thus, evangelicalism is a coalition of ideas and institutions; it is not a unified movement or religious group. With historical roots in Calvinism, seventeenth-century Puritanism, and the influence of John Wesley in the mid-eighteenth century, it was practiced differently in England and America. In England, evangelicalism manifested itself in Methodism, in the foundation of the Salvation Army, and in the rise of the evangelical wing of the Church of England. In America, it was seen in New England Puritanism, continental pietism, revivalist Presbyterianism, and both Baptist and Methodist anti-establishment democratic impulses. Emerging from religious awakenings of the eighteenth century, the evangelical movement by the nineteenth century had taken shape in America, in the British Empire, and in mission fields (Marsden 1975; Noll, Bebbington, and Rawlyk 1994; Sandeen 1970; Stone 1997).

The rise of the United States as a new nation coincided with the rise of evangelicalism, and the evangelical emphasis on voluntary acceptance of

Christianity matched American ideas of individual freedom. It emphasized a personal commitment to Christ, and personal holiness rather than social programs (Marsden 1987b). The eighteenth- and nineteenth-century American evangelical revivalism grew in the same atmosphere that produced American political and economic individualistic liberalism. The basic unit was the individual: ". . . it might be helpful to regard revivalism as in a sense the religious counterpart to democracy and free enterprise" (Marsden 1975:135). It was a religious ethos comprised of voluntary decisions, personal choice, and personal commitment to Jesus. Marsden continues: "Once this personal commitment was made, the process of sanctification was regarded largely in terms of personal purity. Great concern for the welfare of society was often associated with this individualistic scheme, though somewhat as in the free enterprise system the key to collective welfare was to have each individual behaving correctly" (ibid: 136).

With evangelicalism, individual religious experience achieved primacy, and churches and congregations were seen as groups of individuals free to come and go voluntarily. A tendency of American Revivalism was that it lacked a strong concept of institutional authority. It emphasized scripture instead of the church, and the power of the word instead of religious institutions. Evangelicalism was shaped by a focus on revivalism and personal conversion. Marty (1975:71) explains:

In the process, a distinctive doctrine of God and man became normative: God was not a remote sovereign potency but a benevolent loving Father who normatively addressed the human situation in Christ. Man was indeed a sinner, but he was capable of responding to the revivalist's appeals, and once converted, he acquired great potency for doing good. A benevolent empire, full of errands of mercy and agencies of reform and welfare emerged out of the company of the converted.

By the nineteenth century, evangelicals in the United States had established a network of "voluntary societies" that promoted evangelism, founded Sunday Schools, distributed Bibles, founded schools and colleges, and brought the gospel to "needy" people.[5] Nineteenth-century evangelism was guided by a vision of spiritual and moral progress, and evangelicals actively engaged in political and social action including prison reform, temperance, and the abolition of slavery. The civil war in the United States created divisions in the evangelical movement: first over slavery and later as black and white evangelicals split during Reconstruction, 1865-1877. Evangelism was a social movement touching many denominations, including Methodists, Baptists, and Presbyterians, and it had a great deal to do with shaping American culture in the nineteenth century. As industrialism grew in the twentieth century, evangelicals launched a fierce attack on Modernism. After the First World War, anti-modernists formed a sub-movement of evangelicalism called Fundamentalism. Most popularly characterized by their role in the Scopes trial of 1925, evangelicals of this era came to be seen by many Americans as an intellectually repressive religious establishment. Evangelicals, who sought to rescue "the perishing from the sinking ship that was the condemned world" (McLean 1996), saw the Second Coming of Christ as the only cure for the world's political and moral problems. In the 1920s and 1930s, evangelicals were threatened by Darwin's ideas of evolution as well as by Marxism and what they saw to be theological liberals. Negative public opinion practically crushed the evangelical movement. But after the Scopes trial and the ensuing public humiliation that evangelicals faced in the United States, the evangelical movement regrouped. During this time, communism was added to evolutionism as a cause for alarm (Harding 2000; Marsden 1975; Wells and Woodbridge 1975).

The theology of World Vision and that of the new evangelicals grew both out of and in reaction to Fundamentalism. The Fundamentalists of the 1920s were reacting to secularizing tendencies in the United States, and in the process, they developed an anti-modernist doctrine called "dispensationalism." Dispensationalism was a version of pre-millennialism: the doctrine that Christ will return personally to found a kingdom in Jerusalem where he will reign for one thousand years (Marsden 1987b:5). The doctrine provided a general theory of history that anointed the "church age" as the sixth dispensation in world's history, marked by apostasy in churches and the moral collapse of "Christian civilization." It predicted the rise of modernism and emphasized the need to fight it to preserve faith and purity. Fundamentalism's anti-modernist interpretation of the Bible insisted on the inerrancy of biblical scripture. Every word was the perfect word of God. Fundamentalists interpreted cataclysmic biblical prophecies literally.

New evangelicals, in contrast to fundamentalists, repudiated both the doctrinal and the cultural implications of dispensationalism while remaining loyal to some tenets of fundamentalism. Theologically, they stood for a moderate form of classic Calvinist Protestantism (as opposed to dispensationalist Bible teachers). They saw their duty as twofold: to transform culture and to evangelize. The primary means of cultural transformation was intellectual reform. New evangelicals emphasized intellect and higher education and thus, broke with the dispensationalist-separatist right wing of fundamentalism. By the 1940s, evangelicals had failed to take over major denominations in America, and the movement continued its efforts to develop a firmer institutional base.[9] Meanwhile, evangelicals worked through international missions and radio series such as Charles Fuller's "The Old Fashioned Revival Hour." The Fuller Theological Seminary was founded in 1947 in Pasadena, California, by Carl Henry, Harold Ockenga, Edward Carnell, and Charles Fuller, all of whom were major figures in the evangelical movement at the time. It was a home for new evangelicalism; its founders began publishing *Christianity*

Today in 1956.[9] The new evangelicals believed in many components of early evangelicalism, including the inerrancy of the Bible, active evangelism, human depravity and individual conversion, and the efficacy of atonement via the death of Christ. Most significantly, they emphasized theological scholarship and social concerns. The Fuller seminary came to symbolize a move away from the doctrinal and moral rigidities of fundamental evangelism.

The new evangelicals founded World Vision International as "an organization dedicated to childcare, social ministry and medical ministries in Asia" (Linder 1975).[11] When Carl Henry organized a commission for evangelical social action in the National Association of Evangelicals (NAE) and called for the application of Christianity to every aspect of life including the social, World Vision was one example of this philosophy in practice. Fuller Seminary was initially founded because Charles Fuller decided to establish a "College of Missions and Evangelism" rather than a seminary. Ties between Fuller's mission school and World Vision, the mission organization, ran deep. In 1954, one of World Vision's board members was Carlton Booth, Professor of Evangelism at Fuller Seminary (Gehman 1960). In 1966, the Missions Advance Research and Communications Center (MARC) began at World Vision in association with Fuller, as the research and publishing arm of World Vision. Fuller's School of World Mission trained World Vision staff, and World Vision staff taught, and continue to teach today, at Fuller Seminary. There was such cross-fertilization between Fuller and World Vision that a World Vision employee said in a 1994 interview, "The idea of World Vision was started in conversations in the basement of Fuller Theological Seminary."

In the 1960s, while counter-cultures and radical theologies were forming in the USA, so was the resurgence of a global evangelical Christianity. In 1967, the new evangelicals sponsored the World Congress on Evangelism—part of a transatlantic movement with missionary ties. In the 1970s, World Vision made a formal commitment to "development" (Irvine 1996). In 1974, the Lausanne Conference reaffirmed the urgency of World Evangelization with the necessity of "social and political concern for aiding the poor and victims of oppression" (Marsden 1975).

By the 1980s there was little holding evangelicalism together, especially after the scandals of Jim Bakker and Jimmy Swaggart. American evangelists had built empires; they were all serving Christ, but they were rival empires. Despite this, the basic features of the evangelical movement remained, especially a disregard for the institutional church. The organized church (except at the level of the congregation) played a small role in evangelicalism. Even local congregations seemed to be comprised of individuals who were sovereign and free to leave and join churches as they pleased. A central feature of evangelicalism came to be the denial of the authority of traditions: non-Christian religions as well as denominational Christianity were the subjects of critique. An informal, almost anti-institutional sense of church prevailed, with a lack of a denominational church base; evangelicalism was a transdenominational movement. Marsden (1987b) notes an important link between individualism and evangelicalism, which works through independent agencies and "parachurch" institutions. He writes:

> Through offering warm fellowship in local congregations, evangelicals emphasized that the church was made up of individual converts. Often these individuals would be so filled with zeal to proclaim the gospel that they felt compelled to move beyond ponderous denominational structures. They did not usually repudiate their denominations but simply set up their own extradenominational agencies in order to promote the cause more efficiently. Individualism, then, combined with the spirit of American free enterprise, has shaped transdenominational evangelicalism's distinctive institutions.

While World Vision is an ecumenical organization that hires staff members from many denominations, the philosophy that drives the institution was described to me as evangelical. Whether this was interpreted in the conservative, fundamentalist sense or in a more radical form depended on the spiritual orientation of the individual. Nonetheless, as an institutional ideology, evangelism is dominant. In the United States, evangelicalism experienced rapid growth in the US during post-World War II prosperity. World Vision was launched during this time. It was an era that simultaneously associated material goods with "the good life" and certain American ideals, and fostered an atmosphere of Cold War fear and suspicion. This unique historic moment bred a distinctly American vision of the world which was both moralistic and materially prosperous—two qualities which survive today in the philosophy of World Vision.

World Vision's transformation from an internationally focused nonprofit to a multinational partnership began in 1950, with the first branch office opening in Canada (it was officially incorporated in 1959). Support offices were added in Australia (1969), South Africa (1973), New Zealand (1974) and Europe/London (1978). The opening of national branch offices thus began in the English-speaking West. In 1978, an umbrella governing body known as World Vision International was created to include an international board of directors, a larger international advisory council, and a corporate headquarters. The current governing board includes members from both support (financially contributing), and recipient countries. Each of the national support offices (there were 60 at the time of this research) is incorporated as an independent nonprofit organization under the laws of its respective country, while the network as a whole constitutes World Vision International. As a network, World Vision International crosses national boundaries. It is a global, supra-national organization.

The purpose of World Vision, as described in its annual reports, is to provide emergency relief, economic development, and evangelistic activities to more than 94 countries worldwide (World Vision 1997a). World Vision International has grown to become a multi-million-dollar NGO ($290 million [$239 million cash/ $51 million Gifts in Kind,[12] annually] in 1993). The majority of World Vision's support (roughly 70%) is derived from individuals in "First World/developed" nations who "sponsor" children in "Third World/underdeveloped" countries. The corporate mission statement, approved by the board of directors, serves as a starting point for my analysis of the way the institution presents its role to the public. World Vision's annual report (1993) stated:[13]

> World Vision is an international partnership of Christians whose mission is to follow our Lord and Savior Jesus Christ in working with the poor and oppressed to promote human transformation, seek justice and bear witness to the good news of the Kingdom of God.

The statement continues to list the ways in which the mission is carried out, namely through "transformational development," "emergency relief," "promotion of justice," "strategic initiatives," "public awareness" and "witness to Jesus Christ." The evangelistic perspective is perhaps most overtly depicted in World Vision's publicity materials. A "History of World Vision"[14] (World Vision 1994) proclaims:

> Jesus' great commission has been the driving force behind World Vision's projects for more than three decades. Active demonstration and open declaration of God's love and truth are key objectives in all World Vision projects, whether they are in childcare, emergency relief, community development or church assistance.

Religious objectives are both the driving force and the principal aim of the humanitarian work conducted by World Vision as an NGO in Zimbabwe.

CHRISTIAN CARE AND GLOBAL ECUMENICISM: CHURCH UNITY AND THE SOCIAL GOSPEL

Although similar in practice to World Vision Zimbabwe and sharing with it common objectives of Christian humanitarian service, Christian Care Zimbabwe was not connected to the history of American evangelicalism. Instead, as the development arm of the Zimbabwean Council of Churches, it grew out of the ecumenical philosophy of the World Council of Churches. European church leaders founded the World Council of Churches (WCC) in 1937. However, its beginnings were delayed by the Second World War, and it was not until 1948 that representatives from 147 churches gathered in

Amsterdam to form the WCC (World Council of Churches: A Half-Century of Service 2000). The WCC is founded on the philosophical objective of uniting different churches. Its philosophical underpinnings are traceable to missionary movements of the late 19th and early 20th centuries that encouraged Christians to pray and work together across denominations. The WCC is primarily Protestant and includes evangelical denominations. It does not include the Roman Catholic Church, although it works closely with the Catholic Church, which sends representatives to major WCC conferences. The goal of the WCC is interchurch cooperation.

Roots of the ecumenical movement began in 1910 with the World Missionary Conference at Edinburgh. The logic of "cooperation and unity" between churches was linked to the idea that unless the churches in Europe (at "home") were united, missionary efforts in "the field" would be bound to fail. The ecumenical movement was influenced by nineteenth-century revival movements that inspired students to go into the missionary field (cf. fundamentalist or evangelical movements), and by the "Social Gospel" movement that "cherished the idea of a world being gradually transformed into the Kingdom of God by human endeavor" (Vermaat 1989:2, Bell 1979, Duff S.J. 1956). After 1961, theologians from Africa, Asia, and Latin America began to transform the WCC's approach to society and politics. In the 1970s, the WCC was deeply influenced by the liberation theology movement in Latin America. In the 1980s, the WCC actively sought to support liberation movements in southern Africa—a source of controversy within the organization (Vermaat 1989:65–76). The WCC's specific engagement with economic development began in the 1950s (Bock 1974). Because the World Council of Churches grew out of the international missionary movement, it had to some extent been involved in "development" activities before the 1950s. However, the 1950s brought a new awareness of global inequalities and the WCC sought to address these problems with a Christian economic ethic of assistance. The WCC focused on technical assistance, like World Vision and many secular institutions of that time.

The philosophical histories of Christian Care (via the World Council of Churches) and World Vision set the groundwork for their economic development work in Zimbabwe in the late 1990s. The institutional "missions" of each organization (cf. artifacts, Riles 2000) outlined institutional objectives and provided guidelines for the activities and efforts of NGOs and their staff members. For example, Christian Care's mission statement from their 1995–96 Annual Report stated:

As we enter the twenty-first century and we are confronted with escalating social, economic and political problems, the vision of Christian Care, as an arm of the churches in Zimbabwe, is to spearhead a Christian approach to community service.

Our Mission is to improve the quality of life and the self-supporting capacities of disadvantaged people in Zimbabwe regardless of religious affiliation or ethnic and racial identity.

The improvement of quality of life will be achieved by ensuring access to
basic needs, giving special attention to gender, environment, and human
rights by building upon initiatives and knowledge available in the communities. This will be done in partnership with communities, donors, churches, and other relevant organizations.[15]

"Mission statements" such as those quoted above, continually re-written, echo
earlier eras and the social movements that spawned the NGOs.

PART 2: PRODUCTIVE LENS

THE ZIMBABWEAN ECONOMY AND THE CONTEXT FOR RURAL DEVELOPMENT

In the late 1990s, faith-based NGOs such as World Vision and Christian Care
were at the forefront of providing economic development for Zimbabwe. The
national economy during this time generated an increasing disparity between
the few that benefited from neoliberal economic restructuring and the majority of the population for whom structural adjustment policies meant daily economic hardship (Bond 1998; Potts 1998). It was in this setting that the work of
NGOs in development increased in prominence. In the year 2000, an estimated 11.3 million people populated Zimbabwe, located between South Africa,
Zambia, Mozambique and Botswana (World Factbook 2000 as for statistics
that follow). In the 1990s, the Zimbabwean economy was plagued by rising
inflation (32% for consumer prices in 1998, 59% in 1999). In 1999, the unemployment rate was estimated to be 50%. 1996 estimates of labor-force break-
down were 66% in agriculture, 24% in services, and 10% in industry.
Approximately 60% of the population lived below the poverty line in 1999. Life
expectancy was reduced from 56.2 years in 1990 to 49 years in 1995, and 40.4
years in 1999 largely due to AIDS (World Bank 2001). Many of these figures
continued to worsen as the Zimbabwean economy spiraled downward in the
late 1990s and early 2000.

Agriculture employed the majority of the population, and supplied its
primary exports such as tobacco. Although agriculture constituted only 20% of
the GDP, agricultural production was more important than this figure suggests,
as GDP failed to take into account non-market-oriented subsistence production. Thirty-two percent of agricultural land was divided into 5,100 large-scale
commercial farms, which produced most of the nation's market surplus. Small-
scale commercial farming made up 4% of agricultural land (approximately

9650 farms). Resettlement schemes, part of the Zimbabwean government's land redistribution program, in which the government bought land from large-scale farms,[16] constituted 8.6% of land. National parks made up 14% of land. Communal land occupied 42% of the nation and housed 51.4% of the population (statistics above Government of Zimbabwe 1997). Most NGO-sponsored development projects focused on subsistence farmers in the communal lands. During the time of my research, the number of large-scale farms was decreasing due to the government's redistribution program. This process since 2000 has become violent and highly criticized internationally. Primary crops included maize—the national food staple—as well as tobacco, wheat, coffee, sorghum, groundnuts (peanuts), cotton, sugarcane, tea, and sunflowers. Livestock included cattle, sheep, goats, pigs, and poultry. Environmental issues of concern to NGOs included recurring droughts that constricted the economy and threatened food security, deforestation, soil erosion, and land degradation.

TYPES OF DEVELOPMENT PROJECTS IN ZIMBABWE[17]

Drought periods (1982-83, 1987, and 1991-92, 1994) have plagued the region, reducing agricultural projections and food security. During these frequent droughts, Zimbabwe's self-sufficiency in food production was threatened, agro-based manufacturing fell, and water shortages resulted in decreased production in mining, energy, and industrial sectors. In communal lands, drought resulted in livestock and maize losses, and hunger for rural Zimbabweans. Constraints to drought relief for NGOs included poor rainfall, decreased farm-holding sizes, and soils that were low in fertility and deteriorated due to excessive cropping. Rangeland productivity decreased due to overgrazing, and high rural-urban migration by male household members resulted in a shortage of farm labor. NGO approaches to drought relief included rehabilitating, upgrading, and building small dam structures to alleviate surface water shortage, assisting women to improve household garden plots, creating community-based agribusiness dealer networks (to market agricultural inputs to farmers and market agricultural produce by smallholder farmers), and providing credit and loan schemes to solve the problem of a limited cash economy in rural areas. NGOs assisted (and trained) communities in conserving primary water supplies by protecting water springs, constructing deep and shallow wells, drilling boreholes, and building pumps. NGOs also initiated irrigation schemes, and provided training in soil and water conservation.

A shortage of doctors warranted community-based health care in rural areas. NGOs assisted in AIDS awareness and family planning, and provided training courses in hygiene education. Water sanitation in rural areas was also a target of NGO activities. NGOs worked to provide clean water, to build toilets, and to sink wells for household use. Farm workers on commercial farms experienced limited medical, educational, and sanitary facilities; this specific population, in addition to rural subsistence farmers, was also targeted by NGOs for assistance.

Credit and loan programs and micro-enterprise development were two other types of NGO effort in the late 1990s. Credit outreach programs guaranteed loans to farmers and small business owners in collaboration with Zimbabwean banks. Micro-enterprise development programs involved the provision of technical assistance (credit education), loan analysis, management training, and training in technical skills. Income generation and employment was encouraged in fields like tailoring, carpentry, arts and crafts, retailing, poultry, and cropping.

In the 1990s, World Vision Zimbabwe was involved in water and drought relief projects similar to those described above (World Vision Zimbabwe Annual Report 1994). In addition, health and sanitation projects included building health clinics, installing radio communication systems for health centers, and constructing toilets. Agricultural interventions included constructing irrigation schemes and warehouses to store agro-inputs, and distributing fertilizer to subsistence farmers. Livestock restocking and management schemes involved introducing livestock in certain areas, and providing training in cattle management. Funded primarily through child sponsorship (a topic dealt with at length in Chapter 3), World Vision Zimbabwe also initiated programs with a focus on "mother and child health" that included providing vehicles, drivers, and nurse aides to form a mobile clinic team (lead by Ministry of Health officials), and offering pre- and postnatal care including family planning and growth monitoring. Other programs focused on education, initiated supplementary feeding programs in response to intermittent droughts, built classroom blocks and teachers' houses, and purchased benches, desks, and school supplies for children. Rural projects were structured as either small scale "Community Development Projects" (CDPs) or larger scale "Area Development Projects" (ADPs). In addition to its rural programs, World Vision Zimbabwe initiated small-scale urban schemes to assist homeless women and children. Many projects encouraged industry. For example, World Vision provided sewing machines and training in basic dressmaking skills, and assisted in the formation of soap-making and shoe-making businesses. All of World Vision's programs included an evangelism component (which will be explored in Chapter 2).

Christian Care operated in a manner very similar to World Vision's and sponsored the same types of projects: drought relief, supplementary feeding, food production and processing, water and sanitation, health care, animal husbandry, and livestock management (Christian Care Annual Report 1995-1996). Both Christian Care and World Vision have been, at different times, involved in assisting refugees from neighboring countries such as Mozambique. In this research I focus solely on the development programs of World Vision and

Christian Care and not on their emergency and relief work, although the two often go hand in hand, with development activities often following emergency relief efforts.

Both Christian Care and World Vision Zimbabwe are national programs of transnationally financed NGOs. In addition to a "national office" for each NGO, there are smaller regional offices that work to manage the daily operations of development in concert with local development projects and field staff. I conducted this study partly in the national and Harare regional offices of World Vision and Christian Care. Unlike World Vision, which was funded primarily by child sponsorship, Christian Care was supported through grants from its international member churches (through the World Council of Churches in Geneva. See Appendix 2 for a list of Christian Care's member churches in Zimbabwe). The two organizations were similar in practice and orientation. As outlined above, both NGOs began their international work in the 1940s and their work in Zimbabwe during the liberation struggle (Christian Care in the late 1960s, World Vision in the early 1970s).

PART 3: REFLEXIVE LENS

THE METHODOLOGICAL CONTEXT FOR STUDYING CHRISTIAN NGOS

How did I, as an ethnographer, enter into this historical and economic context of faith-based economic development in Zimbabwe? My research for this book began in California in 1994 with preliminary interviews in the International and United States offices of World Vision International, located in Monrovia, California. These initial interviews were structured loosely around the link between evangelism (the urge to change people's spiritual convictions) and the development and relief work of the organization (the urge to change people's material conditions). I was curious about how people in different positions within the organizations viewed their work and the work of Christian, humanitarian assistance more generally. In retrospect, I was prepared neither for the journey I would embark on nor the conclusions I would reach. As a secular (or, as I would sometimes explain, cultural) Jew, I was suspicious of evangelism; I assumed it to be coercive. Evangelism did not have as neutral a hue as the relief development work for which organizations such as World Vision were well known. My conversations with staff members in the California offices were provocative, and I was unsettled by how much I had in common with the employees I interviewed. Based on ideals of helping the less fortunate, the humanitarian aims of the staff of WV International were not far from my own. Although the economic and geographic scale of World Vision surpassed the small not-for-profit arts organizations I had worked for in New York and Los Angeles, the daily challenges of working for World Vision paralleled some of my experiences in the non-profit world. The passion with which people spoke about "the field" where development took place was fascinating. "The field" was where I should go to understand the work of World Vision, I was told, not offices in the United States. The head offices in the West were not part of "the field." In the United States offices of World Vision, employees I spoke with were from all over the world, and many of them had worked for the organization in different capacities, offering multiple views of the work being done. From secretaries and management, policymakers and planners, evaluators, leaders, and field officers, I began to cobble together a picture of World Vision's work. Carried within the experiences of employees of WV International in the United States were stories from the field. Each interview alluded to perspectives not heard yet spoken for.[18]

My choice of Zimbabwe as a field site emerged through a series of accidents. One of my informants during early research with World Vision in California was a woman who, at the time, had been recently hired as the human relations manager for World Vision in Africa. A Ghanaian, she had worked in human relations for World Vision in Ghana and was being promoted to a regional position. We had a wonderful interview, and I liked her a great deal. I liked her spirit, her sense of humor, and the stories of the field that streamed from her mouth. She told me how World Vision was moving its Africa Regional office from its base in the California International office to a new site in Harare, Zimbabwe. She was herself planning to move there in a few months, and spoke of Harare, of Africa, and of World Vision. Perhaps due to our rapport and the fluidity of our conversation, I promised that I would visit her in Harare and told her that I was considering conducting my research there; the sentence jumped off my tongue before I could stop it. She was gracious and welcoming, and after that initial verbal slip, Zimbabwe it was.

In the summer of 1995, I visited Zimbabwe for two months to survey the NGO landscape in Harare. There were NGOs everywhere. NGOs were as much a part of the environment as foliage, or pavement, or cars. In radical contrast to my experience in the United States, NGOs and development were a significant part of the lives of most Zimbabweans, as was Christianity. When I described my project to people in Zimbabwe, it made perfect sense to them. Of course, they said, Christianity and development: no confusion, no mystery, no clarification of terms necessary. In 1992, there were almost 300 NGOs operating in Zimbabwe.[19] From the late 1980s to early 1990s, South Africa and Mozambique were sites of global concern. They were also environments that lacked amenities and comforts for NGO staff. A lack of infrastructure was prohibitive in the case of Mozambique (it was also a Cold-War battlefield), and apartheid created severe limitations for NGO operations in South Africa. Harare became an ideal base for NGOs operating in the broader region. Geographically beautiful, safe, relatively "well developed" compared to other African nations, clean, with roads; Harare was an NGO-worker's paradise. With NGOs flooding the landscape, it was no accident that my project was meaningful to so many people there. There were quite a number of organizations on which I could focus my research. I returned to the United States inspired, with seven letters of support from assorted NGOs, both secular and religious, stating that they would be happy to host me as a researcher.

When I returned to Zimbabwe for research in 1996, turning promises into research sites was a renewed challenge. It was one thing for an NGO director to say yes to a phantom researcher on the other side of the planet, and quite another to allocate staff time and energy to her questions. I returned to Zimbabwe and to the seven organizations with my project. People were busy, organizations were under siege with internal problems, and the requests of an anthropologist curious about religious ideas took on a different tenor. I was confronted by questions: What can you do for us? How is this going to help us? After two months of interviews with directors of different NGOs in 1996, I decided to focus on World Vision Zimbabwe and Christian Care. My research is not one of straight comparison. Although the two organizations differed in historical orientation (as described above), much of their work was similar. Many employees I interviewed had worked, at different times, for both organizations as well as for secular and government development organizations. The distinctions between the NGOs were less apparent than the similarities. Christian NGOs (both World Vision and Christian Care) did not offer development that was purely instrumental, or formally rational. They suggested an enchanted development, which added meaning to economic endeavors of pure calculation (of markets, or micro-enterprise development for example). Both organizations were involved with very similar types of projects; sometimes they even collaborated. They shared agendas, and occasionally resources and staff, with other Christian NGOs in Zimbabwe, including Lutheran World Federation, Opportunity International, Mennonite Economic Development Association, and the Catholic Commission for Justice and Peace.

While on official "attachment" (internship) with World Vision and Christian Care, I continued to interview, and "hang around" with the staff of the other NGOs mentioned above. I stopped by, conducted interviews, and attended training sessions. Boundaries between the organizations dissolved as I learned that people had previously worked for more than one NGO, or that NGO workers attended joint meetings on issues of national concern, such as advocacy for women or economic justice, in forums spearheaded by the Zimbabwe Council of Churches and the Catholic Commission for Justice and Peace. On the advisory boards of World Vision and Christian Care were the executive directors of other NGOs. Paths crossed in multiple directions. For example, the head of the NGO subdivision at the World Bank in Harare had previously worked for the Lutheran World Federation. I met him during my 1995 visit when he was an NGO employee. In 1996, he was working for the World Bank. It was a dense professional world. The range of my informants extended beyond the walls of the two institutions, and beyond the walls of

NGOs in general, to include those whose work and lives intercepted NGO activities. Christianity was a part of all of these activities.

SPIRITUAL VULNERABILITY

The first time someone tried to convert me and I actually considered it, I was sitting in church in Harare with a friend. Somali by birth and the director of World Vision's Gender in Africa program by profession, this friend had become very dear to me. She was happy to take me to church with her. We attended a charismatic church called Hear the Word that, coincidentally, was founded by the first director of WV Zimbabwe.[20] World Vision no longer had direct ties to this church, although it was popular with WV Zimbabwe staff because of its charismatic service. It was early March 1997. My friend arrived in the morning and we drove in her new white car to the church in Avondale, a northern suburb of Harare. A sea of parked cars on a grass and dirt lot surrounded the church. The first morning service was just concluding and songs wafted out of the building followed by hundreds of people who flowed into the parking lot. Hear the Word was held in a school auditorium and the room lacked any architectural adornments to mark it symbolically as a "church," except a large red plastic banner hanging over the stage with "Jesus is Lord" scripted in gold letters. The stage was set up for a band, with a drum set, synthesizers, and an organ. In the center of the room was an island of a sound system. A man sat at the controls mixing the music, as the members of the audience flowed around his equipment and seated themselves on carefully arranged symmetrical lines of folding chairs. On some aisles there were signs that said, "reserved." These were for the church staff: women in green dresses and men in suits and ties with white shirts. These uniforms gave the environment an appearance of organization and control, despite the exploding spirit of its charismatic service. The sense of order attracted and intimidated me: it was visibly apparent who belonged and who did not.

As churchgoers slowly streamed into the auditorium and seated themselves, I noticed a woman standing below the stage. She bowed her head as the pastor placed his hand on it; he was praying. Another man, a staff member in a suit, stood behind her with his hand gently placed at the space between her shoulders. Not touching her, he was there to catch her if she fell during the faith healing. My attention was drawn to this quiet and intense scene between three people, almost private, as hundreds of others walked and talked toward their seats, apparently without noticing the small trio. The music commenced, verging on rock and roll; it was loud and exhilarating. A uniformed woman stood next to an overhead projector that was angled towards a large film screen in the corner of the auditorium. Projected on the screen were the words of the songs. A religious karaoke, the words facilitated participation. Soon the congregation was singing and swaying in choreographed unison. After the hymns, the wife of the pastor, a young white woman with a South African accent, sang a solo. She had long brown hair with bangs, and her figure was conservatively clad in a secretarial-style red and white dress. The audience sported jeans and dresses; some men were in shorts, and others were in suits. Church was a place to be seen, and the younger and more fashionable members of the congregation were dressed as if heading for a disco. The crowd was racially mixed— something unusual in Zimbabwe at that time, when distinctly segregated social geographies for blacks and whites were still ensconced. Nevertheless, there were far more black than white Zimbabweans attending the service. The singing came in waves, crescendos and climaxes. Hands flew into the air, elbows straight or bent, reaching for God in an ecstatic, Durkheimian collective effervescence. Each song was about Christ—the leader, the shepherd— and how he died for human sins. Hear the Word Christianity was the worship of Christ—a human interceptor in place of a distant God, manifesting an accessible and material religion. There was no literal mention of God in the songs, only Christ: Christ was Lord. The focus on the humanness of Christ stood in contrast to my experience of Judaism's elusive and all-powerful supra-human God. That day, the sermon of Hear the Word focused upon the life of Christ as a parable. Missionaries and NGO workers suddenly made sense to me as walking examples of Christ's life. If it was impossible to emulate the life of a supra-human God, it was possible to emulate the life of Christ. In contrast to a God larger that the human ability to comprehend it, Christ represented and embodied model humanness.

The pastor was American, and his sharp American accent shocked me. He preached the Gospel of Prosperity (Gifford 1990, especially in reference to this particular church), and said, "James 4: 'Ask and you shall receive.' . . . Matthew 21: 'If you believe you will receive whatever you ask for in prayer.'" He spoke of links between the act of asking for and that of believing in, via the promise of hope. In the sermon, there was a direct correlation between the attainment of one's wishes, belief in Christ, and material success. The pastor told a story of a woman who was too poor to send her daughter on an exchange program in Germany. In the story, the woman repeated "affirmations." She wrote sums of money on pieces of paper and hung them above her daughter's bed. She sent out a mailing to request funds from friends and family. She sent a press release to a radio station. A veritable business formed; this woman was organized (oddly enough, the story took place in southern California). The woman's wish came true and money flowed toward her. It was a miracle with a moral: "Just think," the pastor said, "this woman wasn't even religious, just think if she had believed in Jesus. . . ." The undercurrent of his story was "just do it, try hard and you will succeed," the American dream in which anything is possible for the individual. The individualism of the gospel of prosperity ignored any structural and political constraints that might impinge upon material success (Gifford 1990).

At Hear the Word, the key to understanding verse was believing. "Believing" and "asking for" ostensibly led to "Getting what you want" and "Putting action to your affirmation." The pastor quoted the Bible: "John Chapter 5 verse 14: 'Have confidence in God. If we ask anything, we know we have what we ask for of him.' John 14:12: 'Jesus is Lord' (reciting the words printed in the red plastic banner hanging above the stage). Chapter 15:7: 'Ask whatever you wish and it will be given to you.' James Chapter 1:5: 'If any of you lacks wisdom we should ask God.'" Faith, through Jesus, conjoined asking with receiving from God, the supreme giver. Giving from God was holy and supernatural, and Jesus was the bridge to the material world. As God in human form, he was close and benevolent, not distant and punishing. Jesus embodied the power to give, modeling the potential for faith to have material consequences. The causal relation between faith and life was exemplified by faith healing, in which humans channeled divine energy. It was a relationship that extended into the world of giving, tithing, and service: "God says tithe, God says give." The pastor continued his sermon. When the pastor stopped preaching he asked if there were any new visitors in the congregation. I raised my hand, and in a flash there was a woman beside me, sitting in the seat that said "reserved," with a card for me to fill out my name, my address, and whether I was interested in home visits and Bible-study groups. The women in green dresses efficiently circled the congregation handing out cards and pens from plastic buckets in a very precise and institutional manner. Another plastic bucket was passed around for people to tithe.

Then, the pastor asked in a tender and delicate voice if anyone in the congregation was ready to make a commitment to Christ: to be born again. A cascade of Christ-seekers glided down the aisles toward the stage. He asked repeatedly, "Anyone else?" After each question, a handful trickled down the aisles. Their movement was accompanied by great applause. The group clustered in front of the congregation was congratulated and then ushered to another room. Although I had been "witnessed to" individually a number of times in the course of my research, this was the first time I had observed a group conversion. I felt an urge to follow the group, out of curiosity to see what happened when someone was born again. I feared my friend would push me forward, or even ask if I wanted to go. Although I was deeply intrigued, I could not overcome the ethical inhibitions I had surrounding my non-Christian identity. Could I, with integrity, pretend to become Christian? I had been straightforward with my friend about being Jewish. I sensed it confused her, but my honesty helped me maintain the slim boundary between my research and me. This church service, although not sponsored by an NGO, was indeed part of the scope of my research. It was a space of faith, a realm in which belief was articulated. The sermon of Hear the Word echoed many of the same sentiments shared by Christian NGO staff: the Christian-ness of development, the scripturally motivated urge to help others. Ethnography often traverses varied terrains of inquiry: multi-sited, reflexive, trans-local. My fields of ethnographic inquiry consisted of the urban offices of NGOs in Harare, sermons in church, development sites in rural Zimbabwe, administrative NGO offices in the United States, and eventually a field of self-inquiry.

Two weeks later on Easter Sunday, I went to church with my friend, the World Vision employee, again. She came by early in the morning and we drove to Hear the Word, which was crowded and familiar. The red vinyl banner "Jesus is Lord" hung again above the stage. Surrounded by ecstatic songs, I felt the joy of being part of a group. The congregation and the singers and dancers on stage performed wildly with the abandon of rock musicians. The pastor spoke of giving: "Life is blessed from giving. . . . The church isn't after your money, God is." He spoke of the virtues of tithing ("God said: 'Tithe 10% of your income'). He spoke of salvation, of "living for another world, not this one . . . it is eternal life." The other-worldliness of Jesus' being born again was a model for all to follow. With Jesus in their hearts, those seated were encouraged by the promise of an after-life.

The pastor described a guest speaker from the 700/Club who was to visit in the near future. An American guest singer sang a Sinatra-style, slow gospel song. There was a short play about the devil (who was a woman) and her two servants dressed in red and black. Jesus, portrayed by a black Zimbabwean in white sweat pants and a white dress shirt, rose from the dead and defeated the devil. The guest preacher was from the American South, an evangelical and a self-proclaimed "missionary and a statesman." He spoke with the fervor of a southern Baptist, using the tactics of quick, fluid, mesmerizing speech with selective repetition. He told of the story of Jesus' crucifixion, the Easter story, as a launch to healing; of being spared from death as he prayed in tongues as a missionary in Mexico and Panama. These were stories from "the field," Indiana Jones survival-at-all-cost stories as fantastical and exciting as an action film. The guest preacher had worked for 29 years as a "third-world missionary," evangelizing and leading pastor's seminars and evening evangelism rallies. "I've got good news for the blind man, the hungry man, the deaf man," he said. "God creates manna when faith demands it. . . . I know that God is good . . . God is a good God . . . His word is absolute truth." His charismatic soliloquy rippled with poetic rhythm, songlike; certain words were repeated with a cadence that was soothing in its percussive regularity. He continued, "Christians are Christ-like ones, giving bread to dying men . . . Jesus is the delivery boy from God's bakery. Giving living bread to dying men." The audience put their hands in the air reaching for spirit; many had their Bibles and pens out and were taking copious notes. "The good news is hope and help. . . . I'm here to tell people there is hope and there is help." Jesus was a bringer of miracles. To believe in him was to believe in miracles and possibility: of wealth, of health, of desires met. "Life in abundance, that is Jesus." The preacher told stories of faith healing, and of raising a dead child to the living through prayer; he told how his wife was warned she could not have children and then subsequently bore four. In the encounter between science and faith, faith was the victor. The way he spoke made anything seem possible, as long as one spent an enormous amount of effort believing. The effort rested on faith, not in the performance of miracles, which existed in the realm of the supernatural. Through faith, one approximated the Godly. The pastor quoted Joshua 1:8: "'If you do talk like God, think like God, act like God, you will have success and prosperity. Be a doer of God, the word of God.'" The Christian ethic had a distinctly humanitarian component, compelling people to "do" in a holy way.

As with the last service, the pastor concluded with a question. Was there anyone who was ready, for the first time, to be born again? Our heads were bowed, so we could not see the people who (apparently, as the pastor would say "God bless you" or "Good for you") were raising their hands. I felt the same terror as weeks before, that my friend would ask me to go forward when the pastor suggested that people "turn to their neighbors who might need some help in making this choice." It was an individual choice. However, this time my curiosity to follow the converters had escaped me. As I was examining my fear, my friend turned to me and said gently, "Let me know if you want to go." I quietly mumbled "no thank you" as the moment I had been anxiously anticipating slipped past me. I wondered if my friend felt uncomfortable, and debated whether I should talk with her about it. Eventually I did. We streamed out of the church with the crowd and I asked if she had ever gone to the front of a church and been publicly born again. No, she said. We both acknowledged that such an act would require a great deal of courage. We ended the conversation on this note, the space of ease growing between us. There it was, an attempted conversion by a friend on Easter Sunday. I remembered a colleague joking how it was my job (a loyalty of sorts, to the discipline of anthropology) not to convert to Christianity. Such distance was useful for objective research. There I was, drowning in emotionally murky water that was difficult to wade through. I was caught up in the energy of the sermon and the singing along with everyone else, but at the moment when the congregation repeated after the pastor, "I take Jesus Christ as my savior, Jesus is my Lord," I could not bring myself to say the words. The falseness prevented me from even mouthing the words. I was paralyzed by the line I was determined not to cross.

The emotional journey of this research twisted allegiances in ways I could never have expected at the outset. I found myself living in reaction, as I tried to understand the "Christian" worlds of my informants. Driving home after a slew of interviews in World Vision's California offices, for example, I found myself listening to music I would normally never enjoy: heavy metal music, "satanic" music. The music expressed my claustrophobia and the frustrations inherent in the limitations I encountered. I could not speak my own mind about issues such as homosexuality and abortion. Discussing morals all day in Zimbabwe, hyper-attuned to the "good" and the "evil" that the discourse of Christian development perpetually defined, my own morality was sealed up and bottled. Stored away. Morality was a topic for my "informants." The internally self-imposed censorship pushed me to an artificially-constructed neutral zone, something similar to the political "neutrality" that NGO workers strove to produce in their development work (which I will discuss in Chapter 4). My opinions seeped into interviews, and when asked directly how I felt about, say, feminism or the role of women in Zimbabwe, I did not hold back. Yet those moments were rare. Most of the time, I was a listener and a documenter. The conversion moment with my friend was a marked contrast. I found myself suddenly curious about experiencing this moral space out of the zone of neutrality. For the first time, I heard my own voice loudly in dialogue with the "Christian" message of conversion. I wanted to see what was behind the door for those who decided to be "born again," yet my own ethical inhibitions about intellectual honesty made that impossible. My honesty had become my research strategy and my limitation. In interviews, I was invariably asked about my beliefs, whether I was a Christian and why I was not. I was frank about my position: I was not Christian. However, the more I lived in the space that Christianity came to inhabit during my fieldwork—the space of faith, as it were—the more it became an attractively alive place. The contradictions disturbed me. They forced me to live through the good and evil, to have them embodied in me, the researcher (cf. Harding 2000). I experienced, first-hand, the tensions I was studying: the hopes, the despair, and the frustrations. For years afterwards I attempted to tease out linear sense from stories and experiences. I was haunted by the people and their expressions of faith, by the ghosts and spirits of the intensity of their emotion, by the intimacy and trust with which some people confided in me about their spiritual lives. To write about faith seemed to betray it, to simplify it, to reduce it to generic social processes. That I was (and am) not a Christian and thus not a "believer" situated me as a researcher. Yet it did not stop me from experiencing religion as it was lived. To witness how the socially observable aspects of religious belief were reinterpreted, negotiated, and made part of belief itself was to experience religion as a political performance (Mudimbe 1997). It was not easy doing my research, especially when I had intellectual disagreement with what I was being told about the world, and how it should be changed.

Studying faith provoked the unexpected, and I reacted to what was presented to me at times with fear and horror. I was not convinced my reactions were my own, they seemed so odd. For example, one evening after being preached to during an interview with the director of Hear the Word Church (who, as the reader will recall, was the first director of WV Zimbabwe and ran the church that sponsored the service described above), I was browsing in the bookstore of a church, and I experienced a most profound desire to steal. The impulse was not brought to fruition. I did not steal. But I wanted to, and I had never wanted to before that moment. Perhaps being surrounded by so much "goodness," I came to embody its opposite: transgression. Through this experience, it became clearer how good and evil were locked in an embrace in Zimbabwe. They were mutually constitutive. I also came to experience how religion had disciplinary effects. The interview that produced these reflections had both excited and frustrated me, perhaps because I felt it was so out of my control. I left the interview with the conviction that my informant had not answered my questions; instead, he had told me what he wanted me to hear. Throughout the interview, the director of Hear the Word Church emphasized his personal relationship with Jesus. As he walked me out of his office, he mentioned it again. This was his message for me to take home. As much as I was interviewing him, he was bestowing upon me his evangelical message. He was "witnessing" to me. I knew he was evangelizing to me and I was helpless. I had no words of protest. I was paralyzed and polite. The "goodness" he offered related to the life of Christ. It had a particular quality that reminded me of interviews I had conducted in World Vision's offices in the United States. No black Zimbabwean minister, perhaps due to cultural differences, ever pressed his views upon me with quite the same unyielding persistence. The emphasis was disturbing, super-good and super-sweet. I wanted to do evil things. To steal, to be pornographic, to shock directives to conform and to join. It was a visceral reaction: flight. I wanted to run. I could not help but hear echoes of the radical right in the USA, and the gospel of prosperity as promoted by Hear the Word. After the interview, I walked around the building to the church bookshop in search of some information about the church. Two black Zimbabwean men in the bookshop were reading Bibles silently. Jimmy Swaggart was on a video monitor, preaching. I noticed a wall of videotapes available for rent to the church video-club members. One wall had the category "salvation." It was as I reached for a pink highlighter pen sold for highlighting Bibles, that I was frightened by the urge to steal it. Before coming to Zimbabwe, I never wanted to steal anything. What was happening to me? I enquired about the church and one of the young men made a phone call and then went upstairs to fetch an information sheet for me. I was impatient, and wanted to flee, but I waited. I noticed a wall of audiotapes that displayed music for church services. Another aisle of the bookshop offered Christian self-help books: two were written by Kenneth Copeland, the founder of the gospel of prosperity, from Orange County, California, where my research began. The books seemed ridiculously expensive for Zimbabweans (z$156 each. At the time of my research, z$10: US$1). The cashier returned. I paid for the pen. He wanted to talk, and asked me if I had ever attended the church. We chatted about the videos and how one went about becoming a member of the video rental club. I walked home to my apartment, as it was slowly getting dark. I felt claustrophobic as the pressure of conversion, along with the dusk, descended. This was once space of inquiry that would not leave me.

INSTITUTIONAL ETHNOGRAPHY IN NGO LANDSCAPES

The day I arrived to officially begin my fieldwork in Harare in 1996, World Vision's Africa office was completely deserted. I signed in with the guard, and noticed that the front reception area was closed. I stood listening to staff talking in the tea/kitchen area, not knowing what to do. I knocked but no one heard me. Finally, I caught the attention of a woman in a pink T-shirt and black jeans and requested to speak with someone that I had met on a visit the previous year. The woman told me to go upstairs, which was also deserted, in stark contrast to the year before when the office had been full and buzzing. It was disturbing. Things in the NGO world changed in quick cycles that mirrored fiscal trends. The whims and directives of donors determined the lives of NGO employees—whether a project would or would not be funded, whether there would or would not be staff, whether to shrink or expand an office. The woman I was looking for, a secretary, was upstairs, alone, in a big empty office. The office had been officially closed in late October, but a skeletal staff was kept on to see through the dismantlement. Donors did not want to fund middlemen, the secretary explained. They wanted their money to go directly to the people in need. It was true: who wanted to pay for bureaucracy? It was not as appealing in its urgency as a starving child, or a family in need. The secretary was hesitant when I said I wanted to interview her about the changes that World Vision's Africa regional office was going through, and she said she did not have the authority to speak. These were sensitive matters. Later, I learned that there had been an institutional drama. The dismantling of the Africa office was conducted by two men flown in from the United States who fired the staff and closed the office. It was so sensitive and political that the matter was taken to a Member of Parliament and it was almost debated in Parliament. No wonder the secretary was cautious. The hand of the state was even involved with the dismantlement of NGO activities. While I was sitting with the secretary, the financial director came in and handed her a letter. She read it and started laughing hysterically. The financial director was laughing too. It was her letter of termination.

Here today, gone tomorrow. I had chosen Harare as a site of research partly because organizations such as World Vision had multiple offices in the city: there was the Harare office and the Africa office, for example, each overseeing different aspects of the NGO. And in a year, the NGO had structurally re-constituted itself. The Africa office was becoming the Southern Africa Regional Office to be based in Johannesburg, losing its separate status. When I first began the project in 1994, the Africa office was in California and was packing up to move to Harare. During the time it took to organize funding for my research, the object of my study had changed completely. How does one go about studying organizations that pride themselves upon constant change, upon being responsive to urgent situations, and upon lacking a center? A transnational NGO has many loci, in forms that resemble tentacles of a Foucauldian capillary power, an apparatus with bureaucratic effects. Organizations such as transnational NGOs are simultaneously located in many places, and demand a multi-sited ethnographic approach (Marcus 1998). However, in the course of my fieldwork, even the conceptualization of multiple sites was inadequate. Some of the sites were not actual places. The "real" action did not take place at office sites, rural sites, donor offices, but in the relations between such spaces. The productive power of NGOs is in movement, as a conduit of resources, power, and ideas, often transforming and being transformed by those to whom communication is directed. In writing this ethnography I have been confronted continually with the challenge of representing the mutable and transient.

The foundation of my research became the morally laden landscapes that compelled me continually to rethink my own moral orientation, especially as I came to understand and respect the evangelistic fervor by which I was at first intrigued and even frightened. Attempts of informants and friends to convert me reinscribed my difference. I was other—a Jew, a member of a shared Judeo-Christian theological heritage, but not Christian. For Africans who had studied the theology of the Old Testament, I was recognizable. While many of my informants had never heard of (or met) a Jew, one field officer who was a former employee of WV Zimbabwe and employed by the secular NGO CARE at the time of my research went to great lengths to tell me how excited he was to meet me, his first Jewish acquaintance. He spoke of the affinity we shared. Jews had also struggled for a homeland. The superimposition of an identity that is assumed by others yet foreign to the ethnographer is a common enough aspect of field research. At times I was taken aback by it; at others I took advantage of slippages of identity. Nonetheless, my own spiritual identity became an increasingly important locus of comparison during fieldwork. As much as I, perhaps unrealistically, would have loved to be less "marked" as an outsider, my Jewish-ness (not-Christian-ness) provided a conceptual dimension to each interview: it was the relief that marked me as different, and endowed me with the potential to become Christian. My not-Christian-ness wove itself into my research as it oriented conversations and inspired heated discussions. Faith emerged as belief, as belonging, as personhood, as an internally defining membership in an external and transcendent group. The Family of God, for example, was a metaphor of kin that simultaneously rose above culture and developed roots (or, in missionary parlance, was "inculturated") to achieve local depth of meaning. The more time I spent learning to see the world through the dichotomous evangelistic categories of those who were converted and those who had yet to convert, the more I saw Christianity take a form that was not dichotomous. It was mutable and dynamic. The boundaries of what were sometimes described as discrete realms (of tradition and Christianity, for example) were continually being redrawn. Analogously, the boundary between the converted and the unconverted always had the potential to shift once someone was "born again."

When I first began conducting interviews in the California offices of World Vision, there was a distinct difference between the way "the field" (the project sites of Christian development for those in need) was described to me by those who had been there and by those who had not. Similar to the moralizing and naturalizing distinctions between "the country" and "the city" (Williams 1973) or between a modern Europe and the lost paradise of Africa for nineteenth-century missionaries (Comaroff and Comaroff 1991), employees of World Vision constructed the object of their aid, "the field," as a sacred place. When speaking with employees in the California office about World Vision's work, the conversation veered to sites of Christian development. When I broached the idea of researching World Vision's office with my initial contact, the director of Holistic Development Research in California, he was skeptical of my interest. Why would I want to speak with people in administrative offices? "They're not interesting, they're just accountants," he said. The conceptual interstice between the "office" and the "field" was vast. Each of the employees I spoke with in the California office who had worked in the field desired to return. The field was described to me as a truer place, closer to the poor and the needy. Those who had not been to the field dreamed of going, and those who had made trips to visit projects or children they had sponsored spoke fondly of the pilgrimage. Notably, the ability to travel reflected the position of the employee: all executives interviewed had been to the field, while none of the secretaries or support personnel had had the opportunity. An evaluation associate in WV USA's office who had worked for the company for 14 years expressed this general desire in a 1994 interview: "I am still struggling with wanting to get out in the field but haven't got too far."

The field as a site of engagement was revered in the United States office. Correlatively, the power of donors and international sponsors to direct projects was a focus in Zimbabwe. At each interview (whether in California, Harare, rural sites in Zimbabwe) I had the sense that the "real" and important work of the organization was happening somewhere else: at project sites, in the Bulawayo (southern Zimbabwe) or Mutare (eastern Zimbabwe) offices, in the lives of sponsors who gave money to the organizations to give to the poor, in donor offices such as WV Germany or WV USA, in the Geneva headquarters of the WCC or the United States headquarters of World Vision, or even in other country offices such as World Vision Zambia, or World Vision South Africa. The space of inquiry was lived in reference to elsewhere. The trajectory of research led me from administrators in California, to field officers in Harare, to "beneficiaries" at rural project sites. Meanwhile, my research took me in between, to the relationships and interconnectedness of sites, and to the imagined places of desire, possibility, and transformation that united them.

NGOs acquired their being in the becoming of everyday correspondence, progress reports, field-visits, and donations.

NGOs present specific ethnographic challenges (Riles 2000). The initial challenge was to get "in" to the NGO, and to receive permission to conduct research. Religion was not a trivial subject for Christian NGOs, and both Christian Care and World Vision considered my project seriously. With the permission of the director of WV Zimbabwe (who eventually gave his secretary the task of scheduling many of my interviews), I was "in." But how did I know I was in? The interviews that were arranged by the director had the aura of staff obligations. It was impossible for an employee to say no, and I suspected I was receiving a particular, director-sanctioned image of the institution. As time passed and I became more unremarkable in the hallways of the NGOs, I met new people, invited myself on field trips, and saw other sides of the NGOs. Research in offices meant that my "informants" had limited time for interviews, and discussions were put on hold for months until we met in hallways or at Friday devotions. With office doors closed and meetings scheduled, there was no central spot to sit and wait, to visit with elders, or to lounge over a meal. Some NGO staff were initially threatened by my presence and assumed I would either take their jobs or expose their poor performance. The power relations of studying multiple dimensions of an organization provoked a continual reassessment of my loyalties. No interview escaped the politics of loyalty. Was I going to report what was said to senior management, who had given me the go-ahead to conduct research? Were the donors to be alerted? Who were my subjects? Were they the beneficiaries, the employees, field workers, management? I traced this power that hailed me as one of "them." Elusive and implicit, it settled-in hierarchies and whispered through institutional reports. Power within NGOs determined who wrote reports on what, what categories were of use and thus documented, and which questions of accountability would propel the reports from the field to donor offices. Because many NGO workers were mobile, I was constantly reassessing the margins of my field site. The field, indeed a mythic place (Gupta and Ferguson 1997c), included travel in Toyota pick-up trucks to and from rural projects, offices, irrigation schemes and gardening cooperatives.

The most fertile research spaces were the intervals between physical destinations. When I got into a truck with a field officer and we were barreling down dirt roads without a notebook or a tape recorder, NGO staff told me what they really thought about the organizations they worked for: their bosses, the scandals, the injustices, and many things I promised never to write about. During these hours, rattled by poor roads, I heard the stories that did not fit into annual reports or project analyses. In Harare, as I poured through archives of annual reports, institutional histories, origin myths, I came to understand the partiality of such documentation. More often than not, people were missing from the confines of the reporting. Where was the religion? I would ask.

Such reports, presented to donors to account for expenditures, only reinforced the importance of money and fiscal flow in defining the NGO to "a public." Arteries of NGOs were the flow of financial resources that directed organizational decisions, but what NGO-life meant to those whose lives were affected was a different subject: it was the subject of my ethnography.

STRUCTURAL VULNERABILITY

In setting out to study NGOs ethnographically, I anticipated paying attention to the supra-national socio-economic circumstances that made humanitarian aid possible and necessary. I did not anticipate that my perception of the categories of those who give and those who receive would be altered by brief acts of violence. The first event was a theft that happened the first day it rained in late November 1996. It had been extremely hot, and the lack of rain had built up tension in Harare. Everyone I spoke with commented on the heat and lack of rain, looking at the sky with disappointment. No rain for the crops that fed the nation meant potential drought and hunger. With the rain came relief from the unrelenting dry heat. The rain was important for the rural areas, and for the Harare population that visited relatives in their rural homes weekly or monthly. Such were the porous boundaries between rural villages and Harare.

Since the theft, I have thought about the five men who mugged me, grabbing me from behind with such violence and desperation. I suppose, in retrospect (always in retrospect), if they had asked me for my money or my things—what I had in my bag that day: a month's rent, a tape recorder with fresh interviews, a notebook full of field notes, a love letter, my address book— I would have relinquished the objects without so much self-reflection. Perhaps, somewhere tucked away in my backpack was a corner of security, my sense of place. The event was destabilizing. People are mugged all the time all over the world. People are mugged in the United States, but I was mugged "in the field": the virtual and sacred space of research, where the emotions of the anthropologist are not to impinge on her observations. Was I not guilty as well? Stealing, or more politely borrowing—perhaps being given—the experiences of others for academic fruition? The men who mugged me made me reflect about the economy in Zimbabwe, about the "festive season" and how the pressure to give and receive at Christmas-time made crime rates soar in Harare. Watch out for *tsotsis* (thieves) during the holidays, I was told. The holiday season, November-December, just before the rains, was a dangerous time. My muggers (my informants) made me rethink need and desire. Perhaps through this disrupting occurrence I became emotionally invested in my topic. I was certainly hailed after the mugging as someone who needed care, a "victim," structurally vulnerable and in need of help. I was not alone even among the small cluster of foreign researchers that I had befriended: most of them had also been mugged. It was not just the experience of foreigners either. The father of the family I was living with at the time was pick-pocketed that same week. In Zimbabwe, desperation and poverty distinguished those who had objects to be stolen from those who longed for them. The incident propelled an intensity of emotion and shock that was to overflow the confines of my field notes; I was made a vulnerable observer (Behar 1996). Too vulnerable. The mugging took place only three weeks after my arrival in Zimbabwe. After being mugged, and due to a certain conspicuousness that I suddenly became aware of as a foreigner without transport (few white Zimbabweans walked on the street or took public transport), I moved from the northern suburbs of Harare where I was living with a family to an apartment building in downtown Harare filled with retired Rhodesians, wealthy black businessmen, and foreigners like me. Baines Avenue, a street lined with jacaranda and flame trees around the corner from President Mugabe's house, State House, was part of an urban neighborhood of hospitals and hotels. I joked about living in this elite neighborhood. Although I could walk to NGO offices from my flat and in this very way was in physical proximity to the NGOs I was studying, this was not a community in the strictest sense. It was an urban setting, a busy street, filled with the anonymity of city life (for similar urban research challenges see Ferguson 1999). Urban anthropology meant getting information from people who were not my informants: the young man at the photocopy shop who suffered gracefully through pages and pages of photocopies as machines broke down and lost toner, the Zimbabweans whom I met walking or waiting for public transport, ready to chat about politics or the weather. My Shona tutor, Lazarus, who patiently taught me a language that I used to make people laugh. "*Anogona kutaura chiShona!*" ("You can speak Shona!") people in the NGOs I was studying would shriek, while breaking into hysterics. The rural folks I met while observing field officer visits were less impressed by my Shona than were the NGO staff in Harare. Rural villagers were more accustomed to anthropologists who came in with field languages to polish, to stay awhile. I, in contrast, was attached to the Zimbabwean development workers, coming in and out for a week each month.

In a country like Zimbabwe with 70% of its population rural, the term urban anthropology is misleading. City life is lived in reference to the rural homes; people have families in rural areas. In Harare, a public holiday means the town is deserted. Everyone goes "home" to his or her village. The organizations I studied were based in cities, in Harare and in other countries from which funding was sourced. Still, the NGOs were oriented toward the rural areas, the project sites, the needy beneficiaries, and the poor. Rural poverty was the beacon for institutional directives. Humanitarian organizations were invested in helping the poor.

As the category of "informant" changed with my experiences of the street after my mugging, even the accounting for my research was shaped by phantom experiences of elsewhere. My stolen credit cards were used during the entire year, until I was able to cancel them. I followed the lives of my assailants as they bought clothes at department stores, filled their cars with petrol, took what must have been small villages out for meals at the fast food— and thus very fashionable—restaurant, Chicken Inn, and purchased fertilizer at the Farmer's Coop. My stepfather remarked that I was doing my part in helping the poor. The mugging experience began as a footnote, subterranean in my fieldwork as I tried to push it away. However, as a dramatic personal embarrassment it became deeply informative. In interviews I was prayed for as the victim. Mugging left its traces, and the incident shaped my vision and me. To NGO staff, I became more human, and in need, vulnerable. NGO staff members who had been cool or distant spoke with me more delicately. They felt sorry for me and I, destabilized, probably looked worse for the wear. The story of my mugging flowed through the NGOs, from directors to secretaries: "I heard about what happened to you" they would say, "Shame." To people on the street, and probably NGO workers as well, I had been a "have." And then, transformed by an incident, I was a victim, someone who needed otherworld-ly assistance, who needed luck and care. I was grateful that people took the time to care, that people prayed for me, that I was studying Christian organi-zations whose job it was to be caring.

The "caring" of NGO staff provided another perspective on the inti-mate "becoming" of born-again Christianity. Months after the mugging inci-dent, someone attempted to pickpocket me as I was walking to an interview. Again, I was rattled. Perhaps because of the early experience, I was jumpy as I walked down city streets, and when I felt someone pulling at my bag I grabbed behind me—clutching the hand unzipping my bag—and screamed. It was an intensely crowded downtown street the day before Zimbabwean Indepen-dence Day, and it seemed as if everyone in Harare was shopping for goods to bring to the rural areas for the holiday weekend. The thief acted irate and inno-cent, and yelled at me for accusing him. Soon I was apologizing for accusing him before scurrying to my interview with a senior staff member of Opportunity International, another Christian NGO in Harare. I arrived at my interview shaking and I recounted the incident to my informant. After the interview, which took on a very different character perhaps because of my obvious vulnerability and emotional crisis, my informant began to pray for me. The interview ended, officially, but we kept talking. He stopped and said he would pray for me, and bowed his head and started speaking to God on my behalf. I bowed my head as well. He asked God to protect me, as I was in a dif-ficult place where I could be exposed to forces that were new and could be harmful. He asked God to guide me, and prayed for ten minutes. I was shocked by his act of caring, touched, hailed, and unraveled again. After being prayed for in a moment of crisis, I had new empathy for Christian develop-ment, and an understanding of why one might convert. When confronted with spiritual and structural vulnerability, the personal contact and intensity of prayer was disarming. I was fused with the recipients of aid, if for a moment, no longer a wealthy foreigner; I was in a desperate situation, without hope, fearful and not knowing where to turn. The moment of crisis was immensely provocative, filled with the potential for new things, ideas, and influences. The hope offered in that moment of crisis carried with it the potential for embodiment that was appealing. Through a glimpse of the process of being prayed for, at first overwhelming, I resisted before receiving. I had carefully reified my identity as "not-Christian," Jewish, and thus different. Being prayed for presented a moment in which I was aware of the transformative potential of Christian faith and the power of what I had been "investigating." During previous interviews when I spoke of faith, of what it felt like, it had been safely abstract.

The comfort in Christianity, hope from crisis, was expressed by numerous people when I asked about their conversion experiences, and why they became Christians. There was a direct correlation in these explanations between well-being and living well. For example, one World Vision staff member, when asked what it meant for her to be Christian, explained the importance of the relation of faith to love. While this is something I have heard plenty of in the clichéd biblical references of popular American Christian literature, she went on to explain, "Christianity is personal." She described faith as "a warm feeling" —as an experience very much like love, involving safety, comfort, and well-being. Having much to do with interpreting "the good life," faith was a missing component in "living well." Development, even secular development, deployed this as its subtext. It was the undercurrent of humanitarian aid. Christianity in development discursively linked faith to love, to hope and success, to well-being, to peace of mind and body, and to a utopian absence of struggle. It identified conversion as a process, embodied in human form through the potential for transformation. Perhaps my being mugged was not so unusual an ethnographic event. Field research is like searching for anthropological truth-values through the land mines of people's understanding of the ethnographer. The constant threat of "mugging," of being robbed of one's precious possessions, of one's cultivated objectivity and guarded truths, informs and challenges the status of the anthropologist as pure observer. This real-world hermeneutics, this fusion of horizons, is more than a mere methodological tool: it becomes the only way to understand a phenomenon.

CHAPTER 2

Theologies of Development:
Faith, Holism, and Lifestyle
Evangelism

MOVING FROM THE PERSPECTIVE OF THE ETHNOGRAPHER TO THE ethnography itself, I now concentrate on faith and development as they intertwined for employees of World Vision and Christian Care. Faith framed NGO work in administrative offices where development was conceived and managed, and at rural project sites where development took place. Faith was such an important part of the work of the two NGOs that for some of the key actors involved, economic development was a religious act and a manifestation of Christian faith. The theological basis of Christian development[1] for World Vision and Christian Care is distinguished by two concepts: holism and lifestyle evangelism. I document how faith was lived and critically theorized in terms of these concepts by employees of the two NGOs. My analysis focuses on faith at rural project sites where evangelism appeared as a unifying and hopeful social force, and faith in NGO offices where it disciplined, at times with divisive effects, the personal and institutional conduct of life.

This chapter, and this book more generally, focuses on World Vision and Christian Care as sites where similar discourses of faith and development occur. While the two NGOs share a great deal in terms of Christian, humanitarian philosophy and overall objectives, such as the eradication of rural poverty, they have different histories and different Christian orientations. To summarize what I have discussed in the previous chapter, World Vision is a transnational, evangelical NGO that operates in 94 countries worldwide, including Zimbabwe. It was founded in the late 1940s in the United States and is funded primarily through child sponsorship, the practice whereby sponsors send monthly remittances toward the assistance of needy children. World Vision began its work in Zimbabwe in the mid 1970s, assisting orphans from the liberation struggle. Christian Care, in contrast, is the development arm of the

Zimbabwe Council of Churches (hereafter ZCC). Linked to the global ecumenical body the World Council of Churches, it began its work in Zimbabwe
assisting political detainees during the liberation war. Christian Care and
World Vision both work in collaboration with local churches and with the
Zimbabwean state. Christian faith is presented in a different hue in each
organization. While World Vision has specific corporate rituals that provide
structure for the faith of its employees and the recipients of its aid, Christian
Care's faith base is less formal, arising from structural linkages to local churches that constitute its membership and governing bodies. The structure of
Christian Care was in transition during my research, as churches were being
given renewed institutional power, and church leaders held positions on local
governing councils. Despite differences in history and orientation, Christianity
provided a dynamic rubric for development in both NGOs: faith was the frame
through which employee performance was evaluated, and through which
employees evaluated each other. Faith also provided the logic for the development work of the two NGOs.

LANDSCAPES OF THE POOR AND UNREACHED

The development work with which this book is concerned is Christian development. One premise of Christian development is that there are two categories of people: those who have been evangelized, and those who are unevangelized or unreached (who have not had the gospel preached to them). These
categories mirror those that divide the world into developed and undeveloped
groups of people (cf. categories of "development" in Ferguson 1994). I found
that for employees of World Vision (more than Christian Care), the world was
divided into two realms: evangelized/developed and unevangelized/undevel-
oped. It was through acts of development that the world could be reached,
touched, and transformed. This discourse is not unique to World Vision and
Christian Care. In the *World Christian Encyclopedia* (Barrett 1982; Barrett,
Kurian, and Johnson 2001),[2] charts and maps designate areas of the world
according to their exposure to Christianity (a spectrum of "evangelized" to
"unevangelized") and their degree of "human need."[3] This encyclopedia, frequently cited to emphasize the shift in global Christianity from Europe to the
rest of the world, documented more than 300 million Christians in Africa in
year 2000, and anticipates over 600 million by the year 2025 (Barrett 2001:12).[4]
Thus in the work of faith-based NGOs, the landscape of need is determined
through a synthesis of relative development and exposure to Christianity.[5]

Addressing this dual need, religious and socioeconomic, spiritual and
material, is what World Vision calls "holistic development," a concept I will
address in detail below.[6] Links between spiritual and material poverty were
actively theorized by employees of World Vision and Christian Care (and
ZCC). For example, a senior researcher at WV International published a call

to action for Christian development workers in the journal *Missiology*[7] (Brandt 1995). The article provided guidelines for Christian development agencies working with the "physically and spiritually poor," to distinguish between economic and spiritual poverty. Brandt explained that although Christian agencies served the poor "through deeds of compassion expressed in development and relief programs," he asked if these activities were "distinctively Christian." Noting that the alleviation of material poverty is also a goal of secular organizations, he articulated the difference between secular and faith-based development as being one of motivation. Key to his argument were the emulation of Jesus Christ in processes of development by development workers, and the attention to spiritual as well as material poverty. Brandt argued:

> It is fair to say that a Christian development agency tries to emulate Jesus Christ. He brought people to the kingdom of God by meeting their pressing needs. Many needs of the poor around him were physical, such as illness and hunger. A different kind of need, found in all income groups, was spiritual poverty. We believe that a prerequisite to entrance into the kingdom of God was—and still is—the admission that we are spiritually poor (repentance). (1995:260)

Integral to both Brandt's article and the work of Christian Care and World Vision is that working with the "poorest of the poor" requires an attention to poverty that is both material and spiritual. Brandt's conception of poverty adds the dimension of "spiritual deprivation" to a common secular list of five development indices: powerlessness, vulnerability, bodily weakness, financial insolvency (material poverty), and social isolation (Chambers 1983 cited in Brandt). Such depictions of poverty frame development for World Vision and Christian Care. bringing development to the poor is a Christian act that involves the body and the spirit.

Economic development, when linked to Christianity, engages theologies of religious and economic salvation. In fact, there is a body of missiological literature on this topic (Bradshaw 1993; Elliston 1989; Lingenfelter 1992; Verstraelen et al. 1995; Yamamori et al. 1996). The attention placed upon this-worldly problems by salvation religions such as Christianity tends to provoke an aggressive, sometimes revolutionary urge to transform the world, and the concept of a "Christian approach" to economic development has been discussed widely in missiological circles as a cross-cultural approach to conversion that utilizes development (Balleis S.J 1992; Bradshaw 1993; Elliston 1989; Miller 1989; O'Gorman 1992. See also the journals *Missiology* and the *International Bulletin of Missionary Research*). Possibly because of the dogmatic tone and evangelizing aims of missiology, secular academics tend to dismiss theological approaches (a notable exception is Van Ufford and Schoffeleers 1988; for debates between missiologists and anthropologists see van der Geest 1990; Bonsen, Marsks, and Miedema 1990; Stipe 1980). The purpose of taking missiology seriously in the context of this research is not to reinforce the evangelizing endeavor, but to acknowledge that this literature can explicate some of the theories of development articulated in the institutional missions of World Vision and Christian Care. For missiologists and employees of World Vision and Christian Care, economic development presumes a religious calling to serve the poor (Yamamori et al. 1996). Justice and morality offer an ontological connection between religious doctrine and vernacular practice. Some scholars have gone so far as to argue for a "theology of development" (Gundani 1988:243; others have tackled the topic directly: Phiri, Ross, and Cox 1996).

NGO THEOLOGIES OF HOLISM AND LIFESTYLE EVANGELISM

Holism

Articulated explicitly in the work of World Vision (and implicit in the work of Christian Care) was the idea of holistic development. World Vision International espoused a "holistic" approach that "bridged the gaps" between the spiritual and material worlds, and between the rich and the poor (Bradshaw 1993). By presenting Christ alongside boreholes and irrigation schemes, World Vision provided a moral, and Christian, interpretation of economic transformation. Economic development served a dual purpose: to introduce Christian beliefs to individuals, and to "redeem" the earth's "God-given potential." Redemption, another key concept, was defined as "restoring the elements of creation to fulfill the purposes for which God created them" (1993:16). Material improvements had the potential to be explained as gifts from God, making development work "intrinsically evangelistic" (1993:41) and economics "intrinsically spiritual" (1993:116). As economic development merged with the religious transformation of cultures, it entailed, and enabled, spiritual conversion. Bradshaw, an employee of the Research and Development department of World Vision International at the time of this research, emphasizes that development projects were interpreted according to what he calls "worldviews" (1993; cf. Hiebert 1994). Even when not overtly Christian, processes of development were intended to change belief systems and practices, whether in relation to God or technological improvement. The development work of World Vision argued for the integration of economic and religious beliefs. In the work of World Vision, improved material conditions described in the phrase "good living" (i.e., a better standard of life) were directly related to "good living" in the sense of virtue and adherence to a Christian doctrine.

Zimbabwean employees of World Vision also described their efforts as "holistic," combining spiritual and material transformation. One of WV Zimbabwe's associate directors (responsible for coordinating local fundraising and overseeing the sustainability of development programs) said, "Holistic [development] in our sense is that we want to change the situation there from the social point of view, economical point of view, and spiritual point of view." Such integrated, or holistic, development is an expression of evangelical holism, in which religion concerns itself with all aspects of life (Pieterse 1992:18). Evangelical holism posits that it is God who "provided the soil" for development or who "is going to help us to prosper" through development activities. For example, the Director of Sponsorship Ministry and Funding (WV USA) explained to me in 1994: "We are planting this seed. We will water it, or the rain is going to water it, but ultimately God is responsible for bringing it up. You see you can bring scripture even into everyday life; that's the whole essence of integrated Christian development." In the "gap" of causality, between the seed and the sprout, is located the world of faith. By tethering spiritual and material transformation, he continued, " . . . even where you are not necessarily buying a Bible for somebody but . . . buying seeds, you are introducing God, and saying how God can be involved in that situation." In the eyes of many World Vision employees, part of change in a community included a Christian, spiritual interpretation: as rural communities saw their crop production improved, they saw God involved in the process.

In African Christian faith, the realms of the spiritual and material cannot easily be separated: development is both spiritual and material.[8] For religious NGOs as well,[9] holistic development was the preferred solution to any problem: it aimed not solely to take care of people's material needs, but also to feed them spiritually. It was precisely in this manner that humanitarian practices of economic development were connected to religious ideas. As compared to missionaries of earlier eras who strove to save people from savagery, World Vision and Christian Care workers strove to save people from poverty. For World Vision and Christian Care, economic development was a primary objective, yet development applied to the whole person: the full human, material and spiritual. The Secretary General of the Zimbabwe Council of Churches (ZCC) stated that there was little difference between material and spiritual development. He explained that development did not necessarily mean physical development, as it could include going to school to develop one's mental capacity as well as putting in an irrigation system to develop one's capacity to feed oneself. He saw the two "capacities" as being difficult to split apart. The Director of the Church and Society program of ZCC, a woman who had been working for ZCC since independence in 1980 (17 years at the time of our interview) also found it difficult to distinguish between development and evangelism, which was a problem when donors sought to finance development exclusively and not fund evangelistic activities. Some donors sponsoring ZCC's development programs said they would not fund mission and evangelism. She ruminated on how difficult it was to distinguish where one started with evangelism as a conversion idiom (building faith) from the development work that included the ability to make material choices. She said, "If development does not have to do with confidence, making choices, and values, then I don't know what development is." In her view, the work of the postcolonial church was to "engage in a sustained effort to bring total salvation for all and the total elimination of poverty." The church, she said, should promote what she called "abundant life" through development. Abundant life meant moving towards "self-actualization and sustainable development." It involved salvation from poverty. She believed that one of the most significant declarations Jesus Christ made was, "I came that they may have life, and life in its fullness." ZCC strove to bring this abundant life, "quality life," to its constituency through development. It was through development that teaching abundant life was possible: "What do we teach?" she asked. "The Word and that which enables abundant life to happen, and that is development." Through the concept of holistic development, spiritual and material poverty could be supplanted by a rewarding Christian life. This brings us to the next concept, "lifestyle evangelism."

Lifestyle Evangelism

For World Vision and Christian Care, evangelism merged with development via a process that I call "lifestyle evangelism." The Director of Human Resources for Africa, a Ghanaian, explained in a 1994 interview in Monrovia, California that evangelism involved living a life in the manner of Christ, and providing an example for non-believers. In order to do this, field workers for World Vision should:

> Establish cordial relationships with the village folks, you know, come down to their level, do so because Christ did that. Christ did not, as it were, impose. Christ came down to the level of the people, and was like them so that our people spend time in the community, live in houses that are provided by the people . . . through what I've said, their lifestyle, showing love to these people, building relationships with them. Building relationships, which will serve as a bridge to bring them over to your side, just loving them. It's not terribly easy to love some of those people, because they are so set in their ways sometimes.

Living a Christian life was key to the success of lifestyle evangelism. The assistant to the director for WV Zimbabwe described how evangelizing was done through the example of handling people in a Christian manner. Faith, he clarified, was not an appendage: it was an aspect of development that framed the work done. It was an attitude or an approach. I asked him one afternoon over tea in his office in Harare how World Vision differed from other organizations, and he explained that it was the way World Vision employees interacted with the people they served. Such questions were asked inside the NGO as well:

"What makes a borehole drilled by World Vision different from a borehole drilled by any other organization?" He responded to his own rhetorical question, of how different World Vision was from other development agencies, with what he saw to be the core of World Vision's mission: "to follow Jesus Christ and to encourage others to follow him—whether it's in the drilling of a borehole, we can relate that to scripture and we can also challenge people to follow Jesus in that way."

A project coordinator for Christian Care also spoke in these terms. Although Christian Care was not an evangelistic organization per se (it identified itself as ecumenical, and as the development arm of ZCC it left the evangelizing to its member churches), she said that the organization being Christian made a difference in the way she approached her work, that a healthy community had a healthy mind and spirit. Development brought NGOs into communities and in so doing the communities identified with the NGOs. The process of identifying with communities, of becoming part of them, was the first step in gaining their trust in development, and in change. She felt that she became part of the communities as she assisted them and in this way shared the Christian aspect of the NGO. Faith entered her work every day: "Before I even go out into the field, I put everything before God because it is his work that I am doing. It is not my work, not Christian Care's work." It was God's work. She believed that if she identified development with Christian Care instead of with God, people would fail to realize that "salvation is brought about by development activities." She thought impoverished communities, desperate for survival and not knowing where to turn, could see the assistance of an NGO as an answer to their prayers. Development was thus a form of salvation.

There was a practical aspect to conflating Christianity with development according to the logic of World Vision and Christian Care. If one established economic infrastructure without a spiritual basis, there was a danger of it falling apart, especially if household heads did not have a Christian background. If, for example, they spent all the money earned through development on drinking beer, or to acquire another wife (very un-Christian activities), development would not move forward. Here, non-Christian beliefs were seen as interfering with the progress of development, much as Weber considered non-Protestant cultures less suited for capitalist endeavor. The alternative was to "go in with the Christian concept" and change such behavior. A regional project manager for WV Zimbabwe explained that "you are not going in there with sort of a harsh edge to say 'you should do this, you should do that,' but through the way you do things, people transform and they see things in a different light." When World Vision went into an area where people were polygamous, they did not castigate people. Instead, they talked to them in such a way that they could see the "benefits of Christian development." It was a process that often took years to show results. She saw the Christian aspect of

World Vision as something that made its work particularly effective. Although Christianity was a guiding principle and even a motivation, it did not exclude non-Christians from participating in development; in fact, quite the opposite. The regional project manager explained:

When we go into a community, we don't assist them on the basis that they have to be Christian first. That is not a condition. So they don't have to please us for anything because whatever they are, we are there to assist them. We only encourage them to be Christian but we don't sort of decide whether to support if they are not Christian. When we go into communities we are not looking how Christian they are. In actual fact we would prefer a situation where there is no Christianity at all and we are introducing it instead of going into a community where they already know [about Christianity].

Since in Zimbabwe many people were already Christian, I wondered why so much importance was placed on the introduction of Christianity. She explained that although some had had exposure to the faith, it was not deep or long-term exposure. Many of World Vision and Christian Care's rural development projects were placed on the periphery of Zimbabwe. Located in "remote" regions with the poorest soil and the most "backwards" people (the unreached and the underdeveloped), these areas did not have mission schools, and villagers were illiterate; if they had heard of Christianity, they could not read the Bible.

I wanted to know how this worked in practice. While visiting some of World Vision's peri-urban projects, I spoke with a field officer who saw Jesus as a model for his work. He had seen thousands of people convert. "People are stranded," he said. "The world is growing and we can't reach all the corners. We are looking for thousands of people to become born-again Christians through this approach." Instead of providing access to Christianity through preaching or publishing Bibles, World Vision employees introduced Christianity through a style of life encompassing material and religious ideals embodied in development. The Director of Mission and Evangelism (WV USA) described the ability to convert as a quality of the World Vision staff in an interview in 1994. He spoke of their ability to make themselves vulnerable and "transparent":

It's the way we love, the way we care, the way we are ourselves and people get to know us, a certain degree of transparency in us. A lot of our workers live with people in the villages. . . . Their lives are open so that becomes almost like, they become a witness for the kind of life that God wants us to live. A life of truthfulness, a life of love, a life of service, so we emphasize a lot this lifestyle as a powerful tool for Christian witnessing. We have coined a kind of a phrase that is: live a life to provoke questions for which the gospel becomes the answer.

The Director of Unreached Peoples (WV USA) explained that "giving a wit-ness" (evangelizing) was a matter of identity, and was integral to who the employees were and how they behaved. Key to the process was the ability to respond to the questions "How come you love us?" and "How come you serve us?" with the response, "Well, God cares about you. God loves you, and Jesus has sent us here. We're serving him and we want to serve you." The Director of Gifts in Kind (1994, WV USA; an Ethiopian and the former director of WV Ethiopia) also affirmed that "Christianity is a life." Proclaimed by deed and not by word, it was embedded in all social processes and interactions as well as embodied in all objects of the material world. Christianity was delivered through the process of identifying oneself with the recipients of aid. He said:

The power of love cannot be underestimated. You are actually identifying yourself with them. And people are very intelligent, and dignified. They start asking why, even while you are doing, patching their wounds and clothing their backs, they say why is he or why is she doing this? They don't know me, why are they doing this? They start examining, they start researching on their own, asking questions, and they come to the point of conviction to accept or not to accept what you do, and that is one of the ways we deliver Christianity.

A distinctive component of the work of World Vision and Christian Care was the long-term scope of their projects. Often beginning with emergency relief and transitioning to economic development, the process of completing such projects often took place over many years. This afforded workers the opportu-nity to evangelize by lifestyle. The director of Sponsorship, Ministry, and Funding (WV USA, 1994) explained:

Many organizations will come and drop things and go away. But we live with them, and we share our lives with them, and learn from them. So that by seeing our lives they begin to ask questions . . . and when they begin to ask questions that's when you witness . . . the pressure now is on you as a development facilitator to lead a Christian life, to demonstrate Christ working in your life. They'll interpret Christ by your life . . . I look at myself as an employee of World Vision, but at the same time, I look at myself as an employee of the Lord, an ambassador of the Lord. Because I'm going there not only in the name of World Vision but in the name of Christ because our desire is for those people to come to Christ.

Holism and lifestyle evangelism were two concepts through which the faith-based development of World Vision and Christian Care was articulated. In institutional directives, and in the way these directives were interpreted and carried out by employees, Christianity was incorporated into the development objectives of the NGOs. Faith became motivation and meaning for the development work, providing logic for its expression.

FAITH AT RURAL PROJECT SITES: EVANGELISM UNITES

If, through lifestyle evangelism, employees of religious NGOs sought to minister through their deeds, what did this mean for communities participating in development projects? Moreover, how did the Christian objectives of Christian Care and World Vision interface with the non-Christian beliefs (termed "traditional" by NGO employees) of rural villagers? While staff attitudes toward "non-Christian" beliefs varied widely within each NGO, in general, the relationship between "traditional" religion and Christianity was fluid and accepting. For example, the Director of the Church and Development program of ZCC explained that ZCC acknowledged traditional religion. Placed in the category of "culture," traditional beliefs were aspects of faith to be integrated into Christian ways of life. The staff of ZCC acknowledged that beliefs besides Christianity existed simultaneously with Christian beliefs. Some of ZCC's member churches were more vocal than others regarding speaking out against traditional religion. Some member churches of ZCC went to the extent of saying "you cannot be a true believer in Christian religion if you have not put things right among your own people." In the "field" of development, the engagement with faith did not refer solely to Christian faith. The Director of Church and Development for ZCC explained that ZCC recognized the existence of faith in traditional practices and did not violate these practices; instead, they were respected. "The last thing we want to do is to antagonize the people we are trying to work with," she said. This involved respecting restrictions that traditional faith placed on drilling boreholes in certain sites. This approach differed from that of "technical people," who harnessed water and sunk boreholes without consulting the community about ancestral restrictions. Cultural sensitivity may be an idealized focus for development practitioners, secular and religious alike. However, Christian Care and World Vision went one-step further and used faith to enter into a dialogue with the spiritual beliefs of the community. Faith was part of the interpretation of development and development was an act of faith. The director of Church and Development for ZCC (mentioned above) articulated the vision that ZCC had for relating faith to development as follows:

> We are talking about the goodness of today's church, which is not only concerned about the gospel as it is spoken but the gospel as it is acted. . . .
> Sometimes we minister to people more by what we do than what we say.

So, we are different in that the church has been known to speak, and speak, but we are acting. We are saying we are also an active church, a doing church. We are showing a different kind of ministry and of course if we can win more souls the better, through the water. It doesn't make someone a worse person by believing in Jesus Christ.

At rural project sites, the link between spreading faith and introducing development was formalized. Christian Care worked with local churches and World Vision appointed an evangelism committee at development project sites (this committee was a subset of the local management committee that oversaw each development project). In 1996-97, I met with members of evangelism and development committees at rural sites to discuss faith and evangelism in development. What emerged were two distinct consequences: the empowerment of women (cf. Maxwell 1999) and the unity of churches. Regarding the empowerment of women, at one project, women on World Vision's evangelism committee had been trained to evangelize. Each of the fifteen members was taught how to preach, to keep time, and to relate to other people (as in colonial timekeeping and evangelism, Comaroff 1991). The evangelism committee was also concerned with the more material aspects of development. They made sure that members of each denomination participated in development projects, bringing bricks, water, and river sand for the construction of school blocks. The women of the evangelism committee spoke of how they were happy to have been trained as evangelists. At the time of our discussion, they were teaching churches to tithe and distributing Bibles to families in the community. Women such as these on the evangelism committee populated rural Zimbabwe while their husbands and sons labored as migrant workers in neighboring cities. Their training had empowered them to speak, to preach, and to make arguments. These were the very types of empowerment that development espoused.

The second consequence was a growing unity between churches, which rural project communities attributed to development aid. At another of World Vision's projects in southeastern Zimbabwe (Chipinge area), I attended a community meeting. The project, ten years in scope, was in its third year of support from World Vision, funded by a donor office in Hong Kong. For this project, as with all projects, there was a separate budget for what they called "Christian witnessing," including an annual all-night revival. The evangelism committee consisted of two representatives from each local church and facilitated the involvement of churches in development. This project included the building of school blocks, houses for primary school teachers, and pit-latrines. Future development goals included the procurement of piped drinking water (there were boreholes, but no piped water) and assisting children who were unable to meet their school fees. While these were typical development objectives, the types found in secular and faith-based NGOs alike, other development objectives included the encouragement of Christian leadership in the community. To reach this goal, churches conducted meetings and seminars. The bookkeeper was animated about changes thus far: "There are so many changes. As from previous years, Christianity was in a backward state. Elders believed in what was done previously in old ages but now the people going to churches are doubling from previous numbers." The most significant change in this community since working with World Vision had been the movement to bring people from different denominations together. This was repeatedly emphasized when I inquired about WV Zimbabwe's evangelistic work at projects I visited. A project clerk explained that there was a movement to unite local churches, saying, "We are here for one God." The annual revivals brought the churches together. He explained,

> There was a separation before. Different denominations had never met, but World Vision has gathered them together from evening to sunset; it is the only place gathering together. Now there is communication of churches. People come together as a result of the Christian witnessing. People used not to eat each other's food. Now, because of Christian witnessing, they eat together.

Utopian perhaps, these statements were presented to me as the fruits of World Vision's efforts in the field. Notably, I was considered a part of WV Zimbabwe by the communities we visited. In my discussions at rural projects, World Vision emerged as facilitating a Christian, trans-denominational community. The chairman of one development committee told me that "people have to be united together by the gospel for any development to succeed." During this group interview the bookkeeper added his opinion, that development was Christianity:

> Development itself, as far as I am concerned, is Christianity itself. People understand when [it comes to] project issues—people leave their homes and children to help. It is a sign of love. There is less vandalism and more cooperation and it shows Christianity is part of development.

In addition, this bookkeeper believed the growth of churches and schools encouraged people to live in a certain way, a Christian way. It encouraged people not to steal, and this was related to the development of the mind.

> Christianity develops the mind of a person to see things differently. Since I was born, I have never seen different denominations worshiping together. World Vision is bringing churches together. People used to say, 'That is a church of witches.' Now we have a changed mind. Fear of the other is

lessened; we sit together and eat together. I am not just talking of buildings like this, or water points. I am talking of the development of the mind.

The entwinement of Christianity with development brought members of
churches together: it was a unifying force. The evangelism efforts to unite
churches had expanded the boundaries of the above community, and as a
result, there was more freedom to visit neighboring communities because of
alliances that had been forged between churches during evangelism rallies. At
another project an elderly woman explained, "The coming together of churches is a unity that came into being through World Vision. It used to never happen in the past, and has enhanced development in this area: to construct a
school by working together. We worship one God and read the same Bible."
The act of working together in development did not exclude those who were
not Christian. World Vision was involved in developing the whole community,
as one member explained:

> There is nothing as difficult as making people from different beliefs work
> together—Christian and non-Christian. It is possible here because World
> Vision didn't say they want [only] Christians. They develop the whole com-
> munity and managed to bring the link between the two groups. The com-
> ing of World Vision and the way they introduced the project didn't dis-
> criminate, and [it] helped to develop minds. Even drunkards could be
> assisted by a Christian because of this unity. That it could help everyone.
> They brought a change in attitudes. People make mistakes but people
> understand and people have to come together and work together,
> Christian and non-Christian.

There were challenges to evangelism as well. At many project sites,
there was no formal place of worship and this was considered a significant
problem. The chairman of one project thought the evangelism committee
lacked "adequate knowledge of the Bible" and organizational skills. In this
community, the only member who possessed such skills was an old, blind,
evangelist, who himself articulated a need for organizational training, for workshops in outreach skills, and for direction in how to evangelize. This elderly
man was sent to the community by the American Board Mission in 1943 and
he had since made his home there. He perceived prayer to be one of the most
significant challenges to faith in development. Although people had converted,
some would "backslide." This position was a contrast to the more flexible attitude, described earlier in this chapter, held by NGO employees toward
respecting non-Christian beliefs. Some churches did not believe that other
churches worshiped a true God and they distanced themselves from them.
There was always more work to do in providing unity between churches.

Overall, however, at rural sites evangelism was presented to me as a positive force accompanying the benefits of development. During interviews with development committees, the subject of evangelism would mercurially shift from the challenges of faith to the more material challenges of development, such as the problems of planning projects during the farming season when people were too busy to mobilize and to participate in development schemes. At one meeting (and in one sentence), a man spoke of religious challenges and then complained about the lack of implements for development, and of a lack of transport to the neighboring town where such implements could be found. A woman added her frustration with the lack of tillage facilities and with not having draught power or tractors. She told of how the services of tractors were offered at unfair prices, how government tractors did not exist in this area, and how the local government representative, the Councilor, was not responsive to communication. At rural development projects faith was an idealistic, hopeful, and unifying component of development. It also had material aspects: constructing places of worship and building church leadership. These earthly manifestations of evangelism existed in tandem with what might be considered secular objectives of development: the construction of schools, clean water facilities, and pit-latrines. Both Christianity and economic development were discussed together, as intersecting aspects of change in rural communities.

FAITH IN NGO OFFICES: PRAYER DISCIPLINES

If people in rural projects saw faith and evangelism as unifying and hopeful, faith and evangelism in development meant something quite different in the Harare offices of World Vision and Christian Care. In the office settings, faith became a moral standard by which employees judged each other. As much as faith framed the day-to-day work worlds of NGO employees, the language of faith became a disciplinary tool. Theoretically, it is imperative to reiterate how faith in this context is an action. Faith as such is also a language, a speech act, and a discourse (Gal 1989). As a discourse, faith is much more than a mere description of an act. Faith is not a reflection of power relations; faith is itself a form of power.

In World Vision (and to a much lesser degree, in Christian Care), employees were evaluated on their faith. Faith consisted of expectations, markers and codes of Christian organizational behavior. Through this economy of signs, power, in the language of faith, was expressed through the implicit and unequal political locations of the speakers and listeners. Empowerment arose in the act of conversion as one ceased to be the subject of conversion. In this evangelical context, through conversion one acquired access to power, to Jesus, and to religious ideas first-hand, instead of through an evangelist/interlocutor. In this sense, converting became an act of discursive power. The language of faith structured the possible field of behavior. As the power of the faithful was the power to make others into different subjects, employees of religious NGOs (as evangelists of development and Christianity) had the power to "transform" others into believers. Those who were developed and evangelized embodied this discursive power and possessed the potential to change lives. Power, for employees of World Vision and Christian Care, existed in this transformation, in the power of faith and its implicit potential of transformation. To have faith was to take on discursive power, the power to categorize the world, to claim it, to conquer and colonize, even if it was over the person sitting at the next desk. Perhaps this echoed the missionary power of earlier eras (cf. colonization of consciousness, Comaroff and Comaroff 1991). Faith, in the work of World Vision and Christian Care, meant access to the power of transformation, material and transcendental; it was expressed through prayer.

Institutionally, World Vision strove to assure adherence to a Christian philosophy by having all employees sign a "statement of faith" as a part of their employment contract. The statement declared their shared beliefs as Christians from members of many churches. Although World Vision hired employees of all denominations, the Human Relations Officer for Africa, a Ghanaian woman, explained during an interview in California in 1994 how important it was for all employees in the field to be born-again Christians. The hiring practices were crucial for upholding World Vision's mission for a ministry that was "lived" and not legislated. She stated this concern in relation to human resources. She sought to hire people who had accepted Christ as their savior and who were committed to living out their commitments to Christ on a day-to-day basis in the field. She said:

> When you go into the field, World Vision in the field doesn't operate like a church. It's just that we are doing our work. We want the people through the way we relate to them, you know, and how we talk to them, and through I mean our expression of faith, to see Christ in us. So if we are not able to bring on board those types of people, then we are defeating our purpose. Because we don't mount platforms and try to evangelize that way. We want to do so through our lives.

In addition to the importance of hiring "committed Christians," which was a crucial aspect of lifestyle evangelism, prayer structured mandatory organizational forums. In Harare, prayer meetings called "devotions" were held every morning. Prayer functioned in the corporate structure as ritual reinforcement of a World Vision community, linking employees to each other, and the corporate office to the activities of the field. Devotions, sometimes including guest speakers, were a weekly institutional focal point, reflecting and shaping NGO community life. At the beginning of each fiscal year, an Annual Day of Prayer was held in each office, including national offices in countries where projects were situated.

The role of prayer was taken seriously by WV International. It was included in its corporate origin-myth: of the founder, Bob Pierce, and how "World Vision started through prayer."[10] A monthly "Prayer Guide" was printed, listing a different country to be prayed for each day and details as to what should be prayed for. The prayer focus was on World Vision internationally; for example: "Zambia: Pray for World Vision Zambia as they go through a leadership transition" (August 31, 1994), or economic events: "Brazil: Pray that the government's efforts in launching a new currency after long term inflation will be helpful for the nation and especially the underprivileged" (August 26, 1994). In addition to daily devotions, Fridays consisted of devotions that broke into departmentally clustered staff meetings (in World Vision in both the USA and Zimbabwe). In each office, prayer formed an integral aspect of corporate order, one in which an inspirational atmosphere could be maintained, and problems and concerns could be aired.[11]

In Zimbabwe, the assistant to the national director of WV Zimbabwe described prayer as an important part of faith in the organization, something that brought people together and transcended the workday world of duties and responsibilities. It created a community in which employees were concerned about each other and depended on prayer. He explained:

> We are always praying for each other. Praying even for major decisions, praying for water to be found, or for resources to be found and things like that. So you are not just using prayer but you are saying, 'We are dependent upon prayer.' And I think the founder of this organization was a man of prayer and he at one time did not have money for salaries and he would pray and money for salaries would come.

He had been told that even staff members that had left the NGO said they missed the devotions held each morning before work. Sometimes there were lunchtime prayer meetings, and if a staff member was ill, the staff prayed for the ill member and at times even went to his home or to the hospital to pray. The theme of the Christian family perpetuated this practice: "we try to say we are a Christian family and we want to demonstrate that Christian faith." The Regional Manager of Field Operations also enjoyed this aspect of working for a Christian NGO. She thought that the daily devotions helped staff to prepare for the day ahead, in contrast to the situation at her previous job with the Government of Zimbabwe in the Department of Rural Development. Moreover, as topics from the Bible were discussed in devotions, differences could be resolved amicably. At WV Zimbabwe, daily devotions were structured in staff working groups and focused on themes, like an elaborately organized Bible study. On Fridays, the staff came together for larger and more formal devotions, often with guest speakers, and the devotions turned into staff meetings.

For employees of World Vision and Christian Care, there was an under-lying pressure to be faithful at work. The Christian context of employment could simultaneously provide a supportive "Christian family" atmosphere and offer tensions of faith when others were not behaving "as Christians." Such tensions led to accusations of hypocrisy, and a loss of faith in the organization (although they did not seem to threaten an individual's personal faith). The administrative secretary for Christian Care, a woman in her late 40s, explained how she relied upon her Christian faith to help her face her daily responsibil-ities. She believed that the fact that Christian Care was a Christian organiza-tion manifested itself in her daily job in the way she approached the people Christian Care was set up to serve. Most people I met who worked for Christian Care in Zimbabwe considered themselves "committed to the Lord." This commitment, as with World Vision, was evident in the weekly staff devo-tions every Monday morning, sometimes conducted with pastors from various member churches. Coming together as a group was good for her, "because that's the time we have the opportunity to brief the staff on what is happening in the organization. If there are some people who are not well, if there are some prayers from other people, those announcements are made on Monday morning. If the director has anything to inform the staff, that is when we are informed." As a combined prayer and staff meeting, devotions structured the life of the NGO.

In addition to more institutionally based moral imperatives of Christianity in World Vision and Christian Care, the personal faith of employ-ees emerged in dialogue with NGO theology. Working for a Christian NGO, for Christians, involved a constant translation between the expectations of the institution, defined according to codified Christian principles that directed the work of the NGO, and the religious expectations of its employees. As employ-ees were identified as Christians, they performed as such, and, dialectically, the employees also evaluated the performance of those that did the categorizing. Christian employees evaluated the work of the NGO—and of other employees within the institution—in terms of their own faith, judging, measuring, accept-ing, and sometimes rejecting the actions and imperatives of the NGO. The administrative secretary of Christian Care, for example, spoke emphatically of how faith entered her job in relation to the work of others employed by the NGO. Her belief in God helped her to cope with the people she met each day. However, about other staff she was critical. She discussed how people from the streets of Harare came to Christian Care's offices in search of donations of clothes or food (Christian Care has at times operated as a relief as well as a development organization). She was critical of how her colleagues reacted to the "destitutes"; she accused them of hiding from the destitutes and of being afraid. In contrast to the weakness and lack of faith of her colleagues, she attributed her own strength in the face of destitutes to her belief in the Lord. She said, "Honestly, you have to be dedicated to the Lord and ask every morning when you come that 'Oh Lord, what I'm going to meet today, please be with me.'"

For others, Christianity was a subtle presence in their NGO work. A project coordinator for World Vision, who had worked for the Government of Zimbabwe as an agricultural extension officer (Agritex) before working for WV Zimbabwe, felt that in the secular world, one could not see the subtleness of Christianity, that Christianity was "subtle the way it affects people's lives. It's not that visible. But you will see that it's definitely different where you are approaching people from any other background and where you are approaching people using a Christian background." She believed that Christians were more committed to what they were doing and had "good characters." Because Christian Care was a Christian NGO, she thought people they worked with in communities "would try to be sober for whatever they are doing and they would respect you." It was an earned respect because "when you say,' I am a Christian,' it makes a difference in that people respect you." This respect stemmed from the assumption that as a Christian, one had integrity and empathy: "they know that you have definite feelings for them. You are not just trying to make them work or trying to see your job done, but you have a certain feeling for them, and if they approach you with a certain problem you might be able to appreciate that problem from a Christian perspective, to say, 'this is a person who was created in God's own image.'" Faith also appeared in her job as she negotiated relationships between colleagues and superiors. She thought that she could converse well with others because of her faith, that it helped her to solve problems.

Faith in World Vision and Christian Care was monitored. At WV Zimbabwe there was a staff member hired and appointed to supervise the role of faith in staff relationships, called the Christian Witness Coordinator, whose presence differentiated this NGO from Christian Care. This intensive attention to the act of witnessing and the role of faith in the daily work world of the institution was something that was structurally initiated by World Vision, with a formal position held by a Methodist minister. It was the Christian Witness Coordinator's responsibility to use weekly devotions to focus the theology of the organization, offering monthly themes for reflection as a guide for employees in approaching their jobs. The themes for devotions in 1997 included: "Humility, Patience or Perseverance, Hope, Obedience, Relationships, Joy, Spiritual Warfare, Thanksgiving or Gratitude, Holiness, Peace, Justice, and Righteousness." Faith was diversely interpreted within World Vision. As previously mentioned, for some employees it made the working environment seem more like a family. This was beneficial, and many people said they liked this aspect of working for a Christian organization: they said that it made people more understanding and considerate, and that human relations were important. Some people also acknowledged the difficulty in this: that there was a very high standard of interaction of behavior (being a good Christian) that was sometimes impossible to live up to. Sometimes expectations were too high, and people felt bad about not being able to live up to them, or suspected that those who did appear to comply might not be sincere.

I encountered a number of staff members in the World Vision's offices in California, and in Zimbabwe, who struggled with the concept of evangelism as part of World Vision's mission. International evangelical organizations are filled with individuals who question the work that they do, a fact easily glossed over in publicity materials presenting a unified view of institutional philosophy. Admittedly, those who questioned the morality of replacing a "traditional" worldview with a Christian one were at the more liberal end of World Vision's spectrum of perspectives. The more conservative evangelicals did not question the validity of Christ as the answer.

There was one staff member of WV Zimbabwe in particular who approached faith differently from all others I encountered. He was the only non-Zimbabwean working for the institution at the time of my research, and this set him apart. While his uncommon attitude toward faith in his work did not constitute a problem for the NGO, it provided an example of how faith expressed itself in inter-staff relationships. He considered himself Christian, but in his own way. He was critical of World Vision's Christianity, but admitted that many participated in it enthusiastically. Although many Zimbabwean NGO staff members during initial interviews, painted pictures of themselves as pious, I later encountered other individuals like this one who were skeptical, or who participated in devotions with less passion than others did. However, this particular employee was the most vocal about his discontent. He believed that some staff members used a "holier-than-thou approach" to put others in their place. Once during devotions, a project coordinator brought to the attention of the rest of the staff this man's lack of enthusiasm and requested others pray to help him find his way to Jesus; this he considered a social slight. He considered the uses of Christian faith pervasive and even coercive within WV Zimbabwe. He felt that faith was forced and enforced.

Not necessarily by coercion but by peer pressure, and coercion is too strong. Enforced is too strong. But, because it is part of the routine and everyone follows routine, you are obliged. It's obligation. You are obliged to participate because you get a salary from this organization. I think that, I think there is a whole range of—what is the word I want—of belief here, depth of belief and commitment to that belief. From very very conservative, to very very religious, to non-religious but religious by obligation.

Employees of World Vision and Christian Care, as perhaps in any office environment, maintained personae that they wore in the offices and took off outside of office settings. Faith was part of this persona, part of the office attire, and a performative part of working for the NGO. This is not to say that it was

insincere, but that it was a visible aspect of the working environment that structured staff expectations. Not everyone came to work for World Vision or
Christian Care for its religious aspect, and many worked for NGOs because in
Zimbabwe it was choice employment. There were few jobs in Zimbabwe in the
late 1990s. Getting a job was a matter of survival, and if that job meant prayer,
many were willing to pray.

As much as some were critical of the lack of fervor of their colleagues
during devotions, the non-Zimbabwean employee quoted above thought some
people used faith to mask their lack of ability. He thought that in a few cases,
those that prayed the most did the least. Filling in the lack of performance with
their faith, he said, "They show their faith and preach it more and jump up and
down about it more to fill in that they are not doing a complete job." He said
he did not feel pressure to evangelize because he was not a Zimbabwean
(again, his difference set him apart). Once he was asked to lead a prayer at a
rural development project and had declined. Even during weekly devotions
when the staff broke into smaller groups for Bible study, he felt there was a
reluctance to call on him because others realized he did not pray the way others prayed. His Christian faith and belief systems were "very much on a personal level and one-to-one, and praying out loud to a group of people is not my
style." He encountered tensions over his faith during his annual performance
evaluation. The evaluation form, which employees and employers both com-
pleted, had categories of (self) evaluation: "Needs Improving," "Acceptable,"
and "Very Satisfactory." For "Command of the English Language," he received
a "Very Satisfactory." For "Christian Commitment," he received "Needs
Improving." During an evaluative meeting afterwards, he asked his superior:
"What exactly is commitment? Christian commitment, what does that mean?"
He was asked, "Do you have a church?" and he had replied, "Not yet." His
superior said, "Ok, Needs Improvement." The employee did not fault an evaluation that stated that the quality and the quantity of his work needed improving; however, he was bothered that he could not meet the NGOs expectations
of faith, and that those expectations were not made explicit. He said, "Even
here on your evaluation form you are evaluated as to your Christian commitment, and it's like, who is anyone to determine that?" There were some contradictions. The application form for employment asked, "When did you take
Jesus Christ as your savior?" He had left that question blank because he had
not taken Jesus Christ as his savior. Although he was constantly being evaluated on his Christian commitment, no one ever checked up on the form. He was
ready if someone should ask and was prepared to answer: "I believe Jesus was
a teacher, and had a lot of really great things to say but, you know, that's my
limit on it." Devotions were a struggle for this employee. During the half-hour
each morning when people spoke from their experiences and their lives and
shared their troubles and hardships, he felt it was rewarding. However, the
concentrated focus on the Bible was more than he could take, and most of the
time it was a long, daily, half-hour. As at rural development projects, in NGO

offices in Harare faith was structured as a unifying principle: it organized the workday world as a "Christian family." Faith was also divisive: it provided a rubric and a set of standards through which employees critically evaluated each other and the NGO itself.

CONCLUSION

Faith did seem to make a difference in the development work of NGOs, even if it was not easy to classify this difference as either "good" or "bad." In fact, a far more complicated picture emerged. For many employees of Christian Care and World Vision, and for the beneficiaries of their assistance, faith was a motivating force and a force that brought people together. At World Vision's rural projects, for example, the evangelistic aspects of development brought participants of rural development projects together across denominational lines. It had a unifying effect. In Harare offices, faith provided a work environment that many compared to a caring family. At the same time, in Harare office settings faith was a disciplinary force used to monitor employee performance. Employees also used faith to assess the work of their colleagues. Faith in this context manifested itself both as a pressure to perform, and as a performative aspect of professional life in Christian NGOs involved in rural development. The negotiation of faith by employees of World Vision and Christian Care on a day-to-day basis was part of the work environment. More than mere rhetoric or ideology, faith provided a rubric—as with the theoretical constructs of holism and lifestyle evangelism—through which employees of the two NGOs interpreted the logic of development itself. Evangelism, frequently depicted as a monolithic effort to transform others and the world they live in, was a process that meant different things in different places. For employees of World Vision and Christian Care in Zimbabwe, and for the rural communities with which they collaborated, the project of Christian humanitarian assistance in Africa and the role of faith in this work were fraught with unresolved contradictions. Faith was used in development as both a controlling discourse of institutional power and a discourse that offered the transformative potential for change. In the development work of World Vision and Christian Care, the discourse of conversion was also the discourse of development.

CHAPTER 3

Child Sponsorship, Evangelism, and Belonging

W HILE THE PREVIOUS CHAPTER WAS CONCERNED WITH THE MICRO-politics of Christian theology in the development work of World Vision and Christian Care, this chapter shifts to World Vision and the flow of funds that constituted the NGO transnationally; it deals with one special form of funding in particular: child sponsorship. The child sponsorship program of WV Zimbabwe altered relationships of belonging—both to an international Christian community and to local kin—for sponsors and their sponsored children in Zimbabwe. In this specific process of economic development, which linked donors with recipients of economic assistance, local realities were reconfigured by transnational expectations. Child sponsorship produced unintended disjunctures between hopeful ideas of global humanitarianism and local political economies fraught with inequalities, reinforced by the very humanitarian aid that endeavored to transcend them. This paradox of child sponsorship was unsettling for donors, beneficiaries, and NGO employees alike. As new relationships were built between sponsors and their sponsored children, they disturbed existing relationships between parents and their children, and between youth and elders in local communities. Perhaps most importantly, relationships of child sponsorship entailed differing understandings of what humanitarian assistance meant, to World Vision employees who facilitated and implemented the sponsorship program, to sponsors, and to the communities being sponsored.

THE POLITICAL ECONOMY OF CHILD SPONSORSHIP

Financially, child sponsorship involved monthly remittances sent from sponsors, through World Vision, to children sponsored in countries such as

Zimbabwe; these monthly payments financed World Vision's economic development at rural project sites. Sponsorship also involved rural communities who elected management committees to oversee development projects and, in concert with local leadership (such as elders and headmen), "identify the poorest families in the community" for sponsorship. Children thus identified were sometimes those who had lost a parent, or whose parents were economically marginal relative to the rest of the community.[1] At project sites, sponsorship lasted between one and ten years and was only one component of World Vision's broader development initiatives in health, sanitation, education, and micro-enterprise development—initiatives that also engaged the families of children who were not sponsored. Sponsorship monies funded these broader initiatives as well: monthly remittances sent by sponsors were aggregated in donor offices in nations where sponsors resided and pooled together to budget community development.[2] In contrast to other development organizations that also facilitated rural, agricultural development, World Vision formed personal links across national borders and cultures through relationships between sponsors and their children.

This chapter is framed by two narrative experiences of men in their 20s: a Canadian sponsor who visited the child he sponsored in rural Zimbabwe, and a Zimbabwean who was formerly a child sponsored by World Vision. The cases describe the complex and often contradictory nature of humanitarian assistance as experienced from different perspectives. I explore child sponsorship from within World Vision, through the evangelistic relationships at the core of its philosophy, and through correspondence between European and American sponsors and the children they sponsored. The political economy of sponsorship accentuated localized experiences of poverty, to the extent that the very humanitarian and evangelistic narratives that aimed to transcend geographic and cultural distance through community development generated divisions and jealousies in the lives of sponsored children and their families. I investigate efforts by WV Zimbabwe to make child sponsorship a local practice, with Zimbabwean sponsors for Zimbabwean children. As Christianity and rural economic development struggled to put down local roots, to "indigenize" in Zimbabwean parlance, or "inculturate" in the language of mission texts and theology (Bediako 1995; Pobee 1992; Sanneh 1989), I look at how these processes took place and why they were not successful. Although in Zimbabwe the Christianity of World Vision had become "Zimbabwean," its humanitarianism—as reflected in programs of child sponsorship—had not yet become a localized charitable form.

World Vision was distinguished from other NGOs by its primary source of funding, child sponsorship: monthly remittances sent from individuals in "developed" nations to children in "developing" nations such as Zimbabwe. Sponsorship was organized through an apparatus of offices that formed World Vision's International partnership. Donor offices in places such as the United

States funded development projects through national offices in places like Zimbabwe. Structurally, the NGO was a transnational network of offices in which donor offices communicated directly with national offices without the coordination of a central office.[3] In 1997, World Vision as a transnational organization claimed to, "touch the lives" of more than 61 million people through 4,279 projects in 94 countries (World Vision 1997a).[4] That same year, individuals in the United States sent monthly remittances of US$22 to sponsor 526,694 children around the world. In Zimbabwe, over 30,000 children were sponsored by an estimated 26,000 individual sponsors overseas, including, but not limited to the United States. The majority of resources for the development work of WV Zimbabwe came from child sponsorship.[5]

Child sponsorship connected sponsors in "developed" nations with children in "developing" nations through the transnational flow of financial resources. In a provocative essay on transnational accumulation and shifting class relations in the United States, Rouse (1995) exemplifies how transnational accumulation is distinguished by the increased speed with which "people, goods, money, information and ideas move across the boundaries of the state" (ibid:358, cf. Leyshon and Thrift 1997). This capitalist practice is augmented by the prevalence of humanitarian, not-for-profit organizations such as World Vision that cross national boundaries and coordinate charitable fiscal flows. In Rouse's argument, the speed and flow of capital is correlated to growing inequalities and shifting class positions within the global sphere, often in local arenas. Ideas of helping and humanitarianism, although not capitalist per se, are correlative components of transnational accumulation. Transnational NGOs operate in the global economy, alongside multinational corporations. New forms of accumulation (and humanitarian redistribution) that promise to "shrink the distances between humanity" offer narratives with the liberatory potential to unify people across national borders. Although charitable donations are not capital in the usual sense of the word, those that give still expect a return, this time in terms of salvation rather than profit. World Vision as a multinational business operated in tandem with the logic of global capitalism employed by transnational corporations.

World Vision embodied the shift from multi-national to transnational capitalism, relying heavily on information technologies to facilitate the communication necessary for sponsorship. Whereas at the beginning of my research in 1994, monies flowed from donor offices to an international office in Monrovia, California, which subsequently disbursed funds to national offices and then to the children who were sponsored, the organization in 1997 was structured as an "international partnership" with direct communication (and accountability) between donor offices and national offices that oversaw specific development projects. There was a growing trend in the NGO world more generally to bypass managerial offices to get closer to the "grassroots" or the "poor"; international funding channeled through NGOs was part of the attempt of individuals in wealthy nations to bypass third-world states deemed corrupt and/or inefficient. For example, during my research in Zimbabwe, the World Vision support office in Germany that funded a large development project in northern Zimbabwe was considering installing a satellite dish at its sponsored project locations to facilitate communication and to bypass the Harare office. This became a minor threat to job security for the Harare office staff; however, they were accustomed to frequent shifts in the organizational structure. One informant explained: "the only thing constant here [in World Vision] is change." The institutional shift was a response to changing flows of capital, to the desires of donors to have more direct communication with rural project offices that monitored sponsored children and to eliminate the middle-management of national offices in metropoles such as Harare. The urgent need for workers to have flexible attachments to their professional identities (a phenomenon increasingly prevalent in the transnational capitalism of the late 1990s) was evident in the frequency with which employees of World Vision shifted positions within the institution.

Amidst a constantly shifting organizational structure, an apparatus of staff existed in each national office to document and monitor children, and to translate and facilitate correspondence between sponsors and their children. In addition to national offices, such as the World Vision office in Harare, there were project offices at development sites. Members of local communities were hired to monitor sponsored children, take photos, and ensure correspondence between sponsored children, the national offices, the donor offices, and the sponsors themselves. Technically, the apparatus existed to facilitate relationships and to move monies transnationally. Occasionally, there were glitches. Sometimes children could not be tracked, and donors were disappointed. As with any bureaucracy, there was much effort to keep the machine running, and at times the processes broke down. The national director of WV Zimbabwe recounted a story of a sponsor who came to Zimbabwe from Australia to visit "his" child. When this sponsor arrived, the child could not be located.

> This chap sat there and he really was disappointed that he could not see the child. I mean they had come two times before and they had seen the child, so the child was there . . . And so we had to go looking for the child, and it took a few days and we found the child. But, we sat here with this chap. I cried, literally cried, and he cried. Now for me that was a different dimension altogether, you know, that we were crying about his child. Now to me as a Zimbabwean who is here, that this man who had come all that way, [and] was moved to the extent of shedding tears for the sponsored child—I mean it did something to me. Now when we are talking about transformation that's what it is, the love that so moves you to that extent. . . . You know it is not just these people who are receiving . . . the sponsorship does something to them. But it's a mutual enriching experience.[6]

This story also demonstrates how sponsors can be deeply affected by processes of child sponsorship. While funding may have traced a path from "developed" to "less developed" countries, relationships moved reciprocally. Perhaps anthropologists have not taken child sponsorship seriously because of the difficulty of wading through the barrage of publicity the sponsorship apparatus produces. Journalists, however, are fond of criticizing child sponsorship organizations for their misuse of funds, or for corrupt and inefficient development practices. For example, a series of articles in the *Chicago Tribune* entitled "The Miracle Merchants"(Anderson et al. 1998) lambasted four organizations for corrupt practices. Fortunately for World Vision, they were not one of the organizations chosen for the exposé. This exposé is important, however, because it highlights the concern that results when global efforts to connect people result in mishaps and failure—when children once involved in a program can no longer be located, for example. Although the primary critique of these four organizations referred to an abuse of funds, a lack of "stewardship" (Irvine 1996:273) for donor monies, the global disjunctures on social and emotional levels are just as analytically significant. In child sponsorship, children symbolize explosive moral terrain. Critiques of child sponsorship such as the "Miracle Merchants" represent children embodying both the hope of international assistance and the despair associated with its shortcomings.

Authors (Stephens 1995; Zelizer 1985) have pointed to the importance of studying the social processes through which children are constructed (and deconstructed) as social and historical categories. Zelizer underscores the historical processes that have sacralized children in a definitive shift from economic to emotional value over time, concluding that the contemporary conception of morally valued, non-laboring but economically priceless children is a modern phenomenon. Stephens and the authors in her edited volume, *Children and the Politics of Culture*, examine postmodern contexts to argue that the "child" as a modern category is being eroded by global disjunctures, including war and the economic consequences of globalization and flexible accumulation (cf. Harvey 1989).

Malkki (1997, 1995) extends this argument to examine discursive representations of children in the international community. She argues that international discourses of humanitarianism that equate children with hope for the future stand in contrast to history and politics. Children, as incarnations of utopia in humanitarian discourse, serve as depoliticizing agents in highly political contexts. Positing children as manifestations of humanitarian sentiment in the world community, Malkki argues that transnational representations of children do not necessarily transcend the national; they may depend upon it. In the supranational imaginings of a world community, the world is an ensemble of nations, and children are seen to embody all of humanity. In effect, Malkki argues, children serve the international humanitarian community as embodiments of a basic goodness and as symbols of world harmony: as sufferers, as seers of truth, as ambassadors of peace, and as embodiments of the future. Children are a "tranquilizing convention" in the international community (Malkki 1997:17). One could argue that new forms of transnational accumulation encourage the consumption of "goodness" and humanitarian ideals, while at the same time children are increasingly interpellated as consumer subjects (Rouse 1995).

Rather than representing children as universal and depersonalized, World Vision's child sponsorship offered highly personalized and intimate relationships of friendship and membership in families. The national director of WV Zimbabwe gave a moving example of the depth of these relationships in practice, with a narrative of a sponsor who lost a photo of his child:

> A sponsor in the States had their wallet stolen, and there was a picture of the sponsored child in it. And they really cried, you know, they didn't know how much they were attached to this child that they sponsored, and it was really moving. They missed the other credit cards and so, but . . . the point of the deprivation was the picture and the picture of the grandmother of the sponsored child. Now, this is a good powerful story because it's drawing attention to relationships of people. And to me it has never ceased to amaze me how there is such a strong bond with people who have never seen each other. It's more than the terms in which we explain it. . . . It's mysterious. [Laughs] . . . because otherwise, you see, we can't explain all this inhumanity and despair. . . .[7]

Thus, not only were children tranquilizing agents, they were also panaceas for such "unexplainable" human experiences as "inhumanity and despair." Through personal relationships, as in child sponsorship, the poverty constituting the "need" for development became manageable and pragmatic, something to be solved with a monthly financial commitment. For the national director of WV Zimbabwe, these "relationships of people" were a powerful component of the development work of World Vision. Organizations like World Vision reinforced the category of childhood, to protect innocent children and their sponsors from the harsh conditions of global economic shifts and the injustices that situate some in "developed" and others in "developing" nations. These relationships involved contradictions and ambiguities. Along with the Christian unity they professed, these relationships inspired what Ferguson (1999) has called "global disconnect" (cf. disjunctures, Appadurai 1990). There was a severe gap between the desires produced and the realities experienced through transnational accumulation. Amidst unity and promises of connection, difference was reinscribed and disparity increased. For sponsors, humanitarian expectations of a transnational family were juxtaposed with the prospect of loss—of a child that could not be found, for example, or of the harsh realities of poverty. These prospects were the "inhumanity and despair" that the nation-

al director described, which defined the urgency of development and humanitarian aid.

The personal relationships of child sponsorship, built through correspondence, existed alongside the impersonality of the monetary exchange of
child sponsorship. The Simmelian fact (1990 [1907]) that these relationships
were being purchased through global capitalism reinscribed the categories of
those who had money to sponsor children, and those who must be sponsored.[8]
The personal connection—between individuals in relationships of correspondence—both effaced the global, political and economic context that engen-
dered poverty and sponsorship, and transcended the potential impersonality of
a monthly remittance. If these sponsored children threatened to become commodities, embodying the commodification of goodness and development and
being fetishized as such, the relationships of belonging to a transnational family and to an imagined, global community re-affirmed generic humanity in the
process. Discourses of evangelism built relationships of child sponsorship within World Vision, transmogrifying money in the form of monthly remittances—
a generic and impersonal standard of value—into embodied human relationships with alive, unpredictable spontaneous others.

A SPONSOR VISITS HIS CHILD

In the United States and in Zimbabwe, I spoke with employees of World Vision
about their experiences as sponsors and managers of child sponsorship. Many
also sponsored children themselves. As I began to talk informally about my
project with colleagues and friends from Canada and the United States, I
learned that some were raised in households sponsoring children far away;
child sponsorship was a part of the global ecumene (Foster 1991; Hannerz
1987). The publicity materials of World Vision promoted child sponsorship as
a humanitarian connection that manifested transcendent love for a stranger.
Such humanitarianism in the context of global capitalism spawns relationships
across space, expressed through an inter-continental traffic in meaning and
facilitated by the transnational mobility of missionaries, consultants, intellectu-
als, and NGOs (Hannerz 1996).

My first case, drawn from a series of conversations I had in Harare with
a Canadian child sponsor named Peter,[9] illustrates such traffic in meaning. His
experiences exemplify a basic contradiction between, on the one hand, the discourse of humanitarianism that cast sponsored children as part of a global,
generic, humanitarian family transcending languages, cultures, and national
identities (cf. sea of humanity, Malkki 1996), and, on the other, particular and
personal relationships of child sponsorship that cut across, and threatened to
disable, the fluency of generic humanitarianism. Within this contradiction, the
identities of sponsors and sponsored children were reconstituted. In visiting his
child, Peter moved from the hopeful humanitarian stance of similitude to a

heightened awareness of the enormous disparity between himself and the child he sponsored. Peter was young, in his 20s, and had been a child sponsor for about four years. He was working on his Bachelor of Arts degree in Development at a Canadian university. He was in Zimbabwe with a special program for gifted students, and had been on an internship with a World Vision development project in northern Zimbabwe.[10] Peter learned of the sponsorship program through his church. While this sponsor's experiences may have illustrated what could be termed more general (secular) humanitarian endeavors to help the less fortunate, they also expressed the implicit chiliasm in child sponsorship that promised a global, Christian family transcendent of economic realities.

Peter told me that he wanted to see World Vision's work, especially since he sponsored a child, to evaluate the quality of its impact. He had spent three weeks "on attachment" at the World Vision project, and was arranging to visit the child he sponsored in southern Zimbabwe. The experience of being on attachment at the development project had been awkward for Peter, especially when a World Vision employee solicited funding from him for study abroad.[11] He encountered an odd culture of expectation between World Vision staff and visiting donors, in which he was implicated: at first everyone confused him with a donor, but when they realized he was a student they simply ignored him. He lived in staff quarters, and paid for his own food—and subsequently the staff's food as well, as there was a great disparity of wealth between Peter and the Zimbabwean village development workers employed by World Vision and living at the rural development project. Peter had never written to his child, whom he sponsored in Zimbabwe. "What would I say to her?" he asked me. He showed me the progress reports and photos that World Vision had sent him. He believed in World Vision, and in the project of development, to the extent that he had come to Zimbabwe as an intern for World Vision and was majoring in Development Studies in college. Now that he was in Zimbabwe, he wanted to visit his sponsored child, and World Vision's Bulawayo office was trying to locate her.

His awareness of World Vision began in his church, the Presbyterian Church in Canada. He explained how the church was involved in initiating the sponsorship of children through World Vision. His church also organized a series of fundraising events called "famines," during which members of the congregation would fast for 30 or 48 hours, donating the money they would have spent on food to World Vision. By participating in these "famines," members of his church both raised money to help alleviate hunger and felt what it was like to be hungry, if only for a limited time. He showed me the materials he had received in the mail from World Vision Canada informing him about child sponsorship; they included progress reports on his child. He remembered being told that if he wrote to his child, there would be certain topical constraints. For example, he was not supposed to write about "wealth and natural beauty," although he was not given any explanation why. More concerned with development than with the Christian aspects of World Vision's work, he thought that sending a small amount of money every month ($27 Canadian) was an easy way to participate in helping others. He said he continued because of "convenience." He described how he had often been sitting at home, watching Global TV Canada, and had seen the two-hour World Vision telethon documentary. "I've watched it and said I should call the number, and finally I decided to do it." Now, the money he gives for child sponsorship is automatically deducted monthly from his credit card.

At first, he had misconceptions about his role as a sponsor. Once, his credit card was stolen and he missed a sponsorship payment.[12] WV Canada called him and asked if he wanted to continue sponsoring the child; they said they had covered it for the month he missed. Peter wondered if the child hadn't eaten for that month because he missed a payment, speculatively thinking, "Would she write, 'Where were you in March 95?'" Sponsorship seemed that direct. Now he realized that it was bit of a myth that the child depended on sponsorship so much, and that this fallacy masked the institutional mechanics that really made development work possible.

Peter showed me a photograph of the child he sponsored. He laughed when he described how some people displayed the photos of sponsored children on their mantles with other family photos. He said he thought this was strange and that he would never do this. "What do I have in common with this child?" he asked rhetorically, expressing how absurd he believed the simultaneously abstract and personal connection to be. On the page facing the photograph, the World Vision report read:

> 4-5 years old Chipo lives with her parents in a rural area. Her parents are very poor. They live in a one-room hut, which is too small for their family. The father, although employed, earns so little that it is impossible to meet their needs. Your sponsorship is an important and continuing part of assistance to help this girl and her family attain self-reliance. For this is the development in which World Vision is involved.

Peter remarked that much of the text could be misconstrued by Western audiences. For example, he pointed out that most people in Zimbabwe live in rural areas and in one-room huts, but for many North Americans a rural environment and a one-room habitation imply impoverishment. He added that it was unlikely that his funds directly assisted the family in attaining self-reliance, pointing out that the funds went into community development and not personal gain.

We talked about what it would be like for Peter when he visited his child. At the time of our discussion, he was planning to leave for this trip in a few days. He anticipated being "treated like a God," which at first he was dis-

gusted by. He explained how shocked he was when a senior (foreign) World
Vision staff member visited the project where he was on attachment and was
given a special bowl for washing his hands and a special bowl for eating. This
visiting NGO dignitary ate with a few of the staff while the rest of the staff dispersed; it was the royal treatment. Later that month, Peter called to tell me
about his trip to southern Zimbabwe, where he had visited the child he sponsored. During his story, he referred to the girl as "my child." He seemed disappointed that he was not treated as a dignitary. He was asked by World Vision
staff to pay for petrol, and was not given lunch. In fact, he did not eat all day.
He took the bus home, getting back to Harare around midnight. An entourage
of World Vision staff members joined him on his journey: the project officer, a
sponsor-relations officer, a driver, and a communications officer who was doing
research. Peter was irritated that he was not given better treatment. Although
he was prepared to be "treated as a God," and had anticipated the embarrassment of this, he was disappointed when it did not take place. He described his
first meeting with his sponsored child:

> The sponsor relations officer pointed to a group of kids and asked, 'Do you
> see your child?' and I thought, how am I supposed to know which one she
> is? I was able to tell by the scar under her eye. The kid couldn't speak
> English and I couldn't speak Ndebele, so it was really awkward at first. I
> didn't know what to say to her. She was eight years old; she was shy and
> didn't say much. The communications officer suggested that she show us
> around her houses, which she did. I didn't feel like hugging the girl or any-
> thing; it was uncomfortable. I brought her gifts—a dress at my professor's
> suggestion, a coloring book, colored pencils, and a Canadian flag. When I
> gave her the gifts things got a little looser. . . there was something to talk
> about.

The giving of gifts was a language in which both Peter and his sponsored child
could communicate. He was disturbed at discrepancies between his project
reports and what his child's life was like, materially. Peter had earlier joked
about the generic intimacy promoted by World Vision, but he was surprised to
find that his reports did not represent what he saw when he visited. The gap
between his experience and World Vision's representation of sponsorship was
unsettling for Peter.

> She didn't live in one hut [as the project report had stated]; it was two
> houses and two bigger huts. The father didn't have a job; he is unemployed
> and has never been employed [again a discrepancy from the project report
> he had received]. I asked the staff how children were chosen for sponsor-
> ship and they said they were selected by the community, the poorest of the
> poor. When I asked if it was a random sample . . . they got upset and

assured me that it was the poorest of the poor children that were sponsored.

Peter had an informed and educated view of child sponsorship and the development work of World Vision, and he was himself studying to become a development professional. Nonetheless, he was shocked and dismayed by the complex relationships and the web of expectation that he encountered in Zimbabwe.

Peter cared about his child. He was responsibly concerned when his wallet was stolen in Canada and he missed a monthly payment. However, the subtle discrepancies and tiny inconsistencies between his expectations and actual social realities in Zimbabwe upset Peter. He never wrote to his child, but at the same time he was disappointed that the "relationship" was not what he had imagined. For Peter, the imagined humanitarian community of which he saw himself a member exaggerated differences when he met his child; local disconnections were all too salient. Peter was uneasy with his burgeoning awareness of the structural relations of power and inequality that had created a transnational space for programs of child sponsorship, and he found himself a participant in local practices of place-making and identity, where his identity as a "donor" depended upon a stark contrast to his sponsored child. It was not only donors that experienced these stark contrasts. Sponsorship incited discontinuities in the lives of sponsored children as well. These ambiguities and contradictions—of longing for connection amidst the reality of difference—were part of the political economies that spawned sponsorship practices and World Vision itself.

RELATIONSHIPS OF CORRESPONDENCE

The institutional mechanics of World Vision made child sponsorship possible and productive. In Harare, I interviewed local managers of child sponsorship, specialists and correspondence analysts, who monitored the reciprocal correspondence between sponsors and their children. On one occasion, I was invited to the Sponsor Relations room and offered an opportunity to read mail from sponsors to their children. Although this context did not allow for the rigorous content analysis of letters and packages, I was struck by the way each letter was simultaneously mundane, with bland and superficial descriptions of everyday life and the weather, and intensely intimate and personal, with descriptions of children and grandchildren, husbands and wives, vacation travel, sick pets—all communicated from countries distant from Zimbabwe. Some sponsor packages contained toys. As I opened the envelopes, I could feel the exoticism of something arriving from far away. I could imagine how excited a child in rural Zimbabwe might be to receive a paint set, a toy car, a coloring book, or even a photo of a family in Germany, Canada, or the United States. The subjects in these portraits emerged as exotic and personal partners in the one-to-one relationship of intimate correspondence, the imagined essence of child sponsorship.

Letters were intensively catalogued and edited by World Vision correspondence analysts who literally cut out anything relating to politics or sexuality. This was done both to exclude content inappropriate in the Zimbabwean context, and to allow World Vision to operate in a space set apart from local and national politics: in effect, to be "neutrally super-national" like the names of their sponsors. Because sponsored children were prohibited from soliciting money directly from sponsors, they did not know the address or names of their sponsors; none of the letters I read contained sponsors' names. All correspondence flowed through the central office in Harare, and children's replies were monitored as well. Children were encouraged to write to the sponsors by themselves, and those who could not write received help from World Vision field staff. According to a sponsor-relations supervisor in Harare, a Zimbabwean woman in her mid-forties, most sponsors preferred to receive letters written by the children themselves, "in the handwriting of the child." If the child was too young to write a letter, the project clerk encouraged him or her to send a drawing, to which the clerk attached the child's letter. These letters, she explained, "give a close relationship" between sponsors and children. Some sponsors get upset when they receive letters from project clerks, so such letters were discouraged in favor of letters from children.[13]

A sponsor-relations analyst, a Zimbabwean man in his 20s himself desiring to attend college in the United States, oversaw the Mashonaland West province with five community development projects. Letters for this province crossed his desk before being sent to rural project offices. He opened the letters and read them, logging the contents, and making note of any politically sensitive information. He stated:

> I read the letter to make sure that certain information doesn't pass to the child, like politics. We cancel that piece of information; for example, if they ask about how the president is ruling the country . . . we either cross it out or cut it out of the letter. And about cultural issues—if they [sponsors] ask 'do you have a girlfriend or some boyfriends,' our children are still young . . . We do not encourage sponsors to send naked or half-naked pictures to our children. In Zimbabwe, we encourage children to have girlfriends only above 18. We don't allow children to ask for money from sponsors directly. The support offices are already doing that for us.[14]

He said that sponsors wrote about "family affairs, because World Vision helps the family," and that "religion is a regular question. They ask: 'Do you go to church? What is the name of your church?' Sponsors send Bibles to our children." They also send gifts and sometimes money in surplus of their monthly payments. World Vision's term for these extra allocations was "gift notifications." With these additional gifts, children were directed to pay for school fees, for example, or blankets and clothes for the whole family. At rural project offices, photomontages visually displayed these transactions. When items were purchased with gift notifications, a photo was taken of the items with the child, and then sent to the sponsor, demonstrating the accountability of World Vision.

As I looked at one letter from Canada, I saw a picture of the sponsor's biological children sent to a child in Zimbabwe, and I wondered what the Zimbabwean child would think when she received the photograph. Attached to the photo was a card describing the birth of a new grandchild, the weather in Canada, the schooling of the sponsor's children, and a description of her husband who was preparing to plow their field. The salutation read: "With love, your sponsor; it is a blessing knowing you and your family." There were many letters and postcards that said, "We went here," "We saw this," "This is what is happening in our family."

There was another letter from a sponsor's son to his/her child: "I am glad to know that you are doing well in school, and also that you received my card and contents. Carry it with you at all times and the Cross will bring you good luck." A young couple from Germany, a secretary and an ambulance driver, wrote a short letter describing themselves to their sponsored child. As I pored through the letters with photos, pictures, and drawings enclosed, I was impressed by how much the giving that flowed through World Vision had personalities, identities, a sense of humor, and offered snippets of lives. Some letters had been translated into English by the support office in Germany, and were to be translated again into either Shona or Ndebele, the languages of sponsored children, by WV Zimbabwe at the rural project sites. One letter offered almost unlimited possibilities. It was a birthday card with an image of a bear playing a cello. The card read:

> Dear Nomatter,[15] In this time I send you only a birthday letter, because I don't know which present a little African girl wishes for her birthday. You can write me, which present do you want and if I can send this present by mail you get it. And please don't write you have no wishes. I know that every little girl all over the world has dreams and wishes. Happy Birthday to you and all the best for you and your family.

Some of the letters and packages contained Bibles, or spoke of Jesus; all of them had the sponsors' addresses cut out or covered up. One package contained a *National Geographic World Magazine;* another had barrettes, talk about families, pets, cats that died, drawings, a collection of an entire foreign world, including magazine pictures. Enclosed with one letter was a wedding picture of the sponsors, a small beaded bracelet for the child, and a birthday card. There was a package from the United States with a coloring book that had the sponsored child's computer-generated picture printed on it, and a colored

The Spirit of Development

computer-printed letter written by a 27-year-old from Virginia who worked for a company that "sells machines that people use in their offices to write things on paper" (I suspect she meant printers). She had made the coloring book for the child. I was amazed at the intimacy, the pieces of lives shared, and the worlds translated in these packages that contained mysteries and evoked hopes. Immense creativity breathed in these packages, in the care that had gone into assembling them. I was touched by the letters; many seemed reasonable attempts to bridge the intimacy and strangeness of sponsoring a child in a country the sponsors had never visited.

In addition to correspondence, annual progress reports resembling report cards with photos were sent to sponsors. They had descriptions of community development, the child's progress in school, and the activities carried out in the community by World Vision. For example, one report on its way to Canada stated: "School fees paid to all sponsored children. Bibles given to all Chiraririro Churches." It continued in three separate short paragraphs to describe that a dip tank was constructed, toilets were built, and the school was renovated. In Mashonaland West province, there were more than 1000 children sponsored, and the volume of letters was significant: 50-100 letters per month, doubling during Christmas and Easter. I noticed that on some of the annual reports the "comment section" listed specific personal difficulties: "refuses to go to school on own" or "mentally disturbed." The detail was shockingly specific, and human. Sponsored children (who were between five months and fourteen years) had relationships with sponsors that had the potential to continue for years, through secondary education (A-levels) in Zimbabwe. These relationships were built through correspondence in which sponsors and their children strove to bridge economic and social distances across oceans, languages, and cultures. These distances were traversed physically when a sponsor traveled to visit his or her child, as with Peter, and conceptually through the imaginations of sponsored children who had not yet met their sponsors.

A THEOLOGY OF SPONSORSHIP

Sponsorship involves a fiscal relationship of credit and trust, founded on a belief that the sponsor will keep paying for his/her child. Money, like a monotheistic God, is a unifying abstraction. It has the potential to "reconcile all diversity into a single unity" (Simmel 1990 [1907]:515). This unity, in the case of World Vision both monetary and theistic, embraced and also effaced the cultural differences involved in child sponsorship. Within World Vision, there was a theological link between the unifying potential of child sponsorship and its institutional origin. An early film made about the founder of WV International, Bob Pierce, demonstrated why the unifying potential of Christianity was of such importance to World Vision. In the film, Bob Pierce, an American evangelist, journalist, and the founder of World Vision International, narrated: "Little darlings, motherless, daddyless, homeless, but thank God these are not Christless. For the missionary has opened up to them the wonderful promises of the word of God. . . . Christ offers a dying humanity, a personal God who personally cares for the personal needs of the lowliest individual. . . ."[16] While World Vision had grown and changed considerably since its early years, stories of its beginnings were often recounted during interviews in both the United States and in Zimbabwe as examples of its Christian basis (see also Gehman 1960; Irvine 1996). One story, an organizational origin myth, revolved around Pierce preaching in a mission school in China in 1947. During one of his sermons he suggested to the children in the mission school not only that they "accept Christ," but also that they "go home and share with their parents their new faith." The next day, he returned to the school to thank the missionary who had invited him, and he encountered a crying child named "White Jade" who had been beaten by her parents as a result of proclaiming her faith in Christianity. At this point, "the enormous social implications of Christ's Gospel began to unfold in his mind. The incredibly vulnerable child in his arms was a child of the King. And she needed to be cared for" (World Vision 1994; Irvine 1996). He gave the missionary teacher the contents of his pocket, which was five dollars, and offered to send five dollars every month so that White Jade could live in the missionary school and avoid parental punishment for adopting Christianity. This story of an initial gift and the tension between Christian, humanitarian families and local dynamics of power between kin delineated the template for child sponsorship.[17]

For evangelists, a great part of religious philosophy rests on the development of a "personal relationship" with Jesus Christ. This was a powerful aspect of both evangelizing and sponsorship in World Vision.[18] At development sites, before Christianity and narratives of making Jesus a "personal friend" were introduced, relationships were carefully cultivated with members of communities where development projects were to take place, in order to "build trust" and a context within which people would listen to the gospel. I was told by several people that "Christ has no grandchildren,"[19] meaning it was not enough to be born a Christian: one must be born again. A senior staff member in World Vision's California office elaborated on the importance of being "born again," emphasizing a fundamental "relationship" between individuals and Jesus Christ: ". . . the importance of a personal relationship with Christ [is] that it's not just a matter of going to Christ or being baptized when you are an infant. We believe that people need to be regenerated. They need a spiritual rebirth. They need to be born again. . . . You must be born again before you can see, or enter, the Kingdom of Heaven." In these relationships, World Vision workers became ambassadors of Jesus Christ, God's diplomatic corps for a transnational Christian family. Unlike other religions such as those found in Zimbabwe, which involved ancestors and spiritual lineages that one must be born into, the Christianity of World Vision involved the spontaneous potential of membership, of becoming part of a "body of faith." A policy paper on child sponsorship published by World Vision in 1997 asserted that World Vision clung to the child sponsorship model because it presented a model of living in unity as a body of faith: "Relationships based in love for Christ and respect for others bind individuals who together create a body of faith. By forging a friendship with a child who may seem less advantaged or strong, a sponsor extends the body of Christ and cares for that member as it would every critical part of its own physical body" (World Vision 1997d). The national director of WV Zimbabwe urged me to take note of the importance of relationships in child sponsorship, defining child sponsorship as

> a realization of God's love, which is transcendent. It transcends boundaries and connects people, and what is passed on from the one to the other is really an indicator of the reality of the relationship that is established. And Christianity is about relationships—relationship to God, relationship to each other—and through this program you have that relationship established.[20]

If child sponsorship programs were propelled theologically by an evangelical desire to link people to Christ in a body of faith, it was not only the donors and recipients who participated. Readers will recall from the previous chapter that World Vision staff in their employment applications were required to sign a "statement of faith" acknowledging that they accepted Jesus Christ as their savior (were "born again"). It was the consensus at WV International that staff at the support and field ends of child sponsorship were Christian and working because of a Christian motivation. At the community level, the children participating did not have to be Christians, although their parents had to consent to their involvement in World Vision community activities.

    Whose lives did child sponsorship change? The communities that received boreholes, irrigation schemes, and other more material aspects of development were obviously affected, but individuals like Peter who sponsored children were also being "transformed" according to World Vision. The child's life was improved materially, and the "donor's heart" was transformed by helping others (World Vision 1997b). Child sponsorship instigated relationships that extended "families" across borders. The national director of WV Tanzania described in a policy paper on child sponsorship (World Vision 1997b):

> In almost all sponsored-child homes that I have visited, the children or families can show me pictures and letters from their sponsors. These items are carefully placed in the home and are treasured as part of an extended family relationship. . . . This relationship benefits not only the child, but it

changes the sponsor. Although most donors sign up for sponsorship to 'give,' to a child in need, they experience a great change themselves and 'receive' in the process of forming a child-sponsor friendship.

World Vision asserted that sponsors, too, "often learn a great deal about God's unconditional love and about themselves by caring for a child of a different culture and position—and equal worth to God . . ." (World Vision 1997b). Moreover, while the global family of Christians transcended national borders and political economies, sponsorship worked because of its explicit emphasis on individual agency. Personal relationships initiated by sponsorship gave individuals a chance to feel that they were making a difference in the face of what have may seemed insurmountable: the larger political and economic processes of unequal development, poverty, war, and even natural disasters. As an international sponsorship coordinator who had worked for both WV USA and WV Australia explained, ". . . it seems that the people that we get the funding from can't relate to a big problem and feel like they can have some kind of import. Whereas if you give them one child, they think, yes, I could make a difference in that one child's life." Representations of children as depoliticized agents of universal innocence aroused potential sponsors out of their apathy and slumber: they provided means for individuals to forge real and personal connections with generic representations of African poverty. Instead of merely watching children's faces on television as icons of poverty and despair from afar, sponsors were coaxed into action by World Vision, and found a way to connect on a personal level to what threatened to be, as Malkki (1996) has noted, a depersonalized sea of humanity. With polities sublimated, child sponsorship was made possible and intimate.

JEALOUSY AND THE LIVES OF SPONSORED COMMUNITIES[21]

In the process of directly empowering a child, child sponsorship dislodged the authority of a parent. These shifts of power, some subtle and others devastating, also triggered jealousy. The most common culprits were gift notifications. These gift notifications were sent beyond monthly child sponsorship dues. These gift notifications were sent directly to children and their immediate families, through the national and rural project offices. An irony of child sponsorship was that as much as child sponsorship linked people across nations in the transnational relationships of a global "Christian family," it divided people locally and had an immense potential to inspire jealousy. In Zimbabwe (and in much of southern Africa), jealousy could provoke witchcraft.[22]

One of WV Zimbabwe's sponsor relations specialists, an evangelical Christian man with a slight build and a quiet manner who had been working for WV Zimbabwe for eighteen years, noted how World Vision's early work in Zimbabwe in the 1970s had taken the form of a "child-care ministry" through orphanages. Children had been central to World Vision's programs in

Zimbabwe: they were the intended beneficiaries of development. On the subject of jealousy, he believed that communities had to be taught not to be jealous, and said, "Some things are done for a child; other things are done for the whole community—dip tanks, crèches, boreholes. The community is not jealous because sponsors send things at different times—they get their sponsors as time goes on."[23] However, in the same breath, he told me a story in which the threat of jealousy was paramount. He had been escorting a sponsor who had traveled from the United States to Zimbabwe to visit her child. When they were about to leave the rural project, he noticed that the child's biological mother seemed extremely anxious. He asked her what was wrong, and she said she was afraid they would have big problems later; she was particularly concerned about *zvidhoma* (malevolent spirits sent to harm). World Vision had brought white people to her home, and white people were a sign of affluence; by bringing a sponsor to visit their child, World Vision was making her family vulnerable to the envy of neighbors. I asked the sponsor-relations specialist how he responded to this dire predicament. He said that it was difficult:

It was very difficult for me to really reassure her. Because I knew that I can say, 'Ah don't worry about it, it won't happen', and yet it's a reality that could have happened. Fortunately for her, we didn't hear of any member of the family being struck by *zvidhoma* because of that incident. But to her it was quite a scare. And I at the back of my mind know those things are real, so it was very difficult for me to give her any kind of support or help. Because I knew as a person who is coming in for a day and coming back to Harare, I am in no danger of *zvidhoma* and she is remaining there and [living with] the reality that the *zvidhoma* can come and hit her. So I just say, 'God will help. Don't worry, maybe God will help and protect you because this work that you are doing is God's work so it will protect you.' But you could see that, ok you are saying that, but one [nervous laughter] is scared.

When I probed about possible adverse effects of sponsorship on a community, he said: "Some people have asked the question, Aren't you dividing the community and making a few kids elite?" He explained that the community (usually elders) chose the families to receive sponsorship support from among those they considered to be most in "need." These were families that World Vision described as "the poorest of the poor." Despite the fact that these individuals were socially and/or economically marginalized in their communities and designated by the community to be "in need," there was still jealousy. Sometimes it impeded "development." I asked how jealousy could bring about *zvidhoma* and he explained: ". . . mere jealousy can create a situation where one person sends a *zvidhoma* to the other. Just because one feels the other person is doing well, or you had a disagreement, things like that. Some people

have recovered out of that state but some people have died because of that."
Fear of witchcraft, and of *zvidhoma*, stopped people from displaying successes ostentatiously. For example, he described how some people "can afford to
put up a nice modern house" but they did not, because they feared that if they
did, then "the *zvidhoma* will come and beat them."

This topography of jealousies provoked by child sponsorship was also
reflected in the life of Albert,[24] a young man in his 20s who as a young boy had
been a sponsored child in rural Zimbabwe. Albert was frequently described by
different employees at WV Zimbabwe as an example of a "sponsorship success
story." The national director encouraged me to meet with Albert to "see what
sponsorship can do." At the time of my interview with Albert he was doing well,
financially, by Zimbabwean standards. Dressed smartly in a pink shirt and a tie,
he arrived at the World Vision offices in Harare in a company car and suggested we go to his office at Bath and Tile World in the Westgate shopping center.
He directly attributed his success to having been sponsored as a child and
recounted how difficult his life had been at the time his sponsorship began.
Albert was one of the "poorest of the poor," chosen by his community to be
sponsored. His mother had died when he was very young and his grandmother had raised him. When his grandmother died, he moved in with his father,
his father's second wife, and his new stepbrothers and stepsisters. He was not
well-liked by his stepmother, and remembered sponsorship coming when he
was feeling "let down," as if the "Lord had turned his back." Albert saw World
Vision's arrival in the community as a rescue and a blessing. He said, "Then
came the sponsor and everything looked up. . . . The Lord came to my rescue
in the form of a sponsor and He was there as a provider. It was a great blessing. The Lord never forsakes his own—there in the good and especially in the
bad times, something happens that reinforces your faith. . . ."

Albert had fond memories of being sponsored, although it had been difficult for him to understand the logic of child sponsorship at the time. For him,
sponsorship was "like you're in the dark and you are handed the light. A great
help from nowhere." He had joined the World Vision program through a
Family Relief and Supplementary Feeding program in 1982, when he was ten
years old. When his stepmother heard about it, they went to the local
Methodist church to register together. I asked him about his memories of that
time, and he said, "All I remember is that there was lots of milk on Friday. All
the children would come every fortnight to meet and have Bible lessons at the
church. I remember the milk, then there was washing soap, beans, and other
things to share with my family." He recalled the way sponsorship was explained
to him at the time:

[They said] you will get letters, presents, and this person has promised to
see you through school. It was hard to grasp what it meant. How can someone who doesn't know me come and take care of me? They never met me.

yet they are saying how much they love me. It was a bit difficult to believe.
. . . There were set times to reply to the sponsor. I always wrote 'Dear
Sponsor,' and never knew which country s/he was from. I think from the
USA, but have no way of telling. . . . The sponsors would send money and
World Vision would translate it into gifts. The gifts were purchased local-
ly—soccer balls, etc. The cards were standard World Vision cards. The cor-
ners were all ripped off the letters [where the addresses were] and I just
thought it was World Vision stationery.

Albert's sponsor was anonymous. The letters he received were translated into
Shona, and since Shona pronouns are gender neutral, he did not know if his
sponsor was male or female. I asked Albert how it felt to be sponsored, and he
said it made him feel important:

Personally, it felt great, really felt like I was belonging, that I am a part of
this person's life. But they phased out the program in 1987, and we weren't
told the projects were phased out. They just closed up the offices. I considered it a phase in life, a chapter that had just closed. . . . I remember
lots of luxury cars and lots of important people coming to see the children.
. . . Important cars made us feel important. We felt we are very privileged,
[they were] important people in suits and ties, and we felt special.

However, when the project ended, he lost contact with his overseas sponsor.
He described a "feeling of loss" without the fortnightly meetings or the gifts.
World Vision's program shift toward "self-sufficiency" was experienced by
Albert as abandonment. Then, after five years without any contact, the spon-
sor sent him enough money for his A-levels. This is how Albert came to Harare.
When I met Albert, he was trying to locate his sponsor. He said:

Now I am trying to contact my sponsor. I never had a chance to thank
them in person. The way the whole thing ended was so abrupt. I lost contact with my sponsor during my O-levels. My dad couldn't afford for me to
go to A-levels. My sister got a call from World Vision and they were asking, 'where is [Albert]?' They said, 'We want him to come to the World
Vision offices.' It was 1989, so I came to Harare. They said: 'You are a very
lucky child. Your sponsor has sent you a lot of money.' After five years and
no contact, I couldn't understand it. . . . [My sponsor sent me] USD$550.
I asked, what is the money for? And World Vision said that the sponsor
gave me a choice: if I failed my O-levels, my sponsor wanted me to repeat
them. If I passed them, s/he wanted me to take my As. It paid for 2 years
of high school, and uniforms, and I came to Harare to do A-levels. I am
optimistic. Somewhere in the files, they must have something about the
sponsor's identity.

Albert's stepsisters and brothers did not benefit to the extent that he did from sponsorship, and this created jealousy within his family when the sponsor paid for Albert's education. A lot of children from his school were on the project, including his stepbrothers and stepsisters who, according to Albert, "weren't as bright." He told me of hearing about the extra funds he received from his sponsor for school fees, and about his stepmother's reaction. She had gone with him to Harare to accept the money, and she could not believe it was only Albert who was to receive it; she wanted him to share the money with his stepbrothers and stepsisters. Albert recalled how the sponsor-relations specialist in Harare had to explain to his stepmother what sponsorship meant, and why the extra money was just for him. Despite local attempts to translate the discourse of child sponsorship into the Zimbabwean context, child sponsorship had the propensity to become an individualizing force. The individualizing discourse in the developed world, which generated the success of individual-based appeals, created conflict in Albert's life, and the tremendous gift of an education for Albert made his father suspicious. As our interview was ending, Albert surprised me with a question:

> Do you think there are ulterior motives behind humanitarian aid? My father was concerned with the ulterior motives of humanitarian organizations like World Vision, and its connection with colonialism. My father was feeling inferior about the gifts and money from World Vision. He told me that after I finish school I shouldn't accept any more money from World Vision. He said the sponsor will send you money for an airplane ticket to the US and then you will never come back. They probably can't have their own children and they will want to adopt you. He was afraid of having me stolen.

The work of World Vision brought school fees and opportunities for Albert, but created a division between him and his stepbrothers and stepsisters. His father was Christian, and this in itself was an identity that alienated him from other family members who thought he was becoming too "civilized," perhaps too western. Despite being Christian, his father was suspicious of the work of World Vision. Simultaneously, World Vision opened the world to Albert. He eventually went to the University of Zimbabwe, and saw himself as someone who wanted to help others—to be more "Christian." He was disappointed that he could not find his sponsor, and that the window of the imagined international community had closed after the project support ended. He had changed, but the "belonging" had stopped. Instead, he was connected to something new and intangible—an urge to do humanitarian work himself. Albert had a dream of working for World Vision; he wished to "translate my gratitude so some kid will look up at me and say, 'that man helped me be who I am.'" He wondered whether "the real benefactors, the people who benefit

the most from this humanitarian work, charitable work, and so forth, are not
the people that we are supposed to help, ultimately, but in the end the people
called the sponsors and so forth have more to gain than to lose." He described
what was gained as "the sense of being you feel by knowing you did something
for someone." He too wanted to "be involved with the welfare of others," not
only for his family members or for himself, "but [for] other people, because we
are just one big family." Yet, in Albert's case, instead of constituting a unified
global, and in this case Christian, world, child sponsorship reformed his local
identity, placing it in transnational counterpoint to local tensions and conflicts.
Albert experienced stress between his Zimbabwean family and his perceived
sense of place in a global Christian, humanitarian community.

GIVING AND BELONGING IN ZIMBABWE

Transnational organizations operate in local contexts, and consistent with
recent trends in missiology to "indigenize" Christianity in Africa (Bediako
1995; Pobee 1992; Sanneh 1989), World Vision was trying to inspire local,
"Zimbabwean" practices of child sponsorship. However, the initiatives had not
yet borne fruit. Despite the fact that Zimbabweans gave support and resources
to their extended families, the concept of sponsoring anthropologically "fictive
kin" was met with fear and resistance. Christian doctrines to give to strangers
had not become Zimbabwean to the extent that other aspects of Christianity
had become African. As much as WV Zimbabwe was encouraging rural communities to be sustainable, it was also trying to be locally sustainable itself and
to reduce dependence on partner offices for support. In 1997, when I met with
an associate director of WV Zimbabwe who was also the coordinator for Local
Fundraising and Sustainability for Programs, attempts at local fundraising
were barely one year old. This associate director, a Zimbabwean and a
Christian, had attended a rural mission school before receiving his Masters
degree in Agricultural Economics from a university in the UK during
Zimbabwe's liberation struggle. He had subsequently worked for the
Government of Zimbabwe as an agricultural economist for ten years, eventually becoming deputy secretary in the Ministry of Agriculture before joining
the NGO sector and working for World Vision. He had cause to reflect on
development as simultaneously a local and a transnational phenomenon.

This associate director was working on building what he called a "culture of giving" in Zimbabwe. When I asked if people in Zimbabwe had money
to give, he clarified, "I'm sure there is a wide group of people who might just
barely make it in life, who I'm sure, if you talked to nicely—if you identify the
need and you really expose the need that other people have—I am sure they
are prepared to give. But it takes time. That culture of really giving still needs
to be developed." He believed that in Zimbabwe people had been "trained to
be dependent on others," and he made a parallel between WV Zimbabwe and

the communities they worked with: the potential for self-sufficiency existed, but the community (of villagers, or of givers) had to be mobilized first. He thought that the "dependency syndrome" had changed the way people thought about giving, and this made sponsorship difficult in the local context. In his opinion, it was the less "participatory" approaches to development that appeared immediately after independence in the 1980s that inspired dependency. Reflecting on the dilemma, he called this dependency "the single thing which is affecting us as a nation because we have been used so much to [being] given money from outside," and he said it was not only the poor in Zimbabwe who had adopted this attitude: it was even affecting people with money. The wealthy in Zimbabwe "are not used to giving somebody money," he said. The logic remained: "If you want money . . . you have to go and ask Americans, go and ask Australians [we laugh]. Those are the donors. We can't be donors, we are not donors—that type of spirit." The local resistance to a culture of giving was a contrast to what he viewed as possible in such places as the United States and Australia. He said:

> Like even in your country, if you go to United States, you go to Australia, you appeal—'we know of some hungry people in Rwanda, we know some hungry people in Zaire, refugees in Africa' and all that, you know, people feel touched. Also, for some of them, they are not very rich. Because the statistics we are getting from the United States and Australians on the nature of sponsors, people who are sponsoring our programs here, it's not the top people, the very rich at the top there, it's the middle class.

Alas, Zimbabwe did not have such a sizeable middle class. When I met with an Australian couple who had worked for World Vision in the United States, in Australia, and for the past four years in Zimbabwe, they explained:

> It's less a part of Shona culture to give. . . . You almost have to teach people to do it. They [Shona] help so many people in their extended families anyway that to give to a foreign cause, or unknown cause . . . People say, 'sponsorship is already a part of our culture.' To institutionalize it [giving] is difficult. It's one thing to institutionalize it when . . . Africans are the beneficiaries, but it's probably much more difficult when the Africans are the givers. Because they look around and then say, 'Well I'm already. . . looking out for this wide pool of people.' World Vision uses the developed middle-class country model, and this country doesn't have a huge middle class.[25]

The more I talked with the Zimbabwean staff of World Vision, the more concurrence I encountered. Many people expressed the concern that Zimbabweans were not "giving" in the way that World Vision wanted them to give. As a result of this dilemma, the woman responsible for spearheading a local child sponsorship initiative, a Zimbabwean in her mid 30s, faced a huge challenge. Nevertheless, she was reluctant to declare, "Zimbabweans do not give." She argued that child sponsorship was not yet appealing for many Zimbabweans because in Zimbabwe rural life was an unmarked category, and was worthy of neither extra attention nor money. Other political and economic factors—such as stresses on Zimbabweans to care for their families in the face of rising inflation, HIV, and a growing disparity between affluence and poverty—were more salient. And in contrast to the willingness of donors in other countries to embrace unrelated Zimbabwean children through sponsorship, beliefs about ancestral lineage also made it difficult for Zimbabweans to accept a non-consanguine child into their family.[26] Without knowing a child's ancestral lineage, a concerned parent would be unable to solve spiritual problems as they arose. Here, the individualism of evangelical Christianity, the very theology that initiated born-again relationships, the transnational "body of faith" and the essence of child sponsorship, was met with staunch local opposition.

I asked the Communications and Public Relations Manager for WV Zimbabwe why it was difficult to garner local sponsors.[27] She had been born in Zambia but had lived in Zimbabwe for most of her life. She agreed that selling the practice of sponsorship in Zimbabwe was "very hard." In fact, it had been the topic of a staff discussion the morning of our interview, during which they had reflected on extended families: how people say, "I am already looking after someone, why should I give to children?" She went on to express that "Zimbabweans do not adopt children because cultural things come into play." She clarified that it was important, in Zimbabwe, for parents to know a child's ancestry, especially if the child had been orphaned. She said: "You must know a child's background so you aren't haunted by something you don't know anything about." In other words, if you did not know a child's ancestors, how could you appease them? The concept of a transnational Christian family was lacking something very important for Zimbabweans: lineage. Because of the high frequency of HIV infection and increasing deaths from AIDS, the question of AIDS orphans was becoming urgent for Zimbabweans and for World Vision. It was a concern that WV Zimbabwe was broaching, as attested by the staff discussion that morning. As with the Australian couple mentioned earlier, the Zambian-born Communications and Public Relations Manager did not think that Zimbabweans were "givers" in the Western sense of the term. That they did help each other in times of need was an important distinction between Western philanthropy and local understandings of helping others.[28] She said,

> I don't think we blacks give . . . the giving people in Zimbabwe are the white community, organizing for charity, Harare socialites. A lot of blacks would say, well, I also need help. Everyone is struggling economically.

> Overseas there is always this thing that you are better off than people in
> South America or Africa . . . to sacrifice pocket money for kids, it's really
> nothing, it's fun.

One reason why she thought Zimbabweans were not giving to charity was that
even the African elite did not consider themselves rich (although in Zimbabwe
there exists a tiny super-elite that is rich, even by Western standards). She
argued that African leaders were poor before independence, and that existing
wealth was "new wealth," something to cling on to, not to give to "charity." She
explained, "When you have money you just want to cling on to it. Put it this
way: overseas donors, most are pensioners or working class people. Here there
are a lot of black people with a lot of wealth, but they hang onto it. I don't think
we are giving as we should." I asked if she thought there was an African ideal
of giving, and she did, although it differed from the Western model of anonymous giving:

> You know in the African situation, if someone dies, people give money
> toward the burial. If people get married, people give money toward the
> wedding. I don't think it is in our culture to give. What is the difference
> between giving and helping? Giving is in the sense of really going out of
> your way to do something for someone. Helping, I think Africans do help.
> I think we want to help each other, and we do our best to help. We are will-
> ing to help. . . . African people are very helpful, very generous to visitors.
> If you visit an African home, it is insulting to ask you if you want something
> to drink or eat. We assume that as a visitor we give you a meal, a drink.
> From that point of view, we are very good at that. But when it goes
> beyond—like sponsoring a child. Or, I don't know . . . Good Works; it is a
> different story. On a family or an interpersonal level, you can't beat us.
> There is a lot of back-up support for each other. But with new wealth there
> is new poverty as well, and the gaps are getting bigger between the two all
> the time. People used to be able to fend for themselves, and now cannot.

These descriptions, by one woman whose job it was to publicize child
sponsorship to donor offices as well as to local Zimbabweans, elucidated how,
when help from international sponsors flowed into Zimbabwe, a new impoverishment, a lack of giving, became part of local self-definitions. As the associate
director exclaimed, in Zimbabwe "you can't go hungry, you can't die of hunger
if you have extended family." Because of the extended family, there was indeed
a culture of giving in Zimbabwe, yet he qualified it as giving that is only extended as far as those one knows, within one's own group. In contrast to an extended African family, which could of course traverse national boundaries, the
model of a Christian family expanded to strangers "in need." This was the cul-

ture of giving that was sought by WV Zimbabwe from potential local sponsors, and it was intimately connected with the social imagination of Christianity.

> As Christians the qualification is that in the eyes of God we are all the same, we are all human beings; therefore don't say because this one is my brother I can help, [or] this one is not my brother, because he is your brother in Christ. We are the same in the eyes of God, and therefore I think that's the area we need to try and sort of broaden our culture of giving to cover even those outside our family circles.

In these ways, transnational philanthropy and the expectations of child sponsorship, when cast onto Zimbabweans, redefined the obligations of extended families as non-giving, throwing into stark relief local understandings of what it meant to help others. At the time of my research in 1996-1997, WV Zimbabwe had not yet discovered how to raise funds for its programs in a way that was acceptable to potential Zimbabwean sponsors. That Christianity in Zimbabwe today is African is not disputed. Even so, specific forms of charity, such as child sponsorship, had not found their way into local practices.

CONCLUSION

To conclude this chapter, I offer a final vignette. The scene is a 1997 community meeting at a rural development project in northwestern Zimbabwe. I had traveled from Harare to a development project site in northwestern Zimbabwe with a World Vision project coordinator[29] to attend meetings at her projects in the province of Mashonaland West. At one community meeting, seated alongside four Zimbabwean World Vision employees[30] in a cement classroom block built by World Vision, we faced sixty residents of the rural community seated on rows of wooden benches.[31] This meeting was a formalized dialogue, critical for monitoring processes of rural development. At this project, World Vision had constructed a classroom block, housing for teachers, and 150 pit latrines; drilled five boreholes for fresh water; and donated five sewing machines for the twenty students enrolled in a dressmaking course organized by a local church in collaboration with WV Zimbabwe. After a Christian prayer and formal introductions,[32] the project coordinator with whom I had traveled from Harare praised the community for their development efforts and discussed details of a construction project still under way. The headman (*sabhuku*), the treasurer of the project,[33] the headmaster of the primary school, and the instructor of the dressmaking classes each spoke to thank World Vision for its work. They explained that without boreholes the teachers had for six years depended on drinking water from rivers and shallow wells. With the classroom blocks, children no longer had to learn under trees. The headman thanked WV Zimbabwe for the money it paid on behalf of the sponsored children in the project, and elaborated on the context of development work in the area (perhaps for my benefit, as the visiting anthropologist). He spoke of the farming land, which was of poor quality, and noted that although his community had not intended to live in such a region, he was pleased it had "developed" because of World Vision. Following the formality of introductions, the ensuing meeting resembled a rally, with the songs and rhythms of a revival. The project coordinator was a Zimbabwean Christian woman in her mid-30s. Raised Roman Catholic in rural, southwestern Zimbabwe, she had since joined a Pentecostal church. After secondary school in Harare, and a degree in Crop Science from the University of Zimbabwe, she gained employment in the Ministry of Agriculture as an Agritex officer (an agricultural extension specialist) before joining World Vision as a project coordinator two years previously. She was particularly adept at such performances, and so she engaged her audience, standing, charismatic and emphatic, as the community laughed easily alongside her.

An elderly parent stood up to speak. His voice filled with concern as he tumbled into issues of child sponsorship. He questioned why extra monies were not sent to parents so they could buy things for their own children. The project coordinator replied that such practices existed to teach people in the community to work harder. The elderly parent politely thanked World Vision for its work, paid tribute to his child's sponsor who had given his child money to buy things, and asked World Vision, again, why he could not buy things for his child himself with the sponsor's money. The project coordinator struggled to reframe his query: " . . . the sponsor looks to the needs of the child, not the needs of the family . . . the sponsor asks about the child. The parents may want a cart or oxen but [World Vision looks] to the needs of the child. The parents will benefit from drinking water from boreholes when it is directed to children." The parent became agitated, challenging, "When the sponsor sends money to the child, am I not allowed to buy things for the child?" The project coordinator parried: "World Vision cares about the sponsor's needs . . . when you keep on giving to people they become lazy. It is better to teach someone to fish than to give them fish." Then, depicting the community as a child, she compared the sponsors' role to the community members' own parental delight at seeing their children walking for the first time. Perhaps she also unconsciously articulated the power relations of transnational classes—of sponsors and the sponsored—in her depiction of parent and child relationships. She emphasized that people should not depend on others but should work for themselves. She was preaching development, and in her sermon the parent's question about sponsorship funds and parental disempowerment was left unanswered.[34]

As the meeting concluded and the community dispersed, I was given a tour of another classroom block where a dressmaking course was in session. I witnessed evidence of World Vision's success, and spoke with women who were being taught these skills, yet my memory of the parent's unanswered concerns lingered. We walked a few meters to the project office, another small and plain building of cement, where on the wall hung a large photomontage of local development work; the project clerk[35] noticed my interest and quickly stepped in to narrate the images. When a sponsor gives money, he expounded, the project office sends photos of the objects purchased to the sponsor. This particular poster documented assorted transactions between sponsors and their children involving the extra monies that had just an hour ago compelled the elderly parent to speak up: z$697 from one sponsor (at the time of my research in 1996-1997 the conversion rate was Zimbabwe z$10: US $1) had purchased a blanket, a goat, and a satchel; z$354 bought a goat; z$823 bought one blanket, satchels, suits, shoes, blankets, and Mazoe drink (an orange syrup to be mixed with water). Aware of my fascination with the sponsorship process, the project clerk introduced me to a sponsored child who was about 10 years old. I asked her, "How does it feel to be sponsored?" Shy and courteous, she described how she had exchanged two letters with her sponsor. "It feels nice," she said. "Why?" I asked, and she replied: "Because I am feeling like I am becoming part of their family." Her response—alluding to the unifying and expansive potential of humanitarianism—was a contrast to the response of the parent who asked why he could not be given responsibility for monies sent to his child from a sponsor. When the project coordinator dodged the parent's question, she either publicly ignored or simply did not realize that in the process of empowering a child, child sponsorship dislodged the purchasing power of a parent, and in this sense dislodged their authority.

Hence the double edge of child sponsorship. On the one hand, humanitarian practices had the truly transformative potential to form relationships through sponsorship: to make material improvements in lives via gifts of education and opportunity, and to create relationships with the potential to transcend distance, class, and culture. And on the other, they had the potential to create localized experiences of lack that stood in the face of benevolent attempts to bridge distance, which inadvertently may have been enhanced by humanitarianism itself. The structure of evangelical theology, fuelled by personal relationships modeled after those between believers and Jesus Christ, was the narrative underpinning of child sponsorship in World Vision. Relationships initiated by sponsorship did not end when projects terminated: at the time of this research, Albert was still trying to find his sponsor. Sponsored children became part of transnational extended families. As Albert said, "I felt belonging." To what? A Christian family that transcends consanguine lineage? An international humanitarian community? What survived in relationships instigated by child sponsorship was a cosmological relationship, an abstract emotional configuring of one's place in the world. Photos of sponsored children symbolized the possibility of a loving world, unified through the personal relationships modeled after Christ's, and it was the potential of these profound relationships that inspired organizations such as World Vision to create such programs. Whether or not the donors were evangelical or even Christian, evangelical ideas of loving strangers fueled the theology of World Vision's child sponsorship program.

Child sponsorship involved more than economic resources or the goods and services of development: relationships of belonging were also exchanged in transnational remittances. Practices of child sponsorship took place between individuals, simultaneously masking and making the political economy that situated donor offices in some nations and project offices in others. Child sponsorship was indeed a successful transnational practice for the millions of sponsors who gave monthly remittances to strangers in order to counteract "inhumanity and despair." Sponsorship helped the poor; a sponsor paid for Albert's education. The effects of such efforts, however, were often characterized by a tragic irony, as global humanitarian aid both connected and disconnected individuals and reconfigured communities. The sense of belonging to a global humanitarian community was temporary for most sponsored children, and the "self-sufficiency" that followed development projects did not account for the disrupted relationships of belonging in local contexts, to stepbrothers and stepsisters in Albert's case. The transcendent aspirations of philanthropic practice not only failed to transcend difference, they may have magnified and reconstituted economic disparity. Child sponsorship provided hope for individuals (like Peter) in developed nations; it also created small divisions and jealousies in locally lived lives. Perhaps the development work of World Vision carried the seeds of its own negation, particularly given the intensified experiences of lack and jealousy spawned in processes of sponsorship. Yet such sponsorship did seem to make a difference in the lives of individual sponsors and sponsored children. Sponsorship was not easy to dismiss and not easy to accept. Programs of child sponsorship were unsettling—and in this way, perhaps, they transformed.

CHAPTER 4

The Politics of Transcendence

THE TRANSNATIONAL RELATIONSHIPS OF CHILD SPONSORSHIP discussed in the previous chapter situate NGOs such as World Vision in an international "civil society."[1] Alongside the dynamics described in Chapter 3—between donors and recipients of humanitarian aid—are the political tensions of sovereignty and governance that exist between NGOs and the Zimbabwean state. This chapter is about the national political-economic context of religious NGO-work in Zimbabwe in the late 1990s. My research directly preceded the racialized political struggles of 2000-2001 Zimbabwe, which included state-sponsored violence and farm invasions. Although this chapter does not account for (or explain) the violence of 2000 directly, it does document a bubbling discontent, both economic and political, that was pacified through NGO programs of economic development. NGOs worked in collaboration with the Zimbabwean state to offer these programs while at the same time espousing a discourse that transcended national politics. This discourse, drawing on two themes—a Christian discourse of "A Kingdom of God," and a neoliberal discourse of "free markets"—facilitated what I call a politics of transcendence. However, as my ethnographic examples will demonstrate, the Zimbabwean state at this time was a weak and desperate state—one that depended heavily on the welfare work of World Vision and Christian Care to pacify a nation in economic decline.[2] In 1996-97, NGOs were working to assist rural communities in becoming economically self-sufficient in the wake of reduced social services; the state was weakened at that time by ESAP (cf. Hanlon 2000) and neoliberal programs of economic reform that had drastically reduced welfare service for Zimbabweans (Bond 1991, 1998). Dependent on international forms of charitable aid, the Zimbabwean state was in a precarious relationship with internationally funded Christian NGOs. The tensions run-bling during my research were evident every day in growing violence that was manifested in increased crime, mobs that publicly disrobed women for being scantily dressed, weekly riots at the University of Zimbabwe, and heavy-handed state attempts to quiet them. It was also present in the protests of war veterans, at that time organized against Mugabe, before he agreed to pay their pensions. The analysis in this chapter speaks to debates on supposed "civil society" and the state in Africa,[3] on church-state relations,[4] and on the ways that development has historically intersected with the extension of state power in Zimbabwe.[5] It also builds on recent critiques of neoliberal efforts (like structural adjustment programs) and their social consequences.[6]

CATEGORICAL UNCERTAINTIES: NGOS, CIVIL SOCIETY AND THE STATE

Scholarly debates involving NGOs most often occur over the relationship between civil society and the state. In Africa in particular, as African states are increasingly deemed corrupt by international donors, civil society has become a prescriptive arena for efforts toward democratization and development. Neoliberal economic programs such as the structural adjustment programs of the 1990s championed this approach, funneling donor funds through NGOs (instead of the Zimbabwean state) in an effort to decentralize the state and reduce its power, and its potential power to corrupt. Alongside the demonization of African states, NGOs have become harbingers of "good governance." Neoliberal economic theories discursively locate civil society and the purview of NGOs outside the state (Diamond 1994; Hyden and Bratton 1992). Others have explored how civil society is perpetually engaged with the state, and yet not bound by it. For example, Guyer (1994) explores how even supposedly "local" civil society in Africa is linked to an international arena of networks and resources (see Ferguson and Gupta 2002; and Riles 2000). The "civil society" promoted by transnational NGOs is dependent upon nation-states and extends beyond them. Boundaries between state and civil society are constantly blurred as NGOs and the state simultaneously collaborate on development and compete for international resources for similar services. Binary oppositions, such as state versus civil society, are not of much analytical utility (Ferguson and Gupta 2002). Broad and abstract, these categories fail to do justice to the social complexities of NGO work in practice. In addition, writing on civil society in a binary frame ignores religion. Where do Christianity and religious NGOs fit in to the binary opposition? Are they part of local civil society? The state? International civil society?[7] These distinctions lose their relevance when one examines the activities of NGOs such as Christian Care and World Vision in practice.

Scholars who use the concept of civil society to analyze the work of NGOs sometimes conceive of it as a form of grassroots resistance, rescuing societies from repressive states. This discourse attributes to civil society the normative potential, and the moral authority, to provide ethical and educative influences in resistance to the coercive ideology of the state. Civil society is thus seen as distinct from the state by its very potential to resist it (Bratton 1989a; Clark 1995; Diamond 1994; Gyimah-Boadi 1996; Taylor 1990; Turner and Hulme 1997). The "civil society to the rescue" paradigm is often described in connection with transnational activist movements focusing on the environment, or women, or other issues of supposed "global" concern (Keck and Sikkink 1998). Sometimes civil society itself is discussed as a global force (Walzer 1995). One analytical limitation of the use of civil society in the case of NGOs is that the category of "NGO" is ambiguous (Fisher 1997; Vakil 1997): there are multiple types and variations inherent to the category. The "non" of "non-governmental" could just as easily refer to grassroots resistance to national governments as to an international civil society. NGOs are represented by two conceptually distinct applications of the state-versus-civil-society paradigm. NGOs as civil society either appear in a nationalist and autochthonous sphere of grassroots political advocacy (Clark 1991; Mararike 1995; Moyo 1991; Ndegwa 1996; Weisgrau 1997), or in an international sphere of humanitarian aid (Beigbeder 1991; Clark 1995; Tendler 1975).

In international civil society, criticism of NGOs stems from insider reports of aid agencies (Hancock 1989; Maren 1997). Highly moralistic, and in the spirit of sensational journalism, these accounts take on foreign aid as a massive and evil business linking governments to "corrupt" African politicians at the expense of poor Africans. Such analyses accuse NGOs of exacerbating problems that humanitarian assistance is presumed to ease or solve. Foreign aid itself is portrayed as a monstrous bureaucracy in support of nothing but its own perpetuation, a "self-serving system that sacrifices its own practitioners and intended beneficiaries in order that it may survive and grow" (Maren 1997:11). This scheme, even when it does not name the state, relegates the state to a negative space shadowed by moral ambiguity. The state appears as a consuming and predatory (ergo corrupt) forum, as opposed to a productive and protective one.

Other scholars argue that the work of NGOs in international civil society threatens the sovereignty of states. NGOs are able to cross national boundaries and "have created direct and independent forms of non-governmental diplomacy through networks of their own" (Clark 1995:508; Hanlon 2000; Kilby 2000). Conflicts arise in issues of international versus national governance when, for example, international demands voiced by NGOs for human rights and environmental conservation compete with state control over citizens and natural resources. NGOs have specialized agendas, and tackle arenas that states tend to ignore. Moreover, NGOs use International Governmental Organizations or IGOs (such as the UN) as channels to assist in lobbying efforts to alter government positions. These channels of influence are also found in NGO networks of international civil society and self-created inter-

governmental arenas (Riles 2000). As NGOs have access to international financial and volunteer resources that supersede states, they bypass states in both
global and local arenas. In the process, African states are becoming increasingly dependent on NGOs for the implementation of development and even
other basic social programs. Theoretically, NGOs glean increased strength
from this dependence and therefore have more opportunity to press for far-
reaching political and economic policy changes (Bratton 1989b; Farrington et
al. 1993).

Scholarship on local civil society (one bounded by national borders)
emphasizes small, local, voluntary organizations to argue that the NGO sector
has advantages over governments in addressing poverty. NGOs are seen as the
"natural partners of the rural poor" (Riddell and Robinson 1995), privileging
small-scale projects and a base of voluntarism. In this literature, NGOs fit into
the "associational life that occurs in the political space beyond the state's
purview" (Bratton 1989a:411). It is a local civil society distinct from the state.
For these scholars (Bratton 1989a; Farrington et al. 1993; Riddell and
Robinson 1995) the center of political gravity has shifted in Africa from the
state to civil society. Particularly in studies of development, NGOs are seen as
advocates of civil society in their struggles against repressive states (Bratton
1989a, 1989b; Clark 1991; Farrington et al. 1993; Mararike 1995; Riddell and
Robinson 1995; Wellard and Copestake 1993). Through local civil society,
NGOs challenge the state (Ndegwa 1994, 1996; Rea 1962) and locally interpret
state development programs (Weisgrau 1997).

My approach, in contrast to the above-mentioned analyses, builds on
scholarship that questions the category of civil society. Tracing the logic of the
term to a neoliberal project that conceals its own use of massive state power
and defines civil society in its own image, some scholars have noted how the
concept of civil society ignores existing forms of civic organization in favor of
those that match the agenda of free-market democracy (Beckman 1993; Eyoh
1996; Williams 1993; Woods 1992). These scholars argue that liberating civil
society from the hegemonic grip of the state is a critical component of the
neoliberal economic project, and caution that civil society, as a concept, should
not be applied without regard to specific social, economic, and historical circumstances. Chatterjee's (1990) critique of Taylor's use of the term "civil society" is a notable example. He uses Hegel to argue that civil society is a western
European concept that cannot be released from the particular relation of states
to the bourgeoisie in early European history, something that is not applicable
in other parts of the world and at other times in history—especially in contexts
where the nuclear family is not dominant. Others add a critique of "good governance," arguing that it too is a conceptual product of neoliberal ideological
priorities propelled by the World Bank through NGOs (Leftwich 1994;
Williams and Young 1994). Still others argue against neoliberal concepts of
democracy and civil society that divorce them from the state, and see civil soci-

ety rather through the lens of social movements such as student protests and labor strikes; a theoretical middle ground—again, spatial metaphors intact—between states and local communities (Chazan 1994; Sachikonye 1995a; for a critique of spatial metaphors in civil society-state debates see Ferguson and Gupta 2002). In late 1990s Zimbabwe, NGOs were neither merely part of a transnational humanitarian civil society nor did they bubble up with the spirit of democracy from local soil. NGOs were organizations whose ground could not be fixed, and this was how their power was articulated and became productive.

For example, At WV Zimbabwe's Annual Day of Prayer in 1997, a transnational company picnic where employees of each national office staff united to pray for world events, one of the invited speakers was a board member of World Vision International.[8] This board member was also the Deputy Minister of Agriculture for the government of Zimbabwe. As she addressed the WV Zimbabwe staff, she spoke as the voice of World Vision and the voice of ZANU-PF: "MPs are supposed to be legislators but we are doing development, talking about development, doing your work. . . . One of your responsibilities is for you to pray for your leaders, us the politicians."[9] In this setting, the identity of the NGO board member troubled categorical boundaries between NGOs and the state. She was not alone. If one examines the employment histories of the staff members of both Christian Care and World Vision, one discovers that most of the NGO staff have worked for the state at some point in their careers. At Independence, the Zimbabwean civil service grew to build a new Zimbabwe.[10] Yet, during ESAP, World Bank initiatives demanded a stripped-down state, supposedly to foster a strong civil society. Some of the casualties of this equation were civil servants.[11] A result of ESAP was that employees from the Ministries of Agricultural Development, Information, Education, and Health and Social Welfare flooded the staff of transnational NGOs, pouring into the country to "help with the transition." For good reason, working for an NGO in Zimbabwe in the late 1990s was prime employment for educated Zimbabweans. Hence, categorical boundaries between NGOs and the state bled into each other, a fact demonstrated perhaps simplistically by the World Vision board member who was also an MP.

This categorical uncertainty was also reflected with regard to NGOs and the communities with which they worked. For example, in the development projects of WV Zimbabwe, because of the donor structure of child sponsorship and the labor-intensive apparatus required to track sponsored children and their correspondence with foreign sponsors (discussed in the previous chapter), a project clerk and bookkeeper were hired from the local community to work for WV Zimbabwe. They lived at the project site and monitored the project on a daily basis. They represented the NGO as it was embodied in the local community.[12] These individuals grew up in the rural community, and they worked for the NGO: reporting to it, monitoring development, and keeping the project "on track." They were of the community and of the NGO. A growing trend with WV Zimbabwe projects was the Area Development Program (ADP). In this development initiative, the entire NGO staff lived at the project. Hired from Harare and placed in the community, they became part of the community. World Vision field officers "walked with the people" the way Jesus did; the NGO was "inculturated." It "grew local roots," echoing colonial missionary boards with their native catechists. The ADP structure aimed to eliminate the NGO field officers based in Harare, along with the monthly checkups. However, it did not eliminate the ambiguity of the relationships forged between NGOs and rural communities. Nor did it eradicate bureaucratic structures of accountability and governmentality. The ADP project staff continued to report to donors, to speak on behalf of community projects to local state representatives and donors, and to liaise with local government structures and funding bodies.

Religious NGOs working with communities in programs of rural development were engaged in long-term projects lasting anywhere from two to ten years. While NGO field officers overseeing the development projects and reporting to the Harare office shuttled between the rural projects and urban Harare on a monthly basis, development was also monitored and in effect conducted by local development committees of village community members.[13] At monthly development meetings when field officers made their visits to "the rurals," these complex relationships between communities, NGOs, and the local arms of the state generated political tensions. A project clerk mentioned how WV Zimbabwe project offices were not solely for community meetings; the state utilized the buildings as well: "Agritex teaches farmers here; whenever the District Councilor has something to say, he comes here. . . . "[14] As I will demonstrate below, the lines between NGO workers, communities, and local government were in constant motion, as development became a desperate political platform for the state. In addition to the politics of individual intent—of donors, recipients and families involved in development, examined in the preceding chapter—the work of NGOs was tightly bound up with the politics of the state.

RELIGIOUS NGOS, CHURCHES, AND THE PRIVATE VOLUNTARY ORGANIZATIONS ACT

When NGOs source and allocate international funds, they bypass the fiscal structures of national economies. While dollars given to the rural poor through NGOs for community development constituted a significant portion of the Zimbabwean economy at the time of this research, they did not flow through state budgets. When I asked the National Treasurer on the Executive Committee of Christian Care, formerly an employee with the Ministry of Information, how the government tracked the activities of NGOs, he replied:

"The Ministry of Labor governs the Private Voluntary Organizations Act, under which NGOs have to register, but this is the extent of it—only legal issues. Perhaps in the President's office, under Rural Development, but there wouldn't be any statistics except for the registration of cooperatives [Cooperative Development]." When asked where the government recorded information, he replied, "It would be a waste of your time; these sorts of records aren't kept. Only those that want to form into cooperatives under the Cooperative Act."[15] A gentle comment by a former civil servant who was on the local governing board of an NGO. No records were kept. His experience spoke volumes about how little control African states had over the finances that fuel NGO-driven development.

In Zimbabwe, as in other parts of southern Africa, state governments have attempted to control the efforts of NGOs through legislation (Ndegwa 1994). One dramatic example of this was the manner in which The Welfare Act of 1966 was revised without the consultation of the NGO community in 1995. A new parliamentary act called The Private Voluntary Organizations Act (PVO) sailed through parliament without debate or discussion. While the legislation required NGOs to register with the government (as had the Welfare Act of 1966), it also allowed the government to take over the management of an NGO at will. NGOs reacted to this legislation with shock and horror, especially when the government attempted to take over the Association of Women's Clubs (AWC). Religious NGOs began to protest this legislation and formed an advocacy group to change the legislation called the PVO Campaign.[16] The PVO Act was finally repealed and the regulation allowing the government to take over an NGO was removed. That this issue was taken to the supreme court of Zimbabwe, and that part of the PVO Act was repealed, received no mention in the state-controlled national press. In 1998, efforts were being made to have the PVO Act repealed entirely on grounds of freedom of speech. Between 1995 and 1997, the PVO Act was a site of a struggle between the state and NGOs over resources.

Although the PVO Act, and the Welfare Act which preceded it, did not have legislative jurisdiction over churches in Zimbabwe, religious NGOs were not outside its scope. They were some of the most vocal opponents of the legislation. Religion was conspicuous by its absence in the PVO Act. Organizations such as ZCC and CCJP were exempt from the strict regulations to which the NGO, Christian Care, was subject. Recall that Christian Care was created as an arm of ZCC (the Zimbabwe Council of Churches), set up to handle the political tension that arose from its activities. It was an organization designed to take the political pressure off the churches. In the 1990s, PVOs (aka NGOs) were development organizations that fell under different legislation than church organizations. However, these distinctions blurred in practice. PVOs like World Vision and Christian Care worked very closely and collaboratively with local churches. They registered with the state under the PVO Act, but merged with the activities of local, rural churches that sought development projects for their congregational communities.

Christian Care was involved in a complex manner with local churches: they were both the governing structure of the NGO and its membership. The Harare regional director felt that the interaction between the NGO, and churches in communities where the NGO worked, was not well developed. I noticed that there was no accounting of evangelism activities, or any church activities, in the annual or project reports. This had not been the case with World Vision, which supported evangelism rallies at its projects and meticulously documented attendance. The regional manager explained that it was the responsibility of the Zimbabwe Council of Churches (Christian Care's governing body) to concern itself directly with evangelism. As a field officer, he was responsible for overseeing the technical aspects of development projects. He said, "We would rather have Christian Council do the evangelism and we do the development work. This is why you probably couldn't get that message in our reports. Because I guess that is deliberate." Although he did not consider it part of his job to evangelize per se, he worked with local churches in the field. The churches facilitated the development work of Christian Care by accommodating staff when they made visits to projects, as well as by providing the NGO with background information on communities. Church leaders knew the needs of the communities. As he said, "Because they stay with the people I think they are the frontline in terms of information gathering." Churches also made communities aware of the services that Christian Care could offer. At the time of my research, Christian Care was going through a restructuring that would give more power and initiative to the churches, the "membership" of ZCC. Previously, only churches that were members of ZCC (listed in Appendix 2) could participate in the work of Christian Care. The aim of restructuring was to provide more direct links between churches and Christian Care. The regional director explained that in the new structure, "churches have now been asked to be members of Christian Care in their own right. And I think that way I can see churches playing a more facilitatory role in determining the mission of Christian Care." This was, in a way, a return to the more political and historical relationship that Christian Care had with churches, working directly on issues of poverty and welfare. The churches, through the Zimbabwe Council of Churches, formed Christian Care in order to care for political activists who were put in jail during the liberation struggle. In addition to ministering to the detainees, there was the welfare of the families with which to be concerned. Christian Care was formed to provide welfare assistance to those who were being persecuted during the liberation struggle. The Harare regional director explained how two directives intersected, linking politically with the church to bypass the state, and promoting the Christian mission of helping the needy:

> Because Christian Care's beginnings were in the church . . . how would I put it . . . the church realized that there was injustice within the previous [colonial] government if I can call it that, the persecution of political activists, their being put in jail. The churches then saw themselves as having a role not only to minister to those who had been detained, but also to meet the needs of their families when they were out. So initially I would put it that way, so it was that fight for justice that the churches saw. Because they were observed and seen as religious groupings, they could not administer to the welfare of these people so they thought of Christian Care.

Since its inception as a political welfare organization, the focus of Christian Care had changed. Now it was focused on "economic injustice" as it assisted the poor. The regional director continued: "We are looking at the poor, those who cannot meet their own needs." After the liberation struggle ended, those who had been assisted by Christian Care became the politicians of the new Zimbabwe, and the policies of Christian Care were set by church leaders. They sat on the National and Regional Councils that governed the NGO.

The churches were actively involved in the development work at World Vision's rural project sites: church leaders sat on local management committees of development projects, and NGOs worked directly with churches in providing skills training for development projects (such as dressmaking classes). Both Christian Care and World Vision depended upon their connections to local church leaders in the course of their development work.

In Zimbabwe, not much importance was placed on whether an NGO was religious or secular. This was perhaps due to the historical role of churches in the provision of agricultural development in the region. While I found that Christian NGOs were more overtly involved in challenging the state than secular NGOs, those that did challenge the state were not involved with economic development. Organizations like the Catholic Commission for Justice and Peace (CCJP), Ecumenical Support Services (ESS), and the Zimbabwean Council of Churches (ZCC) employed staff to research government policies and present critical evaluations. Some examples of this were ZCC's Economic Justice program, Ecumenical Support Services' (ESS) PVO Campaign that organized the resistance of NGOs to government legislation, and CCJP's effort to rewrite the Zimbabwean Constitution. Extremely controversial topics were tackled by some Christian NGOs. Secular NGOs, in contrast, were more dependent on the government of Zimbabwe for political (local and national) support. With less rural infrastructure to rely upon (for example, no church base), and conspicuous ties to foreign institutions such as the World Bank and the IMF, secular NGOs largely kept quiet during the PVO debates. This is not as counterintuitive as it may seem. Secular NGOs were reluctant to criticize the government of Zimbabwe lest work permits be revoked. Directors of secular NGOs told me that their job was not to get involved in local politics; they were not particularly concerned by government efforts to control the activities of NGOs. However, when I asked a field worker for Christian Care about why the Zimbabwean government was so concerned with the activities of NGOs, he said curtly, "Why try to control something if you already have control over it?" The state was vying for control over resources and sovereignty, as was manifested in struggles over the PVO Act. Although the economic development that NGOs supported involved collaborative efforts with the state (with local leadership, for example the District Councilor), the funding of development flowed directly from donors to NGOs to the rural poor, bypassing the Zimbabwean state altogether. While NGOs worked "in collaboration" with local state representatives in development projects, donor directives funded NGOs with an eye to reaching the rural poor as directly as possible. With the PVO Act, ZANU-PF took extra precautions to control the flow of foreign aid. In the midst of such efforts, Christian NGOs such as World Vision and Christian Care negotiated with the state through what I call a politics of transcendence.

THE KINGDOM OF GOD AND NEOLIBERAL ECONOMICS

Using the religious discourse of a Kingdom of God and the neoliberal economic discourse of free markets, World Vision and Christian Care were engaged in politics in such a way as to avoid threats of reprisal from a desperate and volatile state. Although categorized as non-state actors, NGOs were directly involved with the state. This contradictory relationship resembles the ambiguity of colonial missionaries as they supported and challenged the Rhodesian state (Ranger 1962; Weller and Linden 1984). Most NGOs involved in humanitarian and development work in Zimbabwe—religious and secular— identified themselves as "apolitical." But Ferguson (1994) and others (Alexander and McGregor 2000; Worby 1998) have shown that development agencies, even when not directly allied with political forces, have distinctly political effects. This apolitical stance of development agencies, the "anti-politics machine," paves the way for the state. Two discourses facilitated this apolitical stance in Zimbabwe: the first was a discourse of the "Kingdom of God" and the second was a discourse of "markets."

Ironically, although World Vision and Christian Care advocated a similar anti-politics, the genesis of each institution arose from highly politicized contexts. Readers may recall from previous chapters that World Vision International (the parent organization of World Vision Zimbabwe) began its work in the late 1940s and was staunchly anticommunist (communist nations did not support Christian organizations). This political agenda continued in post-Cold War attempts to target places such as the newly "free" Soviet Union. A politically "neutral" stance was officially endorsed. For example, in a World

Vision interoffice memo from its California office regarding the subject "Writing for World Vision," the following guidelines were proposed: "World Vision articles should not take political positions. The agency's work transcends politics to meet human need wherever and for whatever reason it exists. Articles should not favor or criticize any Christian group, because the agency is non-sectarian and inter-denominational."[17] In email solicitations to support WV USA's international efforts I encountered the following description: "World Vision is an international Christian humanitarian organization serving the world's poor and marginalized by providing programs that help save lives, bring hope, and restore dignity. This assistance is provided without regard to people's religious beliefs, gender, or ethnic background." I will add political affiliation. World Vision insisted on presenting itself as neutral. Christian Care, as the development arm of the Zimbabwe Council of Churches, also emerged from an intensely political history (as described in Chapter 1) but positioned itself as politically neutral.

The "official" discourse of World Vision International and one that many of its employees had adopted in Zimbabwe was that the NGO transcended politics via the moral order of the "Kingdom of God." The Kingdom of God transcended national boundaries and historic particularities through a universalizing Christian agenda. The Kingdom of God discourse, however, was riddled with contradictions. For instance, its monarchical model and sovereign authority stood in direct contrast to World Vision's democratic structure of a network of "partners" and its mission of "community-based" development. Nonetheless, the aim of transcending political allegiances afforded NGOs like World Vision and Christian Care a particular ease when working in the context of politically volatile situations such as famine and drought, or even with governments on the verge of collapse. One of the six points outlined in World Vision's mission statement was the "promotion of justice that seeks to change unjust structures affecting the poor among whom we work," a goal with obvious political consequences, if not political intent. Mauss (1990 [1950]) has observed that the word commonly known as "alms" is derived from an Arabic word which means "justice." This notion contains the philosophical beginnings of the social obligation to give, and of Western forms of charity. In the case of World Vision, employees were not "appeasing the Gods," but were using the implicit link between gift exchange and spiritual forces to transcend worldly political structures that restricted their mobility and made their work impossible. By placing "God as the leader of development" (a phrase repeated by WV Zimbabwe-sponsored communities as well as field officers assisting the process), it created a transcendent sphere of operation, supposedly immune to local politics.

Although NGO employees described their work as apolitical, every employee I spoke with in both Christian and secular NGOs had something to say about politics. Opinions about political engagement varied widely among

NGO staff. However, a common discursive thread was that NGO workers operated as impartial interpreters, as agents of change. They were neutral ambassadors of an international civil society. If not the Kingdom of God, then the market offered an anti-political metaphor for NGO activities. For example, the director of CARE Zimbabwe (a secular NGO) defined the mission of his NGO as "facilitating markets." In this case, the NGO transcended politics, and the state, through the neutral zone of "markets" and "choices." NGOs gave people options, the director said, "by moving in . . . by creating systems whereby the economies can expand in the rural areas." This involved eliminating "market distortions" created by the colonial state that had restricted the economy of rural areas, and favored the development of a rural labor force for urban industry. One of CARE's primary objectives, as this director saw it, was to liberate market forces through micro-enterprise development programs that made credit more accessible. While this liberation was discussed in terms of breaking down the social and economic barriers that had been installed during colonialism, in practice it involved remaking (or unmaking) the postcolonial state. He explained how CARE was involved in efforts, funded by the IMF and the World Bank, to decentralize the state.[18] CARE was "working at the level of the government":

> The government of Zimbabwe has adopted a policy whereby they are decentralizing a lot of activities down to the district level. Well that's all fine and dandy. You've got to empower the people at the district levels with the skills, the knowledge, and the facilities to be able to make use of that decentralization power that they've just received. So, we are working at the level of the government.

Through an apolitical politics that worked to "build local government" and to decentralize the Zimbabwean state, this secular NGO—in its very attempt to strengthen markets—was weakening the existing state. This approach was not without contest among NGO staff. Some employees of Christian NGOs that I spoke with firmly believed that their efforts should not work against the state. Others strongly felt that their mission was to be the state's moral critic. As much as some saw their work as apolitical, others in the same sphere were critical of that stance. Some, as the Christian Witness Coordinator at World Vision, felt that "NGOs can't afford to be at loggerheads with the government," and that they should never see themselves as working in opposition to the state. If the churches were, as Mugabe proposed in a speech quoted in the local newspaper, to become the moral fiber of the nation, then Christian NGOs were also engaged in taking its moral temperature. There was a symbiotic relationship between churches, Christian NGOs involved in development, and the state. To work in collaboration with the state was the official position of World Vision and Christian Care, as well as every secular development NGO I encountered.

As an example, I offer a picture of a World Vision development project office. Each WV Zimbabwe development project site had an office, consisting of a cement-block house with a desk, chair, bookkeeping ledgers, and a wall with a photomontage. Displayed on heavy construction paper, with visual and textual narratives accounting for the boreholes drilled, latrines dug, and school-blocks built, these montages were evidence of industry and accomplishment. They visually manifested the products of development. In one photo, the national director of WV Zimbabwe resembled a politician campaigning for office, smiling while shaking hands with villagers. This realm of rural development project sites was where local communities worked with local government and NGO field officers to plan, monitor, and conduct "development." The interaction between local government officials and NGO officials commenced during the initial stages of a project. One of the first rituals of an NGO field officer's visit to a rural development site was to stop by the local government office to see either the Rural District Councilor or the District Administrator. This respectful visit garnered permission to continue what NGO staff repeatedly described as "a partnership with local authorities." Indeed, this was a recurring part of an NGO field officer's responsibility. Nonetheless, when I asked members of local development committees at rural project sites how the state, in the form of local government, participated in their development efforts, my question was often met with laughter. Groups of men said "aaaaaaa," and laughed at the ridiculous nature of my enquiry. One group said: "We communicate information to the [District] Councilor, but no response." Another, in the same region, said, "The Rural District Councilor comes through once a month. The MP came once. They convince us with their sweet tongues. At the district level, the council is 60K from here and the MP is in Harare."[19] The state was without resources for development. The "partnership" was a necessary fiction.

This fiction of peaceful partnership and collaboration with the state differed from the more challenging and advocacy-oriented approaches of other Christian NGOs, such as Ecumenical Support Services and the Catholic Commission for Justice and Peace (Dorman 2002; Ndegwa 1996). Notably, NGOs involved in advocacy were not involved in programs of economic development. What was it about development that was both extremely political and required the denial of political engagement? While churches like the Catholic Commission for Justice and Peace were actively challenging some government policies, many churches and Christian NGOs were involved with development work that the government depended upon. This was the contradiction of Christian development NGOs, a contradiction of being on the forefront of politics and striving to transcend it.

Despite discourses of the Kingdom of God and liberal markets that framed the work of Christian NGOs as politically neutral, the development work of religious NGOs was intensely political. Indeed, in the late 1990s their work was a rather desperate platform for party politics. Due to programs of economic structural adjustment (ESAP), the state had limited funds for development. NGOs, on the other hand, provided access to resources. Meanwhile, NGOs relied on permission from local state officials to carry out their projects. NGO employees described their work as being "in collaboration" with local government officials. This dynamic set up a series of tensions in which the state was so weak that it begged NGOs to continue their development work, and simultaneously tried to take credit for it. To illustrate this precarious and political dynamic, I offer three ethnographic examples.

The first event took place in March of 1997, when I traveled with two field officers from Christian Care to visit projects in Hurungwe, northwestern Zimbabwe. After stopping by the farmer-cooperatives that the NGO had assisted, the field officers attended a meeting with three regional officers from Agritex (the Ministry of Agricultural Extension and Rural Resettlement). During the meeting, local government officials asked Christian Care for funds to support a regional plan that would, as they explained, "outline well-planned villages." They said, "The government wants to create well-planned villages. Planning gives direction to everybody." The meeting was a sad affair. The Agritex officers spoke of how the state lacked resources for national level planning, and that the state was broke. The three Agritex officers had not been reimbursed for their petrol expenses in months. Placed in an awkward position, the Christian Care staff were accustomed to such requests from the state, but could not meet its demand, as funding for Christian Care projects was allocated for small-scale projects, not national planning. The NGO employees delicately expressed their regrets to Agritex.[20] In this setting, the state was not only unable to pay for "planning"; it was precariously feeble. National infrastructure was well beyond the scope of Christian Care's programs, which were oriented toward donor concerns of "reaching the poor" as directly as possible, and not toward supporting the Zimbabwean state.

Despite these weaknesses, the state attempted to look strong. My second example is a graduation ceremony in northwestern Zimbabwe at a World Vision development project. Along with speeches, there were praise songs, and a parade of final projects designed by dressmaking students. As each proud graduate-to-be modeled their tailoring, the audience sang, clapped, and danced in the rows of seats. Husbands danced their wives down the aisles. Certificates were distributed to graduates. The students, dressed in blue and white uniforms and clustered on one side of the room, formed a dressmaking choir. They sang Shona praise songs about Jesus and dressmaking.

As a pastor began her sermon, a truck-full of ZANU-PF representatives raced through the door in a dramatic entrance. They came late and stole the show, pulling up to the door in a white Jeep with ZANU-PF stenciled on its side. As they piled out of the truck, their presence was loud and official. The dressmaking choir switched the words of their songs to praise ZANU-PF as the five representatives of the state paraded in and took seats facing the large audience. Embodying the state, the Rural District Councilor introduced the ZANU-PF party member, the construction officer, an Agritex officer, the District Chairman for ZANU-PF, the District Administrator, and a woman representing the chairwoman of the ZANU-PF Women's League, who could not attend. Three government representatives stood up to make speeches; each speech took credit for the development work of World Vision, which was planning to pull out of the project in the coming months. This transition, a passing on of development from the NGO and community to the community and state, was dangerous in its liminality. Local government officials begged the church collaborating with World Vision to stay, and took credit for the development work of the NGO and community. An Agritex officer stood up and encouraged people to cooperate with donors and projects to "raise themselves up." She encouraged the community to believe in God, to work together, and to work with the churches. She spoke of how the district used to be "the most poor in the country." After two years of the dressmaking classes "we are more developed," she said. The ZANU-PF district representative begged World Vision not to leave. His speech was framed in distinctly moral terms, as he urged the community to work with the church, to concentrate on development (in contrast to gossip), and to work in harmony to make money:

> To World Vision I am saying: Don't leave us. We are begging you to keep on helping us, and to [the church]: to keep on helping us and bringing us to God. In the community we need not to gossip but to concentrate on development. Not on this and that which are bad words. . . . I love people who live in harmony. If you are not sick, if you are not in prison, if you are not in bad mental health, there is nothing to stop you from making money.

Harmony and moneymaking, these were the possibilities that NGOs such as World Vision offered. The district representative made promises that extended beyond the confines of the classroom block. After promising to bring the development concerns of the community to the attention of parliament, and to encourage the building of a factory in the area that promised new jobs, he asked World Vision to stay, again, so that he could be re-elected:

> I am going to ask Parliament to come and see what you are doing. Even donors will source more funds to help people who are doing so well. I am going to tell your MP to make a factory here, and to encourage your MP to come and see how things are starting to move . . . World Vision should remain here in the province so I will also be able to remain here as the district head.[21]

The development work of World Vision, in collaboration with a local church, was a key resource for the state. Yet NGO workers spoke of their work as transcending local politics to alleviate poverty in allegiance with the Kingdom of God. This politics of transcendence, distinctly apolitical, facilitated interaction with the state.

My third example is a case in which the anniversary celebrations of Christian Care became a desperate platform for state politics. Christian Care's thirtieth anniversary celebrations were held in October of 1997 at rural project sites. The rationale for setting the celebrations at project sites instead of in Harare (or even in regional offices) was to emphasize that development was for the people being developed. One field officer explained it to me as bringing development back to the people. Aside from the 200 or so community members who came for the particular event I attended, which incidentally involved a free meal, the state was on parade. How, I wondered, was this placing development in the hands of the people? State representation was indeed significant. In attendance were the following local authorities: a Member of Parliament (MP), Chief Seke, the District Administrator, several Agritex officers (from the Department of Agricultural, Technical and Extension Services, Ministry of Agricultural Extension and Rural Resettlement, Government of Zimbabwe), someone from ARDA (Agricultural and Rural Development Authority), a representative from the Ministry of National Affairs and Cooperative Development, two representatives from the Ministry of Health, a woman from the Ministry of Information, and the District Councilor. The local MP, from the central committee of ZANU-PF, arrived two hours late with big fanfare; the agenda of the celebrations had been rearranged in anticipation of his arrival. The MP was dressed formally in a full suit and yellow tie on this hot day. His cell phone rang conspicuously during his speech. He began his speech with party slogans: *"Pamberi ZANU-PF, Pamberi President Robert Mugabe"* ("Forward with ZANU-PF, forward with Robert Mugabe"). Christian Care was "complementing government efforts," he said, and spoke of the challenges of finding markets for the products of the cooperative. Then he began making promises. He promised that 1/4 tonnes of poultry or pig feed would be given to the co-op. He said he had written to a number of organizations for donations, and he handed out bank brochures for the National Credit and Savings Society, in anticipation of all the money the community would ostensibly be making. He said donors from the U.S. would be installing electricity and building houses in the area in December. "From 100 houses will be increased to 150 at Christmas time. Tiles will be manufactured locally so they will place a big order. There will be training for tile makers." The MP was full of promises of good fortune: he positioned himself as a savior. After the MP's speech, a Christian Care staff member gave a t-shirt to the MP with "Christian Care 30 Years of Hope" printed across the front. The invited church choir sang a song whose words translated as "those people who are lazy, they can join cooperatives."[22] The choir sang thanking Mugabe for his support; they sang to thank the MP, they thanked the Councilor for the area, and they sang to thank Christian Care and all the government ministries that supported them. Development in this context was more of a theater for politicians than "for the people." The politicians took credit for the work of the NGO and the community, and used the celebration as a platform for campaigning. Chief Seke was the only individual who was publicly critical of the project. He criticized the cleanliness of the livestock pens, and commented on the small profits that had been reaped.

AMBIGUOUS LOYALTIES

To work in development amidst the delicate and often competing political agendas described above presented difficulties for NGO staff. The apparent contradictions of transcending local politics and simultaneously facilitating the operations of a weak state took particular shape in a project that I had engaged in with Christian Care. Like many contemporary anthropologists, I was self-conscious about the potential I had as an ethnographer to take knowledge from the field and to ignore my own participation in its making. I met with the Harare regional director of Christian Care and asked him how I could assist the organization. Aside from seeking some directive for daily institutional interaction, I had a vague desire to be useful. The Harare director suggested that I review the history of communication and "accountability" within the organization, and make some projections and guidelines for improving communication. There had been trouble in the past with competition between stakeholders (defined as beneficiaries, employees both paid and volunteer, donors, government, and other NGOs and churches). The trouble revolved around who had access to resources, and who had authority to distribute them. Misunderstandings had generated an internal scandal that was being addressed through an intensive organizational restructuring and evaluation. Realizing that there were specific problems that the NGO sought to address, I reviewed relationships between three realms of the organization that I saw competing for authority: (1) the governing bodies of the NGO, including the National Council, National Executive Committee, Regional Council and Regional Committees; (2) the staff, including the National Executive Officer, and (3) external contacts and other stakeholders, including donors, media, government ministries, and beneficiaries. Churches fit in as both members of the governing bodies, and as stakeholders as the membership. My analysis was not very complex: there were frequent struggles over how much power each of the stakeholders had in the organization, and at times these struggles resulted in a lack of clarity with regard to authority and decision-making. The NGO had a decentralized structure (of regional and national offices), which was identified by many in the institution as one of the organization's strengths, as well as one of its weaknesses. Although the NGO had the potential to be in close contact with its constituency (beneficiaries), it was unclear exactly how decisions as to the allocation of resources and power were made. There were serious communication gaps between finance offices and project administrative offices that were manifest in conflicting and competing agendas between those who raised and managed the budget on the one hand, and those who worked in the field expending resources through Christian Care's projects on the other.

As I interviewed employees in Christian Care, I conceptualized an organizational flow-chart that documented what I saw to be vulnerabilities in the institutional structure through which daily institutional practices were carried out. My chart was hierarchical, with power and directives flowing downwards from the National Council, through the national offices, through the regional offices to the field staff and eventually the beneficiaries. Other stakeholders such as regional councils, donors, member churches, and local government extended in octopus-like arms on the sides of the hierarchical flow. I anticipated that my project would be filed forever in a cabinet, lost, or ignored. I was surprised and a bit embarrassed by how seriously my report was received. Not only was my cursory analysis empowered by the strength of my outsider status, it was taken seriously by the regional director and passed on to the national director, and eventually distributed to the members of the National Council at a subsequent meeting. The national director reflected on my analysis in the form of extensive written comments in dialogue with my recommendations. His response analyzed the limitations and potential avenues for improvement in my recommendations. His primary criticism of my analysis was its simplicity. The arrows should move in both directions, he said. My key confusion regarding NGOs and their relation to the state and to civil society (in the case of Christian Care, both the state and civil society were its "stakeholders") was a false assumption of hierarchical flow from donors, through NGOs, to beneficiaries. My analysis relied on spatial metaphors of state and civil society that posited one above the other (Ferguson and Gupta 2002). The world on the ground was far more complex than either my flowchart or scholarly civil society/state debates could reveal.

As mentioned earlier in this chapter, a recurrent theme in ongoing discussions with project coordinators for World Vision and Christian Care was the complicated working relationship that NGOs had with the government (as a "stakeholder" in development). One project coordinator for World Vision said, for example, "We work very closely with the government." He described the working relationship as a process of acknowledging local power structures and local government officials. This was the theme (or fiction) of partnership articulated earlier in the chapter. However, the fact that international funds went directly from donors to World Vision and bypassed the state was something that local government officials would not "go along with." The project coordinator said,

> I think basically what the government people want you to do, once you acknowledge their presence within a community as the leaders of the districts, and so forth, I think you would have done your job very well. All they want is for you to be given authority to work within the community and as you work to report to them about what you are doing, regularly attending their meetings and so forth and so on, it's fine. But of course you will find problems, they will have their differences. You will find people in government circles maybe don't go along with your ideas because they have got their own ideas.

As much as local families were frustrated by World Vision's funding going directly to children through programs of child sponsorship (described in Chapter 3), so was the state. Monies were given to the local management committee, the bookkeeper, and the staff that ran local project offices. These offices accounted for the funds, and filed reports with the Harare office. Project officers visited to check on the project, to review how the money was being used, to survey the accounting in the cashbook, vouchers, and receipts, and to guarantee there was no fraud. The government was not happy with this arrangement and it created conflict. The same project coordinator for World Vision mentioned above explained:

> So we have a problem with government in that government wants the funds to go through their office and that we are saying we give these things directly to the people. So, somehow it creates some conflict that is hidden. Because you will find some that would come out openly and say 'Ok, we are not happy about the way you are doing things,' and I always tell them: this is how we are supposed to be doing things. There is no way we can change, you see. Since you are a donor, you have got the money and so forth, there is no way they can say, ok get out of the community. But it remains a bone of contention, to say, 'Ok, why is it that you are giving money directly to the communities and not through us?' Because they feel they are the rightful persons to do that kind of job. So basically that's the main problem.

These specifically local tensions, between NGOs and the state, were a product of the transnational context of funding in which NGOs operate. This context was highly political. As the Zimbabwean state became weaker, it depended more upon the work of Christian Care and World Vision to provide welfare services for its citizens. The NGO workers were called upon to navigate this precarious political terrain.

CONCLUSION

Georg Simmel writes on how charitable giving serves to support the status quo in his essay *The Poor* (Simmel 1994 [1908]). He writes, "The motive for alms then resides exclusively in the significance of giving for the giver. When Jesus told the wealthy young man, 'Give your riches to the poor,' what apparently mattered to him were not the poor, but rather the soul of the wealthy man for whose salvation this sacrifice was merely a means or a symbol" (1994:153). Simmel elaborates that assistance is a symptom and necessity of socio-structural inequities: "the goal of assistance is precisely to mitigate certain extreme manifestations of social differentiation, so that the social structure may continue to be based on this differentiation" (1994:155). The social aim is consequently to maintain a status quo. The haves constitute the needs of the have-nots; poverty as a social phenomenon is defined by those who attempt to alleviate it. When giving is institutionalized, it is abstracted and removed from its sensate form. When giving becomes the obligation of states and institutions (such as NGOs) instead of individuals, the poor are removed from the functional means-ends teleology of maintaining the status quo. Giving through states or NGOs may not be styled as giving at all. For example, in the early socialist era of independent Zimbabwe, development (and social welfare) was an entitlement. In the neoliberal paradigm of the late 1990s, however, development had once again become a charitable act. While welfare states speak of entitlements, NGO discourse, in contrast, has moved toward a charity model. In this model, NGOs act as agents of the political and funding initiatives of wealthy nations, or "international civil society" (cf. Hanlon 2000). The relevance of Simmel's point to the work of NGOs in Zimbabwe is that once giving is institutionalized it is no longer about human suffering. The effect is that the status quo is reified for those who are giving assistance. The poor, the recipients of aid are simultaneously within and without the group. Akin to Simmel's concept of the stranger—an outsider who is nevertheless an integral part of the collectivity by his very alien status—the social poor are no longer those who lack means or "suffer specific deficiencies and deprivations, but those who receive assistance or should receive it according to social norms" (Simmel 1994:175). It is in this way that categories such as "beneficiaries," "civil society," and "the state" are reified and taken for granted.

As an ethnographer, I experienced ambiguous loyalties that mirrored those experienced by NGO staff regarding party politics. During one rather boring interview about development with a projects officer in the Church and Development Program of the ZCC, the NGO employee made a startling assertion about the importance of Christian development for keeping Zimbabweans peaceful. He said, "Without such assistance, it will be difficult: socially, politically. Our government alone cannot support these projects. If there are no water projects, aspects like hygiene, diversification, micro-projects . . . If people don't have the basics, that will spill into riots, social commotion will result in civil wars. A lack of basic infrastructure and commodities will create gaps in classes and at the end of the day it will cause social repercussions, problems." The development of Christian NGOs was a form of charity funded by donors in other nations, not an entitlement of Zimbabwean citizens. Perhaps such development did serve to maintain the status quo, and keep people from rebelling against the state. In the late 1990s, it was in the interest of the Zimbabwean state to appear to have strong national development, a strong economy, and a sector of small-scale farmers who were peaceful and harmonious. When members of this sector had food in their bellies, they were less likely to riot for food, to complain about government, and to threaten the social order. Perhaps the contemporary land question in Zimbabwe echoes early post-independence discourses of development that expressed a more radical (and political) agenda of social equity and redistribution of wealth. As an ethnographer, it was difficult to navigate the terrain of politics that must be transcended. In the field I did not see myself as apolitical, although I was not sure where my allegiances lay. In discussions with NGO employees I often brought up politics. Yet I was also aware that the subject was delicate and dangerous. NGOs were in a precarious relationship with the state. In order to continue my research, I too had to frame my work as transcendent and neutral. I too, alongside the NGO employees I worked with, soon faced the realities of this impossibility. I was seen by rural communities as part of the NGO staff: rich, white, and able to help, although I was not. Perhaps this simultaneous helplessness and political engagement could only be expressed through a discourse of transcendence.

CHAPTER 5

Participation as a Religious Act

I NOW TURN FROM THE TRANSNATIONAL (CHAPTER 3) AND THE NATIONAL (Chapter 4) aspects of development to more local engagements of NGOs with rural, Zimbabwean beneficiaries. In addition to the religiously-inspired discourses of political transcendence (the "Kingdom of God" and "free markets") described in the preceding chapter, World Vision and Christian Care employ a discourse of participation, which, in the eyes of NGO workers, is considered particularly Christian. It sacralizes the idea of "community" and transforms development into a religious act. Analytically, the discourse of participation contains a specific conceptual and moral grammar that is comprised of seven key concepts: community, participation, unity, divine intervention, potential, empowerment, and responsibility. Critical to understanding this grammar of Christian development is that alongside the construct of a sacred community is the Protestant discourse of individualism that speaks to a God-given potential for change.

Before NGO workers embark on a project of development, the ground of transformation must first be established. The practice of Christian development depends upon a group of people, a village or set of villages (a community), inspired about the possibility of change. A necessary component of Christian development is the willing and enthusiastic participation of those it is helping. The incitement of desire for change and for development itself is a crucial aspect of development. This is first generated in village settings when NGOs arrive with prospects of income-generating schemes, irrigation projects, education, and skills training. The participatory techniques at the heart of development speak simultaneously to donor expectations of democracy and egalitarianism, and to Christian ideals of individual potential. The scope of participation is always incomplete. A village that is included in a development project sits next to one that is excluded. In addition, communities are never homogenous (Gupta and Ferguson 1997b). The structures of such a relational and unequal economy of development are effaced through the participatory techniques of NGOs and their staff, who become invisible agents of change facilitating "development from within."

PARTICIPATORY RURAL APPRAISAL (PRA)

In Zimbabwe in the late 1990s, the paradigm of participatory development (also known as PRA, or participatory rural appraisal) was all the rage. Donors were funding and NGOs were scrambling to implement PRA-based development. In collaboration with the Zimbabwean state (as in Chapter 4), NGOs sought to promote sustainable development that emerged from within communities instead of being imposed from donors and NGO bureaucracies.[1] Decentralized and modeled from the ground up, these methods were a reaction to earlier, more hierarchical approaches. Both religious and secular NGOs used PRA techniques to assess development projects and evaluate their impact. Theoretically, PRA was a set of tools and techniques involving community assessment and data collection regarding what rural villagers identified as their own problems. The process was intended to encourage ownership of development by communities themselves. As the director of the Lutheran World Federation in Zimbabwe emphasized in reference to this approach: "We don't do it for them; we do it with them. They have to come to identify the problem, what it is they want to change in their community. We don't come up with a solution." Successful development was, in the eyes of this NGO director, "when they have realized that they can do it themselves. They can change their lives, you see."

PRA revolved around two linked assumptions. First, that there was such a thing as a community that would do the participating, and second, that there was a conclusion to development, a goal, and an end product to be imagined before participation began. In practice, communities in PRA were collectivities that had been artificially constructed for the PRA exercise itself (cf. development more broadly, Gupta and Ferguson 1997a; Pigg 1992; for extent of involvement being that of elites see Kelsall and Mercer 2000). PRA assumed that there was a unitary, coherent community to be developed, that it would develop itself, and that it would eventually finish being developed. These assumptions had specific limitations in places like rural Zimbabwe, where membership in rural communities was cyclical and fluid due to labor migration, illness, and the generational cycles of families (Ferguson 1994, 1999; Mitchell 1956; Potts 1995, 2000). Following the line of thought of PRA in the context of Christian NGOs, if Christian development was community development, the idea of community was essential for its function. A community was defined as a category: a village, for example, or a ward. But villages in southern

Africa included absent members who lived in cities, and the members who were present to participate in PRA exercises were typically women, children, elderly men and people with AIDS who had returned *kumusha* (to their rural home). Therefore, the community and the participation of its members were to some degree constructs of NGOs involved in development. Community—as was the NGO partnership with the Zimbabwean state discussed in the preceding chapter—was a necessary fiction of development.

The concept of participation has been extensively critiqued (Rahnema 1992). First touted as a response to purported failures of development due to the exclusion of those being developed, participatory development methods advocated the end of hierarchical models in which experts told the "less-developed" how to proceed. NGOs such as WV Zimbabwe received contracts from the state to conduct participatory appraisals and base-line surveys of areas being considered for development funds. The boom in participatory development can be partially attributed, on a macro-scale, to the development market. Donors were funding participatory development, and in order to compete in the foreign aid market, NGOs followed the trend. Participation was an agenda whose inspiration was external to communities, transnational and fiscally inspired. This was the case in Zimbabwe. Even when programs were not participatory, participation was an NGO goal (and claim). Rahnema points out the flaws in conceptualizing development as participatory. First, one does not learn if one claims to know already in advance. Participatory processes claim to discover the unknown, yet in practice they solicit known expectations. "When A considers it essential for B to be empowered, A assumes not only that B has no power—or does not have the right kind of power—but also that A has the secret formula of a power to which B has to be initiated" (Rahnema 1992:123).

The Zimbabwean government, in addition to local and transnational NGOs in Zimbabwe, used participation as a development paradigm.[2] Local government involvement included Rural District Councilors, VIDCOs (Village Development Committees) and WADCOs (Ward Development Committees). The involvement of these local political structures was critical to the success of NGO-sponsored participatory development, and represented limitations to its non-hierarchical aims. In the early 1980s in newly independent Zimbabwe, participation entered the national language of development, mirroring the socialist discourse of the time. The more radical discourse of "people's power" was quickly watered down into "popular participation." By the 1990s, NGOs were the leaders of programs of participatory development. Local government structures not only relied on NGOs for its implementation, they were part of the "communities" being developed. Donors assumed that NGOs did a better job of implementing participatory development than the government. However, I caution readers not to forget that the development work of NGOs in Zimbabwe was inextricably linked to the work of the state (cf. Chapter 4; Bratton 1989b).

In the world of NGOs, the sage of participatory development is Robert Chambers, a champion of what he calls the family of participatory methods. Chambers has written extensively on these techniques (Chambers 1983, 1994a, 1994b, 1994c, 1997a, 1997b). At first called RRA (Rapid Rural Appraisal) in the 1980s and later evolving to PRA, participatory techniques have been adopted by development agencies, governments, and social science researchers. My aim is not to evaluate the effectiveness of PRA, although its techniques are most frequently theorized in the context of making development more effective. Instead, I am interested in the social relationships that are codified through participatory practices. Chambers, in the first of a three-part series published in *World Development*, outlines PRA techniques that include "mapping and modeling, transect walks, matrix scoring, seasonal calendars, trend and change analysis, well-being and wealth ranking and grouping and analytical diagramming" (Chambers 1994a:953). With PRA, experts come "to listen, to respect, to empower." In the second article of the series, Chambers explores PRA's shift of emphasis from "etic to emic, closed to open, individual to group, verbal to visual, and measuring to comparing: and extracting information to empowering local analysis" (Chambers 1994b:1253). With PRA, according to Chambers, the behavior and attitudes of outsiders are also considered part of the process. An important component of successful PRA is rapport between development workers and communities,

> including not rushing, "handing over the stick," and being self-critically aware. The power and popularity of PRA are partly explained by the unexpected analytical capabilities of local people when catalyzed by relaxed rapport, and expressed through sequences of participatory and especially visual methods. (Chambers 1994b:1253)

In the third article of the series, Chambers advocates the "primacy of the personal" in development. He explains, "The most striking insight from the experience of PRA is the primacy of the personal. This is easy to overlook. Responsibility rests not in written rules, regulations and procedures but in individual judgment" (Chambers 1994c:1451). Chambers elaborates his idea of the personal through his development agenda of "responsible well-being" (Chambers 1997a, 1997b). These concepts were part of NGO development practice in Zimbabwe. Many of the development workers I spoke with had read Chambers or attended workshops to learn his theories. Some had heard him speak. His techniques were taught in a lecture/workshop that was held in Harare for development professionals during the time of this research.

Chambers acknowledges that development's agenda is value-laden: "the eternal challenge of development is to do better . . . to make the world a better place, especially for the poor" (Chambers 1997a:1743). He defines development as "good change." The world of development, he says, "has been normative; and it has involved change. So the underlying meaning of development has been good change." In the editorial quoted above and in his book, *Whose Reality Counts: Putting the Last First* (1997b), Chambers discusses the idea of "responsible well-being." The PRA experience, he argues, combines two themes: (1) locally defined concepts of well-being, and (2) personal responsibility, to form responsible well-being (Chambers 1997a:1748). Implicit in the PRA experience are assumptions that there is a local knowledge that can somehow be extracted from a community, and that this knowledge can be disaggregated from the non-local in processes of economic development. For Chambers, and for many of the development practitioners who followed in his footsteps, well-being was not limited to material wealth. Chambers writes:[3]

> The objective of development is well-being for all. Well-being can be described as the experience of good quality of life. Well-being, and its opposite ill-being, differs from wealth and poverty. Well-being and ill-being are words with equivalents in many languages. Unlike wealth, well-being is open to the whole range of human experience, social, mental and spiritual as well as material. It has many elements. Each person can define it for herself or himself. Perhaps most people would agree to include living standards, access to basic services, security and freedom from fear, health, good relations with others, friendship, love, peace of mind, choice, creativity, fulfillment and fun. Extreme poverty and ill-being go together, but the link between wealth and well-being is weak or even negative: reducing poverty usually diminishes ill-being, but amassing wealth does not assure well-being. (Chambers 1997b:9)

The writing of Robert Chambers is in harmony with the discourse of holistic development (spiritual and material transformation, as in Chapter 2) and the primacy of personal relationships (lifestyle evangelism) promoted by Christian development. Chambers attributes the absence of a focus on personal well-being to "academic culture with its anathema of evangelism, its value objectivity, and its search for general rather than individual explanations" (Chambers 1997a:1749). He may have a point. If, as he says, responsible well-being is an individual condition shared by development workers and participants of development, it is also a discursive structure. Much of the work of Chambers and his contemporaries is built upon liberal democratic ideas of civil society and individual well-being in which individuals are the building blocks of communities. Such conceptions of civil society are founded on neoliberal models of governance that rely upon an assumption of individual responsibility (O'Malley and Palmer 1996).

In spite of the applied popularity of PRA techniques, PRA has also received criticism. Authors (Goebel 1998; Mosse 1995) argue that PRA technicians, development workers, researchers, and other outsiders influence PRA techniques. They point out that PRA tends to be technique-led as investigators go to a community with a fixed set of techniques to try out. Other methods, such as informal interviewing, that do not produce visible outputs such as maps and charts, are underemphasized in favor of techniques that generate attractive physical results. In PRA, outsiders determine the rules. Project workers impose ideas of relevance and determine what is accepted as knowledge. Knowledge gleaned from PRA is that which is considered extractable from a community: "In much of the PRA literature, however, there is a general assumption that knowledge is undifferentiated. And that given the right tools, people's knowledge is both recognizable and accessible" (Mosse 1995:576). PRA literature searches for a simplified meaning of reality. Mosse (1995:577) describes this clearly: "On a transect diagram, for example, a tree appears simply as a tree, whereas in real life the tree (or its removal) may be a symbolic statement about gender relations, a statement about land tenure, or a sign of resistance to agricultural intervention by the state. Moreover, which of these culturally constructed 'hidden' meanings is relevant, will depend upon with whom you talk."

Some development workers were also critical of PRA techniques. In all of WV Zimbabwe's projects, baseline surveys—the initial demographic surveys of a community before a development project begins—were conducted through PRA. The process of NGOs determining need through participatory exercises inspired strategic responses from rural beneficiaries: direct replies from "within" to the possibilities offered from "without." Through PRA, needs were codified and classified according to what a community lacked (and thus supposedly desired) and what an NGO could provide. NGO workers were aware of this and critical of it. The agency of communities was both a sought-after goal of PRA and a meddlesome effect. As the assistant to the national director of WV Zimbabwe said, "People in communities give different statistics to different people (government, NGOs) according to what they think they can get from them."[4] For Christian NGO workers, PRA participatory techniques were limited by funding constraints. WV Zimbabwe's Christian Witness director explained the risks of participation:

> As development organizations, we have a lot of constraints, especially if we are not financially independent. We walk into a community and we may glibly talk about participation, etc., but we try to steer them to the structures we can support. When we say we are engaging in PRA, are we really serious about giving people what they ask for? If we can give them a borehole, but they ask for a dam? Are we serious? . . . sometimes as a development organization we don't want to take the risk of really empowering people to the point that they really own the projects. [If we do that] we will be working ourselves out of a job.

SACRED COMMUNITIES AND THEIR PARTICIPATION

A crucial element of participatory techniques is the way that groups of people become communities to be developed. Participation, readers may recall from the introduction to this chapter, requires the work of a community. Although anthropologists have extensively analyzed the derivation of community as a category in local settings (Anderson 1983; Appadurai 1996; Greenhouse, Yngvesson, and Engel 1994; Gupta 1998; Rouse 1991; Thornton and Ramphele 1989; Weisgrau 1997), development workers have left it large-ly unquestioned. The etymology of the term "community," as Williams (1983) has demonstrated, refers to the commons or the common people and usually conveys a positive tone that calls forth utopian political ideals (as with the terms "nation," "state," and "society"). Like the term "tradition" (Spiegel 1989; Vail 1991), "community" defines political constituencies and expresses political interests. The political uses of community (as tradition) can have a double edge. This was evident in the case of South Africa (Thornton and Ramphele 1989), where "community" delineated objects of legislation for the apartheid state, specifically in the relocation of Africans in the wake of industry (for example, determining bantustands, cf. tribal trust lands in southern Rhodesia). Tied to the control of resources, community has been employed as a unifying idea by repressive states and post-apartheid movements (Biko 2000[1978]; Lan 1985). The usage of the term reinforces it as a political ideal. As Thornton (1989:76) has noted in the case of South Africa, the conceptualization of community does not guarantee its existence: "there may in fact be no audience, no willingness to cooperate, no coherent social organization, no sense of belong-ing. Nevertheless, we often assume that "the community" exists and that it will agree, cohere, follow or listen." In participatory development, the idea of community is teleological. Community is both the target of development and its hoped-for result. In Christian development, the term alludes to religious ideas of community, communion, and communitas. Community signifies "a utopian ideal for the future, expectation of heaven and legitimate goal for dem-ocratic politics" (Thornton and Ramphele 1989:75). This vision of Eden has been particularly important in southern Africa where the categories of "tribe," "clan," "tradition," and "village" have been used as a part of political ideology by colonial states, liberation movements, and postcolonial states alike (Robins 1994, 1998; Vail 1991).

Christian NGOs used the idea of community in concert with a moral grammar of participation that included concepts of unity, divine intervention, potential, and empowerment. This grammar was articulated in a series of inter-views with World Vision PRA experts. One such staff member, responsible for implementing PRA with rural villagers, described PRA as "A situation where we want to assume that the only people who can define their own problems are the people who are actually affected by that problem themselves. So we encourage communities to more or less [solve] problems, to prioritize them, identify [them], design more or less relevant plans of action to deal with those problems." That problems and their solutions were to come from within communities is a key point. In order for this to happen, identifiable problems had to be small in scale and solvable: water sanitation, food security, and education, for example. NGOs were neither equipped nor able to tackle structural political injustices, or to attempt large-scale change. This fact is important given the political entanglement of NGOs with the state discussed in the preceding chapter.

Lest critics argue, as I did during interviews, that the types of problems NGOs like World Vision encountered were beyond the purview of the individual, the community, or even the NGO, God was provided as the solution. In these instances, PRA was made possible through divine intervention. As a PRA expert from World Vision explained,

In order for those communities to be able to solve their problems, they can only do it through divine intervention. We believe that man in his own power cannot, has failed to deal with his own problems, with his own problems adequately. So as a Christian organization we believe that we are now injecting the spirit of prayer, Christianity, divine intervention within the people so that that Christianity itself might inspire the community members to realize that since you have tried all possible options perhaps if we also try this one it might help.

World Vision "injected" the spirit of divine intervention into communities so that they could solve their own problems, and this constituted development from within.

In order for an NGO to assist a group of people with participation, development relied on the premise of unity, of a small and bounded group with a single will that worked in unison. One PRA expert explained,

We encourage people to work as communities rather than as individuals, because we believe that for all these years we have been trying to work as individuals and things didn't seem to be working out, so we are now trying the group approach. So that as long as communities can work in unison they will always be able to accomplish, to deal with their social problems.

As much as participatory development presupposed and sought out an idealized group unity where people worked together, unification and the elimination of conflict were spiritual and economic goals of development. Development strove to overcome conflict and inequality. A society with conflict and inequality was not "developed," according to a PRA expert:

I believe, say, a situation where certain people are underprivileged within society, and yet others within the same society are also benefiting and there is obviously a very big gap between the rich and the poor, it gives us an idea that we still haven't developed, socially and whatever. A situation where there is conflict amongst groups and so forth will tell me that we still haven't attained social development. A situation in which people haven't developed spiritually in any direction, if they think they want to be traditional and whatever but there are still spiritual conflicts and animosity and whatever amongst them then we still haven't attained the type of development we are looking at yet at World Vision.

The unification of a community included the politically marginalized (such as women), the government, and NGO-workers. WV Zimbabwe's associate director and coordinator for Local Fundraising and Sustainability for Programs defined PRA as an inclusive process that involved everybody, especially "all the genders":

> We want to include all the genders. You know in the past we used to marginalize women, women don't make decisions in our culture anyway, men have always been the people who are making decisions, who know what the family needs and all that stuff, but we are saying you are all players in this. And therefore women must be given the platform to identify which ones they see as the most critical problems affecting the community as a whole. So, we are involving everybody.

PRA included the government, since local government was conceptualized as being part of the community. Government officials often led PRA exercises, and were trained in PRA techniques. NGO-workers also became part of the community. The associate director and coordinator for Local Fundraising and Sustainability for Programs emphasized how in participatory development, NGO workers became part of the community, and walked with the people. This philosophy was connected to the practice of lifestyle evangelism discussed in Chapter 2. He said,

> The idea is of participatory appraisal. The key word there is I think participatory, to encourage someone to actually participate in the decision-making, or in the process of development. So from the Christian point of view as well, as I said, we are even encouraging our own staff to be witnesses of the goodness of that. That is really participating. You are not just going there and teaching people about God and how good God is and all that stuff. No. . . . You are saved; you are out of it. But you are part of it. You are actually living it. So you are actually participating. So that participatory aspect starts with the actual participating as a Christian . . . the manner

The Spirit of Development

in which you live yourself should really demonstrate to others the way, rather than go there and you are the teacher, you are the qualified, you know it all. So, whatever you are doing there is for your own good, not for me. So, that concept actually starts with us. We encourage each and every one to be a Christian witness. Witnessing is not only talking but in actually doing, in deed, and sign and whatever. Therefore, it really starts there with participatory rural appraisal. We have to really participate and really practice what we preach.

Note that in the above quote, communities must be encouraged. In this way, participation was a dialogue with NGO employees, who were simultaneously out of the community (saved, Christian, agents of change and able to witness to the unsaved) and part of the community.

After identifying the issues that development could resolve, communities defined what they could contribute towards the implementation of the project. Most often, the contribution was labor. If development, for example, meant constructing schools, then the community would fetch water, carry sand, and mold bricks. Communities provided labor through participation, and World Vision provided funding for building materials and other resources. Project proposals were developed by staff in the Harare office and funds were raised from donors abroad. Although development may have been conceived as emerging from within—even with the assistance of divine intervention—it was supported and financed from without. These external factors of support were markedly absent in the discourse of participatory development. Emphasis was placed on initiative that emanated from within communities. As the assistant to WV Zimbabwe's national director stressed, it was the communities that did the initial assessment and took the lead in project design. He explained that in contrast to the way development had been conducted in the past (with outsiders), the orientation had shifted to development from within communities. He said,

The community does the assessment, as opposed to a sociologist or some kind of social scientist coming to do a research on the people and designing a program from the outside. The new concept [PRA] emphasizes the participation of the community, so that the community is the one that ranks the needs that are there in the community, and also ranks the way that World Vision should seek to address them. . . . In the past it was people from outside who did research on them, and came up with that and then verified it with the community and government officers, but this is the community taking the lead and coming up with information, which is used in the project design.

As simultaneous outsiders and insiders, NGO workers transformed communities by "unlocking their potential." One of WV Zimbabwe's senior project coordinators explained PRA as "starting where the people are." Participation was an act of empowerment:

> Like now we are planning to start an ADP [Area Development Program] in Chipinge. Before it goes we will go as a team: everyone, from every section of the organization, goes to help them. The very fact that it is recognizing that people have a potential . . . That's the most important thing about the PRA, because you start from where the people are. . . . Let people plan their own things, let people map their own community, let people tell you their history, where they came from, their present, and what they think about their future. What kind of future are they looking at? That alone is very important because I think you start empowering people from that very start to recognize that ok, these people think and know they understand who they are. Once you start from there, then I think the whole process that follows becomes very easy.

In sum, PRA as a set of tools and techniques helped to involve community members in assessing their own situation, developing their own plans through data collection methodologies that facilitated the articulation of their own problems, and eventually arriving at solutions. PRA was designed to engender participation in, and ownership of, development and to equip communities with skills that would help them to solve problems in the future. In practice, PRA-based development involved extracting a list of needs and desires from a community. The focus on finding solutions within communities effaced the political economy and the NGOs that made development necessary (and possible), in favor of a discourse of self-reliance.[5] Through exercises that included mapping, wealth ranking, geographic and resource allocation charts, seasonal and historical diagramming, and narrative historical reconstruction, the anticipation of development was extracted from communities. This process, filled with utopian ideas of community consensus and egalitarianism, sacralized communities. Communities included the politically marginalized, the government, and NGOs, who were able to facilitate development as both outsiders and insiders.

HOW DEVELOPMENT BECOMES A RELIGIOUS ACT

For Christian NGOs like World Vision, participatory techniques were linked to a theology of "transformational development" that addressed social, economic, and spiritual poverty.[6] For World Vision, PRA was a Christian act. Through participatory techniques, development workers were encouraged to "walk with the people" and "start where the poor are," mirroring Jesus' biblical travels.[7]

Moreover, by encouraging communities to participate, from a Christian point of view NGO staff were encouraged to be witnesses, evangelists of Christianity and development. They walked with the poor and lived development. A World Vision field officer explained that by "actually participating as a Christian, in the manner you live you demonstrate your faith to others. Witness is in deed and sign. PRA starts with us. We practice what we preach with PRA."

Perhaps I have made it clear that for Christian NGOs, PRA was religious. However, PRA was religious for secular NGOs in Zimbabwe as well. When I spoke with the assistant director of a secular NGO, CARE International, it was apparent that even secular NGOs drew upon Christian phenomenology in their work. This CARE employee was intensely critical of the religious ideas that he believed informed development. At first suspicious of my objectives, he was one NGO worker who requested that his interview not be tape-recorded. In spite of this initial resistance, during our discussion (which was frequently interrupted by phone calls) he would motion for me to listen to and to pay attention. He expressed a humored enthusiasm for my research project, and at points during phone conversations he covered the mouthpiece of the telephone, pointed to it, and said to me: "Listen to this, it is religious." He perceived development as a semiotic translation between discursive realms, and described himself as a translator. As such, he experienced first-hand what he called the "contradictory forces at work in development." He later described these forces as competing discourses: religious and secular, good and evil. He spoke of NGOs as fitting in to an "angelic typology." This employee was a Canadian who had received an advanced degree in poststructuralist theory in Canada before working in Zimbabwe.[8] His background made him an anomaly when compared to the Zimbabwean development workers I interacted with. Unlike the Zimbabweans I interviewed, particularly employees of WV Zimbabwe and Christian Care (Christian NGOs) for whom religion had a taken-for-granted association with development, this man experienced the religious components of development as secular frustrations. His opinions were a contrast to the views of every Zimbabwean NGO worker in CARE and elsewhere who mentioned Christianity in participatory techniques with praise and enthusiasm.

This assistant director described one of CARE's development programs as particularly religious. Unlike projects that focused directly on building markets, the small dams program was a "traditional development program . . . with a presumption of innocence, and community coherence." He was critical of this presumption because he did not believe it was possible to rely on "false notions, which can't be defined." Moreover, he viewed such a construction as exploitative. He said,

> Men listen to prayers in order to eat. They will listen and pray, but they
> want the inputs for free, for cheap. People think they are doing good but

they are creating dependency. The real problems are transportation and markets. In the religious typology, seed companies are evil. The World Bank and the IMF are evil. Multinationals are evil and NGOs are good.

Such visions of development relied on what he called a "religious typology." PRA was an integral part of this typology, which he thought was a form of domination. The opinions of this NGO worker—aberrant though they were in the Christian NGO context—brought out the implicitly religious construction of development in Zimbabwe. While overt in his analysis (in part due to his own frustration), religion was implicit in the development work of religious NGOs like Christian Care:

Religious typology is to help the poor, create household livelihood security, create income-generating projects, participatory projects. PRA [participatory rural appraisal] is PRAying [he laughs]. It is so old that even the Pope, Chambers, is there. There is representation all over the world, and a diocese here. All believe in participation as the answer. It is so powerful that we acknowledge it all the time. If it helps you to get a washing machine, ok, good luck. Participation is domination. Most people don't want participation; they don't want to participate to have things work. They want a tap; they want things to work. Management is required with a few people to run it. The pyramids were built through participation, each person carrying a rock to build a dam, that is.

In PRA we use maps. They always look like a child's diagram. Looks like an innocent village in the evil wilderness. Eden before the fall, but we don't go back to the village, and never need to know how to organize resources to put a water system in. Dam projects were started with a religious typology—it was an 'aim, ready, fire' management theory. Then it changed. Rational thinking is religious typology. Religion is based on being blind. We take truckloads of tourists to see these projects. It is a source of revenues for us. . . .

He drew a diagram on a piece of paper and explained it as an "ice hell and a crystal heaven polarized from each other." If one turned the diagram around, he showed me on his piece of paper, one could easily mistake the heaven for the hell. They were the same. Turning the diagram, he explained, was a metaphor for the distribution of power within the dichotomous relationship of good and evil. He continued:

. . . Sometimes you have to get out of your Land Rover and walk to the community in order to be holy. . . . In the religious typology the public is good and private is bad. CARE is involved in privatizing public resources

and the redistribution of incentives. PRA techniques don't capture structural problems. People want private taps. This is in conflict with the religious typology where the holy family comes together for the font/tap.
Every religious program is a health program, an environmental program or
a gender program, but they don't make any [structural] difference.

His virulent critique captured a crucial contradiction in PRA work. In the
quest to sacralize communities, the structures of power that defined the community were effaced. He drew another diagram of a religious development
program with what he labeled a "holy village" of huts circling the center, a
white picket fence around it, a place for women to do their work, and the evil
wilderness beyond. "Women," he explained, "in the religious typology are holi-
er than men. Men will abandon their families; women won't cheat on you.
Most of [participants in the dam] program are women. Women are running
development. Men are forced to be nomadic. They can't go home. The political economy is an economy of necessity. Religious economy is role given. The
field is a holy place."

DEVELOPING POTENTIAL FROM WITHIN

How is the field a holy place? In the participatory development work of World
Vision and Christian Care, the discourse of "development from within" framed
conceptions of community and of personhood. The idea in participatory development that "with PRA people have potential"[9] described a potential for
change that lay within both communities and individuals, not within NGOs. In
the discourse of Christian NGOs, this potential was "God-given." NGOs were
seen as providing a helping hand to assist people in reaching their "God-given
potential." As the assistant to the national director of WV Zimbabwe explained,
World Vision used the Bible to help communities see that they had potential
for development and change:

> You use [the Bible] to try and foster unity in the community. You use that
> to try and encourage the community that development does not come
> from outside. They have the potential, and that potential is God-given. It
> is not man-given, it's God-given. And all that we are trying to do is say: we
> are coming as a helping hand for them to try and reach their God-given
> potential.

World Vision's coordinator for Local Fundraising and Program Sustainability
explained it as a process of "believing in yourself": "The main thrust in development is, you have got the potential. It is really the question of believing in
yourself; the starting point is mobilizing the community." In the above quote,
mobilizing and participation were the same (cf. Kelsall and Mercer 2000) in a
utopian vision of consensus. Development was a process through which the

desire and confidence to change was unleashed from within communities and individuals by NGO workers. In the words of the PRA director for WV Zimbabwe, NGO workers helped communities "to believe in their capabilities, to believe in themselves, to believe that they can do it, and to believe that change belongs to them. . . . They will not change until change comes from within."[10]

The national director of WV Zimbabwe used a biblical example to define development as unlocking an individual's potential in the face of a community. He told me the story recounted in John, Chapter 4, of a woman at a well who had been ostracized by her community. The story explained how Jesus encountered a lonely woman who had been isolated from her community because of her "bad reputation." Jesus did not discriminate against her. Instead, he engaged in a dialogue with her and was not put off by her social status. Jesus strove to unlock the potential of this woman:

He senses the potential she has and that unlocks her as a person, and the proof of the unlocking is that she is now bold or courageous enough to face the people who were ostracizing her, her community. . . . I see World Vision saying we know of the gospel, what it says . . . in terms of people to become who they are supposed to be. That we are in the process of working with people, not stereotyping them or reinforcing the attitudes of communities, but that there's a liberation in it and that's important in the sense of people now realizing that and having hope and working for themselves in that. Now we have got some resources and we've got staff, I think with experience, and we can work on development to change people. Transformation, the word transformation, for people to be transformed and for people to work together to improve their environment and themselves.

WV Zimbabwe workers helped people to become who they were "supposed to be" through development. It was liberating. Human potential, unlocked through Christianity (and WV Zimbabwe staff) was made possible through divine intervention. The key was the spirit of prayer, injected into communities by WV Zimbabwe. It was a spirit that sounded a great deal like American conceptions of success through "positive thinking" and self-fashioning. A researcher of WV Zimbabwe involved in organizing and facilitating PRA spoke of how PRA differed from the charity model in which beneficiaries passively awaited being helped:

As we go into the projects doing the PRA or whatever, you tend to see a situation where community members see you as people who have have just come to assist them. Actually as people who have come to lift them, you actively lift them as they passively follow your strength, that type of thing.

. . . We are trying to change their way of approaching things so that they realize that there is no one who can control their destiny except themselves, none but ourselves can free our mind, none but ourselves can actually change our way of life.

Although NGOs came with limitations as to the types of development they could and could not support, the framework used for participatory development was that communities must be encouraged to find (and believe in) their own potential for change. NGOs from "without" assisted the process of "development from within." The coordinator for PRA techniques at WV Zimbabwe explained how PRA encouraged change "from deep within a community":

The development workers are the ones who are doing one, two, three. But you go through the process of helping them to believe in their capabilities to believe in themselves, to believe that they can do it. And to believe that change belongs to them. No one will change them. It is up to them to make up their minds to change from whatever area A to area B. It doesn't matter how much development workers want to change people, they will not change until change comes from within.

She continued to explain how World Vision used excerpts from the Bible to conduct PRA:

We quote a number of scriptures. I'll just give an example, where Peter and John ask the lame to walk. . . . This lame person is expecting money, but John and Peter say that silver and gold we have none, but we will give you what we have. And what we have is the power of the Holy Spirit. And what we have is the knowledge that you can do it yourself. You are capable. And what you need is to believe in yourself that you are capable in doing a lot in development work. Whether there is money or there is no money, you are still capable of doing your own development work.

In addition to using biblical stories as analogical tools, WV Zimbabwe trained PRA facilitators with an exercise called "Secrets in a Box." One of the advantages of this exercise, according to World Vision staff, was that people could actually see and feel the lessons of development. It was a training tool used to help would-be PRA facilitators (WV Zimbabwe staff who were to go into communities and organize PRA exercises) to unpack things within a community using all of their senses. One staff member who had been responsible for training other World Vision employees in PRA techniques explained:

In the box, before the session, you put all sorts of objects: money, markers, leaves, paper, toys, whatever you can think of. Then you ask a volunteer to look at the closed box and guess from distance about its contents. The second volunteer gets to shake and handle the box but not open it. Again he/she must make a list of its contents. The third volunteer is allowed to reach into the box and feel what is inside and try to make a complete list of its contents. The fourth volunteer is able to open the box and pull out the objects and describe them in detail. It's a bit [of] goofy fun and depending on the objects and the volunteers, it can be fun for the group of participants. The big idea is to get people to think about possibilities and use more than just one sense to learn about a community.

The technical training director for WV Zimbabwe said, "What [PRA] means is that development work in the office is actually shaking what is happening in the communities, and those who may come to visit you—they are just feeling [what the community is going through]." The slogan of PRA was that communities themselves knew best about their problems of development, and they knew best what were the most appropriate solutions. Communities had been surviving through difficult circumstances without the assistance of NGOs like World Vision, and were (supposedly) adept at survival strategies. The logic was that when development workers came to communities, the communities would have plans of how they wanted to implement development. NGOs could boost plans and facilitate the implementation, perhaps offer technical expertise. PRA teased out desires, which were framed as coming from "within" communities and individuals, themselves dependent upon NGOs and donors for the funding that made the manifestation of these desires a material reality. She explained the process of developing a "community vision," a unified vision of change:

During the PRA, you go through this process up to decision-making where we ask the people to vision, to have a community vision. What would you want this community to be like when we leave? When everything else is said and done, what do you see? What vision do we have for this community? What do you see? What would you want this community to be like? What is your community vision? They will say we want this. We will ask them to close their eyes and daydream. Close your eyes and dream what you want this area to be like.

Acknowledging the potential within counteracted a dependency on others and obfuscated the dependency on the NGO.

The process of changing and transforming communities "from within" was not without conflict. The director of the Harare regional office of Christian Care spoke of one project that was very "conservative" and had a difficult time changing its beliefs and attitudes. Specifically, he gave the example of communities where people did not send their children to school, or, alternatively, where people were resistant to using medicine, even in the case of malaria or diarrhea. Change was at times met with resistance. This director explained,

> We should in the first instance accept that change can be resisted. . . . But of course, you get into situations where people say, 'ok, your intervention is causing problems here and we don't want to see you.' . . . Most likely, the most vocal are those who are well off. We will say, 'fine, this is how you see it but we see it differently, and as far as we are concerned, we haven't really done anything wrong.' . . . The biggest problem that I see is where you go in and your activity exposes the negative part of the leadership. That I think is the most difficult. . . . You have to move in and work as an agent of change from within them. Work with the few people that are prepared to take up your ideas, prove your ideas, and then let the others adopt [them]. . . . Then, we can introduce our ideas slowly, get those who accept them, work with them, but not at the exclusion of those that don't accept them, no. But then those that don't accept them will learn from those that accept them.

Community development, if successful, fractured "the community" whose unity was presupposed.

Narratives of "development from within" obfuscated supra-community political and economic relations and the work of NGOs. They fashioned development as a product of bounded subjects—of communities and individuals—and excluded others who were not part of particular development exercises. The narratives also made development the responsibility of those being developed. The Christian Witness coordinator for WV Zimbabwe spoke of empowerment as a form of responsibility. He thought the approach of World Vision—to come in "more as advisors" and people who "listen" rather than solve problems for the community—was beneficial. If NGO workers solved problems for communities, they were not empowering the communities. He said,

> I think that as development organizations we really have to be careful when we are talking about empowerment, that we are not seen to be walking into the villages and giving our people the impression that we have come to save them from their environment. Because for one thing, they live with their environment; they know what is going on there, so why don't we start by finding out from them exactly what it is that they need to deal with. . . . Together with empowerment goes responsibility. Because, responsibility here mean[s] that people are taking it upon themselves to deal with the problems and the difficulties that they face as a community, and that is very very important. To say, 'ok, we are meeting the challenge. We may ask for some charity, as all of us do need assistance once in a while,

but initially we will take full responsibility for the situation that surrounds us and do something about it.'

This "responsible well-being" was indeed Robert Chambers' theory in practice.

FUTURES ARE BLEAK: DEFINING NEED

Did the communities participating in development projects see development as coming from within? During trips to development projects with WV Zimbabwe and Christian Care, I took the opportunity to ask rural villagers what they envisioned for the future. The villagers were not at a loss for words, and did not need "participatory" exercises to express what they considered primary development-related problems and challenges. It was during a few of these group discussions that I saw how NGOs incited desire in rural communities, and how this was necessary for NGOs to do their work. This was how they provoked "development from within." Without the desire for change, the work of NGOs was impossible. Groups of village development committees presented themselves as in need (cf. Gupta's underdeveloped, 1998), consistently saying the future was bleak and thus they needed help from NGOs. Perhaps the future was bleak, and as the violence of 2000 would later confirm, the communities had cause for concern. Nevertheless, villagers certainly knew to whom they should express their desires: it was to the NGOs. Because I arrived with the NGO, I was identified either as one of their staff or as a foreign donor from whom the organizations sourced funds. Even with extensive explaining, this image could not be dispelled, and I eventually accepted the village perception of my role, and began to listen to what was being said to me. Communities anticipated being given something, and responded with requests for the NGO. The identification of a "need" involved an intense manifestation of an awareness of what was indeed possible through NGOs. I felt as if I had asked something that the community was expertly prepared for. At one community meeting,[11] after discussing the local history of development and current problems, I asked what people saw for the future, for their children. They responded in rapid-fire dialogue with a list of complaints (all but those noted as such were comments made by men):

When I look into the future there is no hope. I see the problem of unemployment. Jobs are becoming scarce. It is difficult to get jobs and parents are getting old [woman].

Much of young people go to O-level and then have nothing to do. It would be good to have skills training—carpentry.

The future for our children is bleak. There is a problem of land. Children expect to inherit land but if land is small it is not a solution. We need water to make the best out of small land. Unlike the past where there was so much land.

The problem of a shortage of Bibles; even those who go around preaching some don't have Bibles.

The problem of housing; few can build like the one we are sitting in [square and cement block]. Most build pole and dagga, and this means the continued cutting of trees. Trees are not growing. The future is bleak. Because of poverty, some parents fail to meet secondary level school fees.

There is a problem of accessibility of roads, especially during the rainy season. Sometimes it takes a month for busses to come. We wish for proper roads with proper gravel. Now roads are mostly gravel. . . . Problems are big and resources are small, especially if you have the problem of a sick person. During the rainy season you can't even use a scotch cart and at that time we are attacked by malaria. With malaria, there didn't used to be drugs. Drugs are at the clinic, but the clinic is far. It would be better if we could keep the drugs here. Sometimes drugs are in short supply. There are no phones, no firewood for cooking food. In the future we need solar [power].

It was true, and World Vision, the NGO I had come with, could not possibly address all of these complaints. At another community, on a different day,[12] a dominant concern was that WV Zimbabwe was soon to pull out of the area. The specter of self-reliance was not looked upon positively. And at another village, after having a long discussion with a group of men who represented the building committee of the World Vision development project, I was given a list of requests.[13] At the end of the day, as we were leaving, one man came up to me with a written piece of paper that identified him as the village development worker. It listed his name, underlined, the Village Development Committee (VIDCO) number, and the Ward number and name. The paper said, "Need help," and then gave the following list:

Stationery
Furniture
Room of working (if possible)
Working day and night, but don't have torch.
No raincoat during rain season,
No hats during sunny days
No regular supply of medication to the community
Orphans are not usually recognized by the Government or community as such.

I thanked him, and said I would pass on the information, although I was not sure to whom I could give it. My mere presence had opened a pandora's box. The idea of a "donor in disguise" (Goebel 1998) did not apply here, as I had come with the donors. I embodied the category of donor. The desires were unlimited.

CONCLUSION

NGOs, and the government structures they worked with, vanished in discourses of responsible well-being, of potential, and of development from within. The political economy of NGOs in relation to the state receded as NGO workers and government representatives were discursively transformed into participants in communities they sought to assist. Christian NGO workers saw themselves as unlocking a God-given potential for change. Participatory development, although in reaction to a charity model (development from without), located the "need" and the "responsibility" for change and development within communities and individuals. This discursive practice subdued other discourses of governance and responsibility, of entitlement or the welfare state for example, in which the state was responsible for the well-being of its citizens (cf. neoliberal governmentality, Rose 1996).

This chapter has investigated a grammar of Christian development that bolstered neoliberal economic aims. In the next chapter, I examine how the endeavors of World Vision and Christian Care became increasingly complicated in local settings, as local inequalities and jealousies were inspired by development. NGO conceptions of development from within, including the potential for change and community participation, produced unintended consequences when they collided with local expressions of good and evil, witchcraft and God, person and polity.

CHAPTER 6

Good, Evil, and the
Legitimation of Success

IN THE WORK OF WORLD VISION AND CHRISTIAN CARE, MORAL categories of good and evil provided an interpretive frame for economic activity. Christian development constituted categories—of the developed and the undeveloped, the "evangelized" Christian and the "unreached"—and inspired tensions over these categories. Perhaps all development, secular and religious alike,[1] makes distinctions between human beings and attempts to make new persons in the process. Development discourse is itself relational and morally charged, reconstituting the previously existing ethical ground in the lives of those who do the "developing" and those who are "being developed" (Ferguson 1995). For employees of religious NGOs in Zimbabwe, the danger of witchcraft lurked in this morally charged ground.

In development efforts, the evil of witchcraft was framed by the goodness of Christianity; the two were bound together. Witchcraft interfered with and "retarded" development. Christian development workers simultaneously saw witchcraft in evolutionary terms as "backward" and acknowledged it as part of the lived present. Their trajectory was at first glance teleological, and seemed a reproduction of modernist narratives of progress and "stages" of development. With further scrutiny, however, I saw how the dichotomous cat egories of good and evil, and the apparent contradictions of Christianity and witchcraft, coexisted. Embedded within the development discourse of benevolent progress existed its inverse: the evil of Satan and witchcraft.

In this chapter, I examine these moral tensions from what may initially seem like two competing perspectives. First is the Zimbabwean view of morally correct economic behavior that de-emphasized the successes of individuals. My neighbor in Harare, for example, a young Zimbabwean man, explained how doing well in Zimbabwe was suspect. He said, "In the rural areas, if you

141

are doing very well [economically], people suspect you of doing witchcraft. People will say, in response to someone's success: 'How can he be doing so well when other people are not?" Second is the view of World Vision and Christian Care employees who attempted to make the material successes of individuals morally acceptable as they trained people to do well economically. In the development work of World Vision and Christian Care, the contradiction between these two perspectives was not resolved. Rather, it was given a discursive space for negotiation. Christian NGOs, with their explicit religious agendas, gave voice to moral forces of economic development—to teleological striving for progress, and to the malevolent forces of demon spirits. Unlike so-called "secular" agencies, religious NGOs offered a language to discuss conflicts such as jealousies and witchcraft, and they offered the possible resolution of these conflicts through Christianity.

A BOOKKEEPER'S STORY

At a rural economic development project in northwestern Zimbabwe an employee of World Vision was attacked by a demon. The project bookkeeper, a young man of twenty-eight, had grown up in the community that housed the development project. Elected by his neighbors and hired by World Vision, he monitored the daily activities of rural development, including the initiation of irrigation schemes, the introduction of water and sanitation programs, and the building of schools. Such examples of participation were part of progressive trends in development that were thought to move away from West-centered models and to place the directives of development in the hands of the people being developed. They were manifestations of "participation from within," described in the preceding chapter. One evening, while walking home from the project office, he was suddenly struck by an illness that rendered him paralyzed and unable to speak. After seeking help from doctors who could not cure him, he went to a traditional healer, a *n'anga*, who told him that an evil spirit called a *chikwambo* (pl: *zvikwambo*) had been sent to kill him. During an interview, conducted after he had recovered, I asked the bookkeeper why the *chikwambo* had tried to kill him. He explained, "Now they [community members] say, 'he is developed and he is proud of himself.' It wanted to kill me because they say, 'he is proud.'" The community had elected him the World Vision project bookkeeper. "I grew up in this community and they are the ones who voted for me," he explained. The *n'anga* told the bookkeeper that the person who sent the *chikwambo* was jealous. The bookkeeper said,

In development we are seeing a lot of things, because the first thing, it is hard to bring the community together. There are some of them who don't participate, so to bring them together you have to mobilize people. The way you mobilize the people could even make the *chikwambo* to come to you, because other people don't know they are being helped. . . . People say, "He is doing such and such and we should fix him."

This bookkeeper was grateful to have survived his encounter with a *chik-wambo*. He employed the *n'anga* to kill the *chikwambo*, and he gradually recovered his speech, but the moral tensions underlying economic develop-ment remained.

The story of the bookkeeper's malady was recounted to me repeatedly on separate occasions by staff in World Vision's Zimbabwe national office in Harare. His experience was a social drama held in institutional memory, cast and recast as an emblem of the link between religion and development. His experience marked the social and spiritual dangers of economic development, as well as the appropriate (Christian) moral stance necessary to combat them. When the story was told to me by World Vision field officers, it was narrated as a straightforward series of events: the bookkeeper at the development proj-ect had been attacked by a demon; he was physically paralyzed, he found him-self unable to speak; the cause was witchcraft. However, there was a subtext to this story. As a young man, the bookkeeper's status placed him in jeopardy with regard to his community. His new position incurred the jealousy of elder com-munity members who were bypassed for the position. Months after the book-keeper's recovery, I met with him and he offered his story. While recounting his battle with forces of change and community, he expressed a tremendous sadness. It had been a difficult ordeal and things had not become much easier afterward. I sat with him in the cement-block World Vision project office at the rural site, in the company of the project clerk, who eagerly added details and confirmed the bookkeeper's testimony:

Bookkeeper [B]:   I got engaged by World Vision on 26 October 1993. So, I worked from 1993 to today [July 15, 1997] with World Vision. Through working, I got ill. I don't know what happened. I came to work at the office and my hand was paining, and I was failing to even write with a ballpoint pen [the clerk confirmed this, and showed me how weak the bookkeeper was, imitating how his arm was strong, but his hand was use-less]. So I told [the clerk] to help me to do the work. This was in February or March. . . . At the end of the day, when I was going home, I was just beyond a certain river and I could not reason what was taking place. When I got home, I could not speak a word. I was stammering. I could not speak a word—today I stammer. So I had to go to the doctors to have blood tests, and they could not see anything from my blood test, and I had to go to African doctors, *n'angas*. So, when I got there, I was told that there was a *chikwambo*—a short man which is made from medicine, *muti*. He said that is what affected me and it wanted to kill me. He said it was pos-sible to remove it if I paid ZD$250 [US$25]. I wanted to survive, so I paid.

I was given *muti* to wash my face and body, and he said, "I will kill this thing when you are present," and he did. It was like a young crocodile mouth with teeth and ears and eyes just beneath the mouth. He called it and said it would come from my home. We waited for one or two hours and we saw it come. I came to believe that because I am now able to talk. When it came, there were two portraits of a man and a woman, sculptures from wood. He put a black cloth on top of the pictures and we waited for about one or two hours, and when he opened the black cloth, the thing—*chikwambo*—appeared. He said this is the thing that wanted to kill me.

Erica [E]:   *Why did it want to kill you?*

B: Now they say, "He is developed and he is proud of himself." It wanted to kill me because they say, "He is proud, but it is us who voted for him." I grew up in this community and they are the ones who voted for me. After the *chikwambo* was killed, I came to my home. I was still stammering, but after two days I began to speak. In two days I was able to speak fluently.

E: *Where and how does Jesus come into all of this?*

B: I prayed to Jesus because it is He who gave it [the *n'anga*] the power to conquer that. So I praise the Lord for what he did for me, and all members of World Vision, they prayed for me.

E: *Who sent the chikwambo?*

B: An individual who was angry with me. I don't know what has happened to him. He likes to take advantage of the community. It is jealousy. God knows when it will end. So I believe God has the only help. Now I am seeing the community is responding more than before I was ill.

E: *Did your recovery give you more power in the community?*

B: Sometimes I can say so. [long pause].

E: *What is a chikwambo?*

B: It is like a person, started as *muti* [medicinal herbs]. It works like a person at night for people who bought them. It is small, the size of a coke bottle, with hands and legs and long straight hair, like you, *chirungu* [pl. *muRungu*, "person of Caucasian descent, wealthy person" (Hannan 1996:403)]. [We laugh].

E: *Is the chikwambo black or white?*

B: Black. It possesses people and makes them speak. If you don't have any offense it won't kill you—it has mercy or it would kill every-one. . . . They cost a lot of money. Owners cry for *chikwambo* when n'an-

gas kill them. The owner of the *chikwambo* paid z$250 for the one who tried to kill me. The charge of the *muti* depends on the price of the *chikwambo* [i.e., the *muti* cost as much as the *chikwambo* did]. *Chikwambo* come from *n'angas*, not spirits, but from *muti*, herbs.

E: *Is it a big responsibility to have a chikwambo?*

B: *Chikwambos*—they have an agreement, such as each year to kill an ox for me. It drinks blood; if you don't satisfy the agreement, if you breach the contract, you will be in for it. It will kill the owner who doesn't care for it well, who mistreats it. It will kill you and your family. When a *chikwambo* kills you die from bleeding from your nose and mouth. Now I am enjoying because I can read and write and I can even go to football with others and am fully recovered except that I stammer sometimes.[2]

When I was told about the bookkeeper's predicament by the World Vision field officer responsible for this region, she acknowledged that it had happened, but expressed concern that he had gone to a *n'anga* for assistance. God, the Christian God, was where Christian NGO workers were supposed to turn for assistance. For the Harare staff of World Vision, the bookkeeper's acts were examples of how easy it was for rural project staff to slip in belief, to fall from Christianity "back [into] traditional ways."[3] The bookkeeper was not quite "developed enough." Being developed, for the upper (urban) echelons of Christian NGOs, was like being "converted" in the colonial era: it meant being economically successful, self-sufficient, and Christian. Here Christian field workers echoed the civilizing mission of earlier eras. Yet, for the bookkeeper, *zvikwambo* (pl.) were part of a daily reality. They were a threat posed by the community, and they were precisely a product of development. Without his job as bookkeeper, he would not have inspired jealousy from the community. Without World Vision and Christianity, a *chikwambo* would not have been sent to harm him. For the bookkeeper, there was no contradiction between Christianity and his visit to a *n'anga*. A Catholic, he did not see himself as less Christian for treating his affliction with the mediation of a *n'anga's* skills. The *n'anga* was simply able to solve the problem, and God (a Christian God) helped the *n'anga* to do that. Religion, whether Shona religion or NGO-inspired Christianity, was an integral component of development, and of a person's economic successes or failures in relation to the community in which he or she lived This is a theme we have seen in Chapter 3 as well, where witchcraft and jealousy were a predicament encountered in programs of child sponsorship.

CHRISTIAN NGOS AND WITCHCRAFT

Witchcraft has a long history in southern Africa, and recent anthropological scholarship documents its apparent contemporary revival, explaining witchcraft as an effect of particularly modern forces.[4] Revising functionalist explanations of witchcraft as "pre-modern," contemporary writing on witchcraft asserts that it is the result of, and a reaction to, emerging inequalities and class relations spawned by global capitalism.[5] This seemed to be the case in the work of Christian NGOs in Zimbabwe. Witchcraft, apparently stirred up by the very modern forces of economic development, appeared in the work of World Vision and Christian Care as a moral threat and a moral challenge. In the development efforts of religious NGOs in Zimbabwe—and in the context of the Zimbabwean economic decline that made development "necessary"—categories of the supernatural were given new and perhaps ever more urgent expression. In Zimbabwe, along with the "successes" of development manifested in the material improvements of lives, hovered the potential for evil, in the witchcraft that emanated from the envy of others (Ashforth 1996; Bourdillon 1976; Comaroff and Comaroff 1999a; Evans-Pritchard 1958).

My point is not to determine whether or not the tensions of development propagated witchcraft activity. Rather, I am interested in the ways that the particular Christian composite of material and spiritual progress affirmed a discursive and social space for witchcraft. After all, witchcraft is a phenomenon that existed in southern Africa before missionaries and before industrial capitalism, certainly before programs of economic development. What has changed is that Christian development made witchcraft, and the moral issues surrounding its practice, a germane part of economic activity. Throughout this book I have expressed how for employees of World Vision and Christian Care, faith was an important part of development. Whether it was the Christian faith of employees and rural beneficiaries or the faith-based aims that drove institutional missions and inspired donors, faith was a form of power to be reckoned with when implementing programs of development. Discussions of witchcraft were no different. The ways that witchcraft and other malevolent elements of the supernatural (evil spirits, for example) intercepted rural development were very real aspects of drilling boreholes and building schools, of community involvement, and of political and economic change. NGO employees acknowledged the spiritual challenges of development with as much seriousness of purpose as they did the material ones. Moreover, the occasions when such spiritual dangers were discussed (for example, during development committee meetings or project coordinator site visits) became opportunities for development workers to bring Christianity into the conversation. Christianity could combat these forces.

MALEVOLENT ARSENALS

Let us return to the bookkeeper's malady. His narrative is but one example of jealousy emerging from the tensions of success in a context of impoverishment. During my fieldwork, people went to great lengths to ensure I understood the complexities of violence that could occur as a result of jealousy. The "rural areas," I was told, were sites of such dangers of "tradition" and of *muti* (herbs, especially for use in witchcraft). Field officers at World Vision in Harare joked that the areas where they hosted projects were the places where one could purchase the most powerful *muti*. Christian development took place in these very sites of supposed "backwardness" and spiritual danger. Moreover, the witchcraft resulting from jealousy elucidated the relational nature of economic life, and the ever-present potential for evil and corruption in success. Demons— such as the *chikwambo* that attacked the bookkeeper—were sent by people who experienced lack or need in the face of another's advancement, and even if not addressed directly, these moral realms were the backdrops for development projects. These ideas fed into the ways that Christianity was used and interpreted in local contexts. *Varoyi* (witches) sent demons to those of whom they were jealous.[6] My research assistant emphasized:

> Shona people don't want to see a person who is above them. When I say 'above them' do you know what I mean? I mean position. If there is a poor family wearing nice clothes and talking and enjoying themselves, they are going to have problems. They [others] just become jealous and say, 'He is living well. *Usiku vanhu vashanyira*' ['At night they, the jealous ones, will visit them'].

Some of the worst forms of *muti* are *zvishiri* or *zvidhoma*. No one can see the *zvishiri* or *zvidhoma* except the *n'anga* from whom it was purchased and the victim of the demon. *Zvidhoma* take the form of tiny people, and survive on the blood of others who must be killed to feed it. I was told these spirits required a great deal of care, monthly feedings at least. Unless fed properly, *zvidhoma* will kill their owners. *Zvishiri*, another form of evil resulting from jealousy, appeared as birds with teeth and also beat and killed people. What is most important in this analysis is the socially relational nature of evil: it results from someone's lack in relation to another's plenty. The violence perpetrated by *zvidhoma* and *zvishiri* is mysterious and brutal, and difficult to discuss due to the Witchcraft Suppression Act of 1899 (Rutherford 1999). This law, still in effect at the time of this research and hotly contested, made accusations of witchcraft illegal; to accuse someone of witchcraft was to risk being sent to jail for defamation of character. People had few "official" channels of appeal in addressing such matters, and this magnified the gravity of such situations (Ashforth 2000). Those I spoke with about these evil spirits were all Christians, and to them these things were all too real. Some explained the situation as a dichotomy of spiritual realms, pitting those on the side of *Mwari* (God; *vadzimu* or ancestral spirits were commonly classified in this realm), against those on the side of Satan (*zvishiri* and *zvidhoma*). My research assistant,[7] for example, called the evil spirits "*vadzimus* [ancestors] of the side of Satan." *Duramazwi: A Basic Shona-English Dictionary* defines *chidhoma* (sing. of *zvidhoma*) as "A wild animal in service of a witch, creature associated with a witch" (Dale 1992:19). In Zimbabwe, *zvidhoma* were known for killing, but not exclusively, as they were also notorious for robbing money and causing other economic misfortunes. My research assistant explained,

> It can be sent in here to rob your money. You find you have z$200 but you have done nothing; your money hasn't worked. I didn't buy anything but I can't trace how I used the money. Which means your money has been taken by *zvidhoma*. If one suddenly becomes rich, then they are at risk of being attacked by *zvidhoma* who will steal their money.

Because of such fears, people had begun refusing positions of leadership at rural development sites. Being a manager or the head of a village development committee, showing success in relation to the positions of others, made one vulnerable to the envy of neighbors, coworkers, and strangers. Sometimes the *zvidhoma* did not kill; they simply beat someone as a warning to instill fear. Someone who had been beaten would be able to see *zvidhoma* while others could not, and this created a culture of fear for those who might otherwise be successful. In contrast to this, I was told that proclaiming a Christian identity could provide protection. "They can send bad spirits to you, but if for sure you are standing on God, nothing will happen to you . . . If you are a Christian, you just believe if God is there, how can He let me be sent *zvidhoma* or something?"

These narratives of good and evil, of God, of success, and of jealousy permeated all my discussions of development in Zimbabwe. And when they were not spoken of in public meetings, they were discussed in private. How did this context of potential evil relate to the development efforts of Christian NGOs? One field officer for World Vision (the one responsible for the *muti*-rich Chipinge area of southeastern Zimbabwe) said that these beliefs hindered development. Fear of being struck by evil spirits affected participation on local governing committees of development projects. However, he added, prayer combated all of this evil. He explained the process as hinging on development education,[8] specifically, on using the Bible and finding a verse that related to development to combat these evil forces. He felt that secular development did not take these components of development into account, and said: "We use evangelism to our advantage . . . The issues and the values brought up are our way of evangelizing, not by preaching. We influence, not change beliefs, through continuous interaction." He added that *zvishiri* was the work of the devil.

At development projects, World Vision held crusades to combat these forces of evil, of *zvishiri* and *zvidhoma*. Every project had an evangelistic component, such as evangelism rallies, and training of church leadership. When I offered the critical challenge that evangelism was seen by some to be coercive, he countered that God is a "God of progress." He did not feel that World Vision's work was destroying African cultures. As an African, and a long-time staff member of World Vision, he felt that he was "bridging the gap to attract people to Christianity. Enlightenment comes; it is a matter of approach. We recognize community spirituality, and questions come up; it is not a simple process. The purpose is to make Christianity attractive, and for that you need to respect [where people are]." That God came first for World Vision made a difference, for him, in the work that was done. While my inquiries into the worlds of *zvidhoma* and *zvishiri* were sometimes met with silence, I found that as much as people denied knowing about this phenomenon, they later shared stories with me. People were overflowing with narratives they had heard, or read, or been told, and it informed the way they approached their development work. At first I anticipated that this would be a sensitive area within Christian organizations, but mostly it seemed something people took for granted as landscape and did not think much about. The Zimbabwean Christians working for Christian NGOs all seemed to agree: "I can't explain it, but these things exist." These beliefs were real for the communities people lived in, and if field officers had not seen it directly, then they certainly knew of someone who had.

On one of my trips to visit rural development projects with Christian Care, I was encouraged by a field officer to ask a group of men about *zvishiri* and *zvidhoma*. We had driven to the site of one community meeting and had arrived ahead of schedule. Our previous meeting had been cancelled due to a funeral, and we had a few hours to spare, so we walked to check on one of the granaries that had been built and to talk with some villagers. We came back to the bottle store and sat for a while, waiting. We talked about *varoyi* and it became apparent that the two field officers from Christian Care's Harare office had had their own encounters with these evil spirits. We talked about what happens when one trespasses moral ground in development work, about the dangers of being a field officer in the context of rural communities and the social realities of jealousy. One field officer explained that some are born to trespass moral ground and others to buy the ability through *muti*. He said, "People don't just die in Africa, there is always a reason, always a story. Even if it is an old person, there is a reason." The two field officers had very different styles of working with rural communities. One believed in what he called "going down to the people's level," while the other adamantly thought one should keep a distance, especially for fear of *muroyi*. He later admitted that for this reason he did not even like to participate in the common greeting of shaking hands.

As I was pushed out of the truck with a supportive nudge by the field officer that encouraged "going down to the people's level," he told me to ask a group of about seven men who were also waiting for the meeting to begin about *zvidhoma*. I assumed this was going to be secret territory that foreigners like me were not allowed to enter, but I was truly mistaken. The other field officer helped to translate the steady stream of stories that resulted. The stories revolved around morality and what happens when one person gets rich or succeeds at the expense of others.[9] The issue of religion in development provided the explanation for why one person achieved success in relation to another: it addressed not *how* one community received a borehole or drinking water, but *why* (cf. Evans-Pritchard 1958). In other words, witchcraft narratives provided clear, qualitative and cosmological answers to what were usually posed as quantitative and apparently "neutral" questions of economic development. The men gave me example after example of *varoyi* in their area. One recurrent theme was the necessity of secrecy, and another was danger and gender. For example, the next-door village was made up of women, all of them supposedly *varoyi*. Apparently, there were no men under 30 in that village, which was attributed to the women's will to stay in control. According to the men who told the stories, all *varoyi* were women. They said they were afraid of women, and afraid of talking about these things in case one of the women walking by might be one of them. They explained that *zvidhoma* were sometimes given in pots (*hari*), inherited, or purchased. I asked why it was only women who owned these demons, and the men said that women were more hygienic, more disciplined, and thus could take better care of them (they required regular feedings of fresh human flesh); these things were hard to care for. I asked whether this stopped people from *budiriro* (developing, succeeding, progressing), and they replied, "You just have to be quiet, humble, help others, and not show off wealth if you want to succeed without coming to harm." People often carried fertilizer or sugar home from the shops at night so as not to provoke the jealousy of other villagers. Leaders were particularly vulnerable to these things; there was an inherent weakness in both socially articulated power and visible wealth.

This vulnerability (cf. spiritual insecurity, Ashforth 2000) made the discussion of jealousy and development difficult at public meetings. On a rural trip with World Vision to Chipinge in southeastern Zimbabwe, I posed a question to a large community meeting about whether they had experienced *muryoi* (witchcraft) in their community.[10] After a long silence, one man spoke:

> People now appreciate the value of working and competing. In the past, those who didn't have, felt those who had, had to suffer . . . Now, jealousy, it could be there, but I'd rather compete with you. With the coming of Christianity, it has changed people's attitudes and [people have] realized those things are not right in the eyes of God. With Christianity, if one falls sick, we now understand we can go to a hospital or go to a neighbor who will pray for you. We used to go to a *n'anga* who created animosities.

When I asked about *zvidhoma* or *zvishiri*, a nervous laughter rose from the group. An elderly gentleman explained, "Those who believe in Jesus

Christ—it doesn't mean anything to a Christian. The power of God is too much for a *chipoko*. *Zvipoko* have a relationship with people who use *muti*. They kill people." Later, while we were driving with some members from the project to check on two boreholes being drilled, several community members confided in World Vision's field officer. They said yes, there was indeed witchcraft in the community and they were very frightened. Because there was someone present at the community meeting whom others mistrusted, silence shrouded the topic. People were afraid that if they spoke about witchcraft and exposed a witch, they would themselves be attacked.

At other sites as well, people would come forward after meetings, singly or in small groups, explaining why there had been silence on the topic of jealousies. At one of World Vision's rural projects, the project clerk confided in us while the NGO staff and I were having lunch after the community meeting. As we were eating, he said there was a problem of witchcraft, but that attitudes were changing: it used to be that a young person would not build a smart house for fear of being bewitched, but that now more people were building such houses. Christian development offered a space for success. Development was entwined with Christianity, and Christianity provided an arena for ethical issues—such as jealousy and inequity—to be discussed and socially negotiated.

In one community meeting in southeastern Zimbabwe, a debate occurred when I asked whether there was any jealousy related to material success in the community. An assertive woman answered that before the development work of World Vision, jealousies were prevalent in the community. She said: "If a person showed progress and positive development, they would send something to attack them. Now, with churches and the coming of development, people are repenting and there has been a positive way of looking at things." A concerned man spoke up in disagreement to say, "Some issues are more complicated. In the community we are living in, you have to work hard to survive. But there are also people who are not working, who are lazy and those are the ones who send things to attack people. Due to jealousy, laziness, people decide to spoil other families' progress. We still have this problem here. Even people who go to church continue to use these things." There was a long, uncomfortable silence after this statement. Then a much younger man spoke up and said, "I am very optimistic on the future. In the past, we used to eat sadza [mealie-meal porridge] without relish. Now we have relish and irrigation schemes. Now we have learned about agriculture and by selling cotton I have hopes to buy a vehicle." A concerned and vocal older man contradicted him: "To me, the future, yes, but it could be difficult and complicated. Once World Vision pulls out, the future might be difficult . . . I still feel that we appreciate the issue of coming together, but I feel if World Vision pulls out, people might not be ready to take over mobilizing on their own without assistance." This quickly became a dangerous spiritual issue. Someone else foresaw the difficulty of evil spirits and Christian development. He said, "There is a major challenge of fighting evil spirits and demons, and they beat up people who are possessed. We continue praying. The major challenge is one of prayer for those with hardships." The issue was one of inequality. This stood in tension with the ideology of "development from within" and the socially homogenizing discourse of community development. Another man jumped in to explain why there might be difficulty in the future, especially when World Vision stopped supporting the development project:

> I still feel the future is difficult to foresee. A current problem is there are some people in the community who are already plucking and eating tomatoes, and others don't have tomatoes. There is work to make sure this gap is reduced. The challenge is to educate people to understand. I fear World Vision might leave before the other irrigation scheme is complete and then some would have before others have a chance. And I fear others might not be able to pluck their tomatoes.

This man worried that World Vision, and development, might leave socially dangerous inequalities in the wake of their departure. Christian development, in its attempt to eradicate the evil of poverty, stirred up volatile, unpredictable dynamics of power and these dynamics were articulated in the "invisible" world of spirits. Here, perhaps, malcontents did emanate from the activities of development, as the voice and breath of modernity itself (Comaroff and Comaroff 1993). The power of development had a moral echo of good or evil; it had value in people's lives. The stakes were high: life and success through a good crop, or even death by jealousy. I am not arguing that the malevolent arsenals were true or false—I assume they existed—and they structured the way people inhabited and moved through their social worlds. Whether they carried their purchases home in secret or in public, it was up to persons to make these decisions, to take these risks. NGOs like World Vision and Christian Care facilitated the productive power of development, which was material and spiritual, visible and invisible.

When I brought up the issue of witchcraft in an interview with one of World Vision's project coordinators, he said: "*Zvishiri*, okay, what a complicated thing—eeee!" He had experienced *zvishiri* through stories told to him by the communities he worked with. One account he had heard described the pressure on a family to share their harvest with *zvishiri*. The *zvishiri* asked for a bucket of maize, which the family was instructed to leave in a particular place. Another story described a village development worker (VDW) who was selling some things during a field day—bananas, aprons she had sewn, and so on. A *zvishiri* came to the woman and asked her to share some of the profits she had gained from her sales, noting that she would suffer if she did not oblige. The project coordinator qualified his stories with such comments as "I don't know how they solved this issue, but this is what I was told. Whether it is true or not true I cannot prove it."

Another story told to me by several World Vision employees was about an instructor for a dressmaking class at one of World Vision's rural projects; she, like the bookkeeper, had been attacked. The event surrounded a conflict between the local management committee (LMC) and the dressmaking instructor. The LMC had complained that the instructor was stubborn and would not listen to them and since they were unable to get along, the LMC had decided to fire her from her position on the project. The woman, in protest, came to Harare to meet with the project coordinator and tell her side of the story. The project coordinator suggested she return to the project and assured her that when he came to visit they would examine her case. When he arrived at the project and tried to discuss the issue, it was a tender subject. As it turned out, the chairman of the LMC was someone who people believed had *zvishiri*. He had been in his position on the development project committee for more than ten years, continually elected because people feared the threat of *zvishiri* in the event that he lost his position. The chairman of the LMC explained to the project coordinator (who had come from Harare to settle the issue) that he would not let the woman stay in the project. The woman's father, a member of the Salvation Army, was also known to have these powers, and had threatened the chairman by saying he would put him in the palm of his hand. "You can fit here, in my palm, you are too small—you will fit here, you see." The woman who was to be fired believed her father was stronger than the chairman when it came to such spiritual powers. The chairman offered a challenge to the girl's father to see who would outlast the other. That this challenge was spoken in public at a community meeting shocked everyone present. The chairman had said, "Who is going to go first? Myself or the father of that girl?" The father of the girl died shortly afterwards. The project coordinator was horrified that he had heard the threat with his own ears. He believed that "these things have an effect on development, a very serious effect on development." In fact, he believed they could "retard development in a most crucial way," because under such circumstances participation from the community became very difficult, if not impossible. In such situations, a person whom the community did not want to lead a project could be chosen as a leader with the assistance of spiritual forces such as *zvishiri* or *zvivanda*. "No one is prepared to fight against this person because they are scared of these *zvishiri*," the project coordinator explained. They are afraid he will attack them with his powers. "So they [the community] will make sure that they just put him there, and whatever he says they will follow. If he dominates, that's fine." People follow out of fear. Fear of being bewitched kept people from developing their homes in Chipinge, where some of this project coordinator's development projects were located. Those who were scared of witchcraft "would rather have their money, keep it, and not develop their home. Because once you develop your home, they will say, 'Ok, this man is proud. He wants to show off and all those kind of things, and then [he claps his hands] those things come, you see."

How did the staff of Christian NGOs deal with these malevolent arse-nals? I asked the project coordinator what he did in such circumstances, and he said he would pray, pray a lot, and then use the Bible in development to combat these forces. He would find a particular verse that related to develop-ment to use as an example. For instance, he had used the story of Peter and John approaching a man who was begging for money. "The disciples were not the type of people that wanted people to remain dependent," and they told the man to stand up and walk in the name of Jesus. The biblical story presented an analogy: World Vision also promised to enable independence," He said,

We would use that as an example to say this is the endeavor that World Vision has, not to continue giving you [the community] funds, but to [help you to] stand up and walk. You are empowered, now you can do things for yourselves which means now you can even help each other within the com-munity without having to wait for a donor from outside to come and help you. So what we are endeavoring for is that you stand up and walk on your own, you people, rather than to remain dependent.

The Bible was used to facilitate a basic understanding that members of the community were valued as human beings. He believed that this understanding gave them confidence. Using biblical reflections, he could teach people that they were created in God's image. He felt that World Vision used evangelism to their advantage, although it was not the sort of evangelism that involved standing before people and preaching. Instead, evangelism included the man-ner in which the Bible was used in community meetings. In these settings, issues and values were brought up and this was, to the project coordinator, a form of evangelism. In this way, and through continuous interaction, he believed he was able to influence beliefs. This form of evangelizing worked better than preaching. Issues such as drunkenness or AIDS could be addressed in a biblical context. Community meetings were settings in which he could "motivate the community to plan for the work that is coming," and in the process, he would find a way of bringing in biblical topics: "That's a way of evangelizing; that way, I believe, is the best. Without having to go to people and say, 'Ok, you people come here and I want to preach to you. They won't come. You won't get anybody." In this way, changing beliefs was a long process, "a very long process," and not something that could be preached in an afternoon. He did not think he could change people's beliefs, but he thought he could influence a change through continuous interaction and education.

I was fascinated by what was emerging as a central paradox—how to teach people to make material progress without it being associated with evil. When I asked the project coordinator about it, he laughed and admitted that he had never tried to tackle it directly. He encouraged people to get involved in income-generating projects so they could "become, sort of free, or to be independent." That was the basic thing he was teaching, but he admitted that it was very difficult and at times he did not know what to do. For example, when he once saw a young boy being attacked by a *zvishiri*, he said, "[I,] just took a look, and I left the people in the community to deal with their problems because I didn't know what to do at that very moment." At first it seemed that Christianity would emerge as an alternate solution, but he admitted that it was indeed a tough question as there were solutions within traditional beliefs that could also solve the problems of *zvishiri*.

For the World Vision project coordinator, *zvishiri* were a real part of his development work. "I think they are real," he said, "because the devil, the devil does funny things. So to deny them, to say ah, those things they are not there, they are not there, no. I don't think it would be the best for us . . . these things do happen because the devil can do miracles in his own way, but some other form of intervention is needed to free people from these problems." The other form of intervention was Christianity, specifically through evangelism. He continued, "If I plan to do water, if I plan to do agriculture, if I plan to do schools, evangelism has to be there," whether in the training of leadership, evangelism rallies, or the distribution of Bibles.

THE DANGERS OF DOING WELL

In Shona, the word for development, *budiriro*, is also the word for physical and material success. Yet, as much as Christianity in Zimbabwe carried with it implicit narratives of faith in action—trust, honesty, and benevolence—the ways development was interpreted in local contexts manifested more than a simple munificent moral outcome. Good and evil were locked in an intimate embrace in Zimbabwe. Trust and honesty implied the potential for their opposites. Desire, greed, and envy were the flip sides of moderation, generosity, and contentedness, and they co-existed, one calling upon the other through its silence.[11]

At the time of my research in 1997, Zimbabwe's national economy was fraught with rising inflation. IMF–World Bank–state collaboration in "structural adjustment," including programs of privatization and market liberalization, polarized economic relations between individuals. Differences between wealthy and impoverished people were exaggerated to new extremes. Development took place in this context, and hailed those who were "needy" and those who must be "developed." Newspapers during my fieldwork continued to document a climate of economic hardship, and this was made clearer through the strikes and protests that spilled onto the streets daily. People struggled to feed their families in the face of rising inflation. With new wealth in Zimbabwe came new perspectives on poverty—ones that emphasized the vio-

lence and frustrations of economic inequality. In this climate of rapid economic change and increasing inequity, Christianity embraced the moral dimensions
of development and made wealth more respectable. It simultaneously articulated inherent contradictions and provided solutions. In the Shona press, the
weekly newspaper, *Kwayedza,* was filled with stories of people struggling to
negotiate the religious and moral terrain of economic development. One article, in March of 1997, described how a dam that had recently been constructed was morally dangerous. It told of children dying while trying to cross it. The
explanation given by the author was that the dam had not been made "Shona"
through ancestral rituals. Since it was still "English" (the product of international development efforts), it was evil. "Good development" in this context
was local, "indigenous" development. It was development from within. It was
development that acknowledged local spiritual realities and the role of the
supernatural, phenomena invisible to secular development agencies. My Shona
tutor and research assistant helped me to read stories in the vernacular press
about people rumored to have killed children in order to help their businesses. One story was about a family that owned a successful bus transport business. People in the village were certain that this family had used *muti* to
become successful. The proof was in their son, who was crazy and acted like a
bus, walking around making bus noises, asking people to get on like a driver.
There were rumors circulating of taxis in town that talked, and said things such
as "Oh, I'm tired," as if the spirits of the children killed to help the owner of
the taxi business were speaking. This witchcraft accusation framed the material successes of individuals as morally suspect.

    As I mentioned in the opening of this chapter, and as the above stories
attest, it was morally suspect to "get rich quick" in the Shona context of late-
1990s Zimbabwe, and Christianity offered protection from public scrutiny in
the face of such success. Christian development fit squarely at the center of
this perfidious moral terrain. Just as colonial missionaries offered refuge to out-
casts, misfits, and accused "witches" by giving them a home and work on mission stations (Hunter 1961), Christian NGOs offered justification and some
degree of protection for individual success. To declare oneself Christian was to
say "I don't believe in *muti, varoyi,* or x, because I am Christian." More importantly, with belief in Jesus, defined as a "higher" power, one could be protected from the malevolence of others. For Christians in Zimbabwe, there was
clearly less social stigma about getting wealthy. Christian business was "good
business" (as in Long 1968). If development promised success, which in turn
could invoke the danger of witchcraft, then Christianity offered protection, but
not automatically; hence the task of field officers. The missionaries of Christian
NGOs, field officers facilitated the interpretation and re-interpretation of
Christianity in development at local project sites.

    I witnessed these dimensions in play at one of World Vision's urban
projects in Epworth, a peri-urban township close to Harare. Because of the low

cost of rents in that area, there was an influx of people who were moving there from rural areas in hopes of finding jobs in Harare. The township was filled with the types of concerns on which NGOs concentrated their work. The small income-generating program that World Vision was involved with was a gardening project for women. I traveled to Epworth with three of World Vision's project officers. It was about 15 minutes from the center of Harare by car, but it looked like a completely different place, part urban, part rural. When we arrived at the gardening project, we were greeted by six of the co-op members, all women. Their children came and went during the meeting, with questions, to offer bread and sodas, or to satisfy their lively curiosities. We sat on the side of their sandy garden. A small thatched shelter provided shade from the bright mid-day sun.

After formal greetings, the meeting began with a prayer and continued with introductions. The chairwoman of the gardening project and a secretary were both taking notes. The cooperative was called the *Madzimai Kubatana Cooperative* ("Women Unite Cooperative"). One co-op member began the meeting by telling the history of the co-op and explaining the difficulties it had encountered with regard to local jealousies. She explained that she had raised z$2000 from selling sugar cane she had grown, but that the money had been stolen. The trees they had planted to serve as a fence for their garden were cut down at night. Business was not easy in this environment. The co-op formed in 1985 with fifteen members, but four members had dropped out because of financial problems or the deaths of family members. These four women had returned to their rural villages (*kumusha*). Most of the women in the cooperative were widows, and they explained they were gardening to send their children to school, to buy food, and to pay rent. Those who were not widows had unemployed husbands. They all lived in temporary shelters.[12]

In 1992, the women met World Vision. A field officer came, saw their problems, and offered assistance. He provided seeds to plant, and a sprayer with *mushonga* (fertilizer/pesticide, also a term for medicine). At the time, they had been using tin cans for fetching water from boreholes; they were given irrigation pipes and training sessions on gardening by World Vision. The training, in collaboration with the government Department of Agricultural Extension (Agritex) and a pesticide company, taught the women to use a rope and pump for irrigation. They were also trained in other gardening techniques such as plowing and planting. The women saw it as an improvement; their harvests had been helped quite a lot. However, the ropes were too long to keep in their homes, so they stored them in the garden. They went to the local authorities, the local government board, to ask for help building a shelter to keep their pipes. They were given permission to keep them, and to build a storeroom, so they then molded bricks. But the bricks were not strong enough: when it rained, the shelter they had built collapsed. It had been constructed in sandy soil with no roofing materials. They next hid the plastic pipes in the grass, but when another neighbor burnt her fields, the fire burnt all the grass and their plastic pipes with it. It was a major setback for the cooperative. The co-op members talked to the woman who had caused the fire, and she agreed to buy the ropes, but could not pay for them. At the time of our meeting they were back to the original mode of watering their garden, which was quite elaborate, using small tins and long ropes to pour water into bigger containers before carrying them to their large garden.

After hearing of their hardships, the field officer made a semi-serious joke: "Thou shalt love thy neighbor." The chairwoman of the cooperative was trying to get reimbursed for the burnt pipes from the neighbor. The field officer, without giving solutions, continued to ask the women how they planned to carry on. The co-op had not reported this case to the police because the culprit was their neighbor, and subsequently they were faced with the dilemma of needing to water their garden without any irrigation system. The women eventually decided that if the neighbor could not pay, they would take something from her house and sell it as payment for their loss. The neighbor had promised to pay in installments, but had not yet come through with any payments. The women thought that the neighbor was taking advantage of World Vision since the pipes were given by a Christian organization, and it had become an issue of local justice. As an alternative to retribution, the field officer offered market possibilities to the gardening co-op. He suggested they buy some used pipes and withdraw their money from the bank for this purpose. The women responded with frustration: "You are talking about a pump but we don't have money due to a lot of rains this year. We couldn't harvest maize and it was destroyed by the rains." So he continued coaching them on capitalism. He advised the women to buy maize from the rural areas and to sell it in the peri-urban areas. He suggested they could make a lot of profit, 50% profit, and gave them an example:

> If you get $300 for the maize and pay $100 for transport, you can get $600—which is 50% profit. You should buy blankets from Metro [a discount membership store] and exchange them for maize in the rural areas. For $65 a blanket, you could sell them in the rural areas for 50kg x 2maize. 50kg of maize are sold for z$200, minus $70 profit if you sell the blankets for $130.

The prospects were intriguing to the women. They explained with fervor that they had also been involved in other income-generating projects. They had been given a sewing machine by World Vision and were producing petticoats for sale. The women complained that when they sold their petticoats locally, they received mostly credit or a few Zim-dollars here and there. The field officer told the co-op that when they did that type of business, they should not sell in their own area. If they sold in other areas, they would get cash. He said that even if they were taking petticoats, they could take them to the rural areas and sell them for maize. Another field officer chimed in to say that people in Epworth wanted to buy maize and to go to the grinding mills themselves, as it was cheaper than going to supermarkets. She thought people would buy the maize if they brought it back to sell. Or, the field officer continued, they could buy soap from another of World Vision's cooperatives, and take it to the rural areas in exchange for maize. One woman concurred, saying that she saw the soap samples in World Vision's office, and that even in Epworth people would buy that soap. The discussion of market strategies reached a feverish pitch. The field officer gave them advice on how to start their own business. He said:

You can get $3 profit. Buy soap for $5.75 and sell it for $8 or so. Start with one carton; just see if it will pay, or if you are losing z$100 or something. You can get $75 profit from that carton. A carton is $125 and has 25 [bars of soap] if you get $200 they you have $75 profit, just start with one.

He started to tell them about another one of World Vision's projects in a neighboring township that was selling soap. "Last month they got $500 each, this month $400. They have about $1000 in the bank and the orders are coming. Those people are going up." Those people were being developed. They were making money; they were "going up" in life. He offered to take the co-op members to the discount store, Metro, after our discussion so they could look at the blankets.

The discussion was a flurry of imagined possibilities. Our conversation turned to my research on Christianity and development work. The women responded to my inquiries with polite diligence. Their responses were long and detailed, and they spoke with each other for the benefit of my understanding.

The chair of the cooperative spoke first:

We as a group feel we should be Christians. As individuals people have different tempers but as a Christian we can ignore these things; for the group to be united we have to be Christians. We follow the biblical concept of work . . . we use our hands to work. We are mostly widowed; some have husbands, but they are not working. Instead of looking for money in bad ways like prostitution, we are working [in a Christian way].

Then a series of women joined in to express their opinions. One said:

Working under Christian principles we can avoid child prostitution and disease. Today disease is rife, and leaves children abandoned. Christianity makes us strong.

Three other women added, one after another:

The link we have with Christianity is the strength we get from God. Prayer is the major thing, and the strength we get from God to do our work. Christianity in this work enables us to have unity—we can feel for each other and carry each other's burdens. We also believe that every blessing comes from God. We have a lot of thieves. Now they steal but we are protected. After stealing, we still remain with what is there. God continues to bless what is there. Everything has a leader and we have made God the leader of our development.

I want to affirm what was said before: we recognize the blessings from the Lord. You eat of your sweat, and God blesses the hands that work. And it is trust and a liability for us to be able to work together; we need to have trust. Trust does not come into a person unless she believes in the Lord and this is why we trust one another.

Since 1985 when we started this thing, we will not give up because of our strength in the Lord. We have seen many other co-ops disband because their expectations were not met. We are still together because of God. The Bible says I should live to teach my children, and by working I am teaching my children how to live a good life. The registration of the co-op has been prolonged, and other members have fallen by the wayside, but we continued because of that trust [in God]. We are showing children how to do things, how we will cope. We are showing them to work, teaching by example.

I brought the group discussion back to the beginning of our meeting. I wanted to know how they interpreted the jealousies of their neighbors in light of their Christian orientation. They responded.

We are facing a lot of opposition because of jealousy: they cut our trees because they are seeing if we can prosper, but because we believe in God we don't give up. . . . They come by night and cut the trees. They have even taken the hand pump from the borehole. The wood is for firewood and building, for squatters. You have to build with tools in one hand and swords in the other. Some of the men in the community are jealous, that's why they cut down the trees, but some are so happy, especially those who have women here to assist the children. It was so hard in the beginning and no men wanted it to happen [the co-op] but now they are jealous and want to join.

The presence of Satan is felt through the people and through jealousy. We don't fight back, but we can feel the spirit of the evil, so we don't confront people.

Their dreams for the future were as follows:

The future is to upgrade our homes, build good houses and have good lives, especially having our children go to school.

Our dream is that the children don't have to go through what we are going through today, but for them to be educated and for them to live a better life. This life should change so our children should not live this life.

The last dream is to be with Christ when he comes so that I can go and rest.

Jealousy, and the evil that resulted from this emotion, was a serious threat to the development work of the Kubatana cooperative. It did interfere with development, and at first glance it did seem to be the result of demons unleashed from development processes themselves. However, as I will argue, the good and evil of development were the results neither of a systemic economic change (modernity, or capitalism, for example), nor of the introduction of Christianity. Here, as in all of the development I encountered in Zimbabwe, development involved the remaking of persons within the context of living communities. This remaking entailed tactics and strategies for negotiating both "visible" and "invisible" worlds. The two were discussed with speedy inter-change, and without the bulky logical imperative of causality.

The mutable moral activity that exists between visible and invisible worlds in Africa cannot be represented as a simple dichotomy. This has been addressed by Kiernan (1982), who attempts to escape the moral dichotomy of "good" and "evil" with an analysis of ancestral relations toward the living in Africa. He examines how ancestors—who ostensibly protect the living—can actually do harm. He suggests that, when studying ancestral relations in Africa, anthropologists use categories that are not morally dichotomous: of "constitut-ing" (protecting) and "allocating" (disrupting) instead of "good" and "evil." Constituting and allocating agents can perform both "good" and "bad" for the living. Following Kiernan, I propose that the important point is not the cate-gories themselves. To understand the ways that the "supernatural world" inter-sects with the "natural world" in Africa, one must release oneself from the assumption that good cannot cause evil. This understanding of certain muta-bility can also be applied to Christianity and the work of Christian NGOs in Africa. The world of Christian development is a protean world, where contra-dictions merely reinforce the necessity of flexibility. Such contradictions for those who study them are not necessarily contradictions for those who live them.

CHRISTIAN BUSINESS IS GOOD DEVELOPMENT

If, as demonstrated through the example of the gardening cooperative, material success puts one at risk of the jealousy and witchcraft of others, how did Christian NGOs make economic success morally acceptable? The mechanics of this transformation were evident at a graduation ceremony at one of World Vision's rural project sites in northwestern Zimbabwe (also mentioned in Chapter 4). Here I encountered the particular discursive conflation of progress, success, and development, with the moral subtext of "good" Christian business.

A field officer, a driver, and I had arrived in the afternoon after a long journey from the hotel where we were staying. It was our second day of visiting community development projects and the third project community on our itinerary. Over 100 people of all ages overflowed the cement schoolroom, buzzing and humming in anticipation of the scheduled event; the air was filled with excitement. It was a joyful culmination of months of hard work by the dressmaking class at the project. The fruits of the class, final projects of dresses and tailored women's suits, hung from ceiling rafters on wire hangers. A reverend from ZAOGA church was in charge of the dressmaking school at the project. He had directed the course that was subsidized by World Vision.[13] He explained to me, as we waited for the event to begin, that the work they were doing in projects such as this one was a combination of preaching and dressmaking. "Even if you are not a Christian, you will be by the time you finish the course," he said happily. He told me proudly of post-graduates who opened shops and cooperatives, and who were employed in factories. These facts demonstrated the success of the project and of ZAOGA's collaboration with World Vision. He clarified, "As Christians we want to help people who are poor. We want them to be more wealthy when they come to God. Most people think that poverty is the will of God and that it is a curse. If we train them to be wealthy, they will know it is the love of God." Our discussion was cut short by the opening of the ceremony, and we were ushered into the classroom and seated in a line of chairs set aside for us, facing participants in the dressmaking school and their family members—the community of community development.

After extensive formal introductions, the event proceeded with a sermon by a pastor of the ZAOGA church. She spoke in Shona, with high-pitched conviction.[14] The ZAOGA secretary sitting next to me took photographs of the proceedings with an elaborate camera. The ZAOGA Pastor stood in front of the crowd clutching an English-language Bible, and preached that everything was the work of God, including the work of individuals. Work towards prosperity was the work of God. She avowed,

God has created people so they can work. The lazy people should not be given food, God says. God created us with the wisdom to be laborers and in order to do better. Some people work and some are idle. People should work with their hands and rid themselves of poverty. But God has given us grace to use our hands and to work. If you are lazy your poverty will follow you around like a thief. Strengthen your hands and legs that are weak so you can do something to prosper. If you don't use your body and hands to work, poverty will follow you until you die. We are to work together because God gave everyone twenty-four hours in the day to work. There is no difference from one person to the next; the difference is in how a person uses their mind. Each person has twenty-four hours. God should bless our work and raise up our lives. I desire that God give me the same knowledge that he gives others so that I can use it to prosper. God gives us everlasting life, not to perish, but to prosper.

After the sermon, a dressmaking choir (noted as such on the photocopied program) stood up to dance and sing, "Surprise the lazy people and show them what we have done" in canon. They performed a short drama about lazy people and a woman who worked hard to learn dressmaking: the woman who learned dressmaking could then sew things for herself and others. They sang of encouraging fathers to support their women to go to school so they could learn to use their hands.[15] The state was present as well in this ceremony: the District Coordinator for the Ministry of National Affairs gave a speech in which she thanked ZANU-PF (the ruling party) and World Vision, and spoke of God-given talents. She declared that we were to use the gifts given by God. A theme emerged: idleness was evil. She said, "People who come to dressmaking school have cleaner homes. Those women who could not come to the course are still at home tidying up. The person who is lazy is very jealous and can even be a witch or a thief." Lazy people had an enhanced potential for evil. Those who worked hard, fuelled with the passion of Weber's Protestant ethic, would find salvation through providence (see also Maxwell 1998).

The dressmaking students modeled their final projects. Farmer-husbands danced with the dressmaking graduates, their wives, down the aisle between the wooden benches toward the front of the meeting hall, to loud ululations. There were more speeches. The director of the ZAOGA dressmaking school said: "With poverty, people have tended to be robbers. People are afraid to go from one point to another, but not of hunger, they are afraid of those who don't go to school. We need everyone to have the opportunity to have some self-reliance projects. We need to help everyone." He encouraged everyone to "have an income-generating project so they will have money," and warned:

When poverty comes in through the door, love flies out the window. In families there are harsh words between wives and husbands because of poverty. Husbands are trying to cover up that they don't have money for salt so they say harsh words to their wives. Children can't stand up straight from a sitting position, they have to turn around bending because their clothes are torn behind and they are embarrassed. Because of poverty, people are running away from homes to towns. Women are trying to entice men for money.

The underlying discourse of this development project was that poverty was evil and dangerous, and success was good, morally superior to poverty, and closer to the work of God.[16] He continued, passionately:

Poverty is in the hands; success is in the hands. A learned person is a person with a course in a special job. I see men sitting around doing nothing, asking for work. I say what kind of job are you looking for and they say 'any job.' There is no such thing as 'any job'—you can't get O-levels for any job. O-levels don't create employment . . . We need to keep on doing things, developing our area and developing ourselves. I am discouraging the thinking that you can only have tea occasionally and good meals only at holidays. People say I will repent later, but you never know when you will die. You can die eating.

The audience was laughing. They enjoyed his humor. His sermon was an engaging pep rally for prosperity. The field officer for World Vision stood up and made a speech as well. Her tenor, in Shona, resembled that of the preachers who had gone before her. She was also preaching development:

You have succeeded and I have succeeded. As the leader of Mash[onaland] West, we have helped people help the needy in a Christian way. World Vision has had nine years with this project, [and spent] up to about z$3 million. We have built dams, sponsored children. . . . We have been united with ZAOGA because we also put Christianity ahead of us, and we don't have a problem in which kind of church, but we want people who worship God. The desire of God is to help people to develop, not to hurt people. We have the same teacher in [a neighboring project] and will have the same success. To the women: you are educated and no one can take it away from you because no one can take away your knowledge. Now you have permanent knowledge. We have developed.

They had developed and they had developed well. Christianity and the work of God not only made development possible, it made development "good." It was contrasted to the "evil" of poverty and its correlative consequences of crime and unhappiness.

In addition to sanctifying life at development projects, Christianity made business "good" in the Harare offices of Christian NGOs. In response to my asking what made NGOs Christian, people said repeatedly that it was the relationship of Christianity to trust. To be a Christian business meant to be a trustworthy business. With a Christian business, there was less likelihood of embezzlement, theft, or other evil associated with personal gain. Christian money was good money. Aside from using the life of Jesus as a motivational model for their development work, NGOs emphasized that to have money, as a Christian business, was to be able to improve one's life in order to help people. It was not associated with wealth at the expense of others (as in the case of witchcraft and *muti*). Since the objectives of Christian development were benevolent, it was benevolent prosperity. For example, an employee from the Mennonite Economic Development Association (MEDA) explained that "the [Christian] environment at work is crucial and influential, [we have] devotions every day in the morning from 8:00 to 8:30. . . . If you are living with Christ, everything becomes very simple. To be productive, [you] need teamwork, there must be peace, which is what we preach every day. The word of God tells us how to approach difficult relationships." Faith, in the work of religious NGOs in Zimbabwe, was described to me as a context, an environment of expectations, and a set of ideal principles that guided the workday world. It delineated the work of development. The topic of faith and development was difficult to discuss with people, and variable in expression. Faith was belief in a supernatural world, in the good icons of Christianity: God, Jesus, the Holy Spirit, and the evil manifestations of its challenge. The MEDA employee continued to explain the relation of Christianity to good business by emphasizing that the work of the Christian NGO should "portray the Christian element of our environment," specifically, "the ability to accept difficulties, being honest, being faithful, being considerate to other people." He said, "Money is to improve your life, not for profit, but to [create] a situation whereby you can help other people." This Christian benevolence in turn inspired others to follow Christianity. He explained, "We are doing a lot in helping the unemployed in Zimbabwe; the way we help people will also attract other people, and at the end of the day people will be interested in knowing something about Christ." The faith of Christian development was evangelical. It involved trust in a Christian business ethic, a Weberian Protestant ethic. The employee from MEDA said, "Trust, being Christian . . . the whole thing rests on faithfulness, and being trustworthy. [Good business means] no kind of cheating is expected, trust is being faithful and honest. Christianity is a kind of communication." Christianity gave principles to business, which might otherwise be seen as greedy or avaricious. "You have to be a person of principles. In business there is a lot of profit, corruption. As a Christian, before you do any transaction you use Christian principles." Christian business was good business—profitable, successful, and morally sound. Christianity, in turn, shaped business—not only the ethic of conducting oneself economically, but the industry of development as well.

Through the practice of Christian principles, of not stealing and of honest bookkeeping for example, Christianity was regenerated in the work of religious NGOs. For the accountant at the Harare regional office of Christian Care, faith in Christianity entered her job and prevented her from stealing. She said, "Here at Christian Care you handle a lot of money. There are donations coming in, and I am expected to bank that money . . . Faith has got to come in because it's that I handle money, otherwise I will be taking that money for my own personal use and maybe return it at the end of the month. That's the use [of faith]." As the accountant, she felt that if there were not Christian principles guiding her work, she might borrow money from the organization. Faith kept her from stealing. Others also spoke of this intersection of morality and economics in the work of Christian NGOs. The chair of a regional governing committee of Christian Care (an advisory board) saw the primary aim of Christian economics and Christian values as being continued support of the church. Church-based loan programs, organizations such as the one he directed,[17] helped people to prosper so they could eventually support the church economically. He explained how the goal of ZECLOF (and Christian Care, and Christian development in general) was to "uplift people from their poverty." ZECLOF worked through churches, and looked at poverty alleviation from the perspective of churches. He said,

> Churches have a way of getting a lot of people together, and besides praying they should also be able to uplift their standard of living . . . In fact, how I understand it is that sometimes if people are poor their poverty can actually lead them to be unable to pray properly. So, if they can be able to raise their standard of living, then they can appreciate religion, because if somebody spends a lot of time trying to find food, they are not going to find time to pray.

Before working for ZECLOF and being appointed to the governing board of Christian Care, the chairman had worked for the Zimbabwean state in a parastatal lending organization that administered small loans to facilitate post-independence development efforts, and worked very much like ZECLOF. However, there was a difference between his experience working for a church-based Christian organization and his experience with the state, which had to do with the association of Christianity with honesty in business conduct. My point here is that the capitalism advocated by development programs, when identified with Christianity, strove to release itself from an association with evil in the Zimbabwean cultural context. Whether or not it achieved these aims is not pertinent. Of significance is that discursively the tendency of capitalism to inspire greed and personal gain at the expense of others was transformed into traits of benevolence and honesty. Not only did these traits redefine economic activity, they reinforced the power of Christianity in people's lives.

Development discourse, with its cult of rational actors and its emphasis on individual progress, with its Protestant ethic inspiring and demanding work and individualism, did not simply unleash evil, like bats out of Weber's iron cage. It also did not inspire evil, as if it were some moral reaction to the conditions of development itself. Rather, development discourse carried within it the moralizing forces of both good and evil, and the language to describe it in these terms. Christian development, with its dichotomous moral categories of "good" progress and "evil" backwardness (read heathenism, traditionalism, superstition, corruption, etcetera) echoed the discourse of progress articulated by missionaries in the colonial era (cf. Comaroff and Comaroff 1997). As we have seen in the case of Christian NGOs in Zimbabwe, the evil of witchcraft was not produced by progress; it was part of the goodness of progress. It was its chorus, its counterpoint. Alongside the evil of witchcraft, the goodness of Christian business and development was articulated. Jealousy and witchcraft, and the tensions of success in Christian development, were bound together. For Christian development workers in Zimbabwe, witchcraft may have interfered with their efforts, but it also provided a space in which to discuss Christianity.

Conclusion

THIS BOOK REPRESENTS A TRANSFORMATION IN MY OWN THINKING about religiously inspired economic development and about international humanitarian aid. In 1994, when I began this project, I was adamantly opposed to and even fearful of Christian evangelists. As an urban and (culturally) Jewish woman from the United States, I did not expect to meet the types of evangelists I encountered in Zimbabwe. Employees of Protestant, Christian NGOs in Zimbabwe, as evangelists, were on the forefront of offering welfare services to Africans; they were the harbingers of liberal democratic ideas and services. Before I began this research, I assumed that missionaries carried with them an essential "evil" in their attempts to "do good." After all, they destroyed cultures and collected souls. In Zimbabwe during the course of my fieldwork, I no longer knew where I stood, morally and politically. I began to respect evangelists and missionaries for their moral conviction, and became wary of development workers for the very things I used to fear of missionaries: their urge to change people's lives for the better. The work of Protestant NGOs was a morally defined form of cultural intervention; it was helping people, and people really were grateful. With disturbing complexity, Christian development workers challenged the dynamic binarism of good and evil. They acted in the manner of ancestors who punished as well as protected (Kiernan 1982), and n'angas (healers) who had knowledge that could be used to harm as well as to heal; their aims at times resembled the simultaneous leveling and accumulating mechanisms of witchcraft (Fisiy and Geschiere 1991). By provoking and combating jealousies (Chapters 3 and 6), and encouraging discourses of individualism and community (Chapter 5), employees of Protestant NGOs assumed the dual capacity to invite and to mend injustices. Christian development carried within it both a liberatory potential and the tragic irony that change could bring its own disappointments (as with child sponsorship, Chapter 3).

There were ways that Christian development was successful. It made the realms of jealousy, morality, and religion explicit in development work. It faced and named "evils," of poverty, inequality, and human suffering. These were political acts—even if their politics were overtly denied (as in Chapter 4). Indeed, the contradictions embodied in practices of Christian development often overpowered its goals of transformation. Nonetheless, Christian development provided a discursive space for negotiation with jealousy and evil spirits, with the material success of some and the impoverishment of others, with moral struggles that could not always be resolved. That the discourse of Christian development was inclusive of unseen spiritual forces (witchcraft, spirits, faith) alongside the very material injustices that made development necessary and possible, made it more powerful in the Zimbabwean context.

The meanings of "faith-based" (Christian) humanitarian aid, and the relationships through which they are expressed, are particularly relevant in the face of new policies being set by the United States (one of the largest international donor countries in the world)[1] regarding faith-based initiatives in the provision of welfare and social services.[2] This book has examined Christianity as it travels across the globe, from the Christian motivation of humanitarian aid in the United States offices of World Vision International, to the African Christianity of World Vision and Christian Care in Zimbabwe. I trust readers have understood that my point is not to translate meanings across cultures, as for instance a vernacular translation of the Bible might do. Rather, I have attempted to show how the faith of Christian development forms sites of struggle over meanings, over transnational financial accountability, and over expectations, met and unmet. The discourse that fuels a good deal of global humanitarian aid is neither neutral nor secular; it is often Christian, and the proselytizing agenda of Christianity—whether implicit or explicit, about converting souls or creating entrepreneurs—is part of faith-based assistance. Faith-based development, unlike "secular development," provides a space in which to negotiate and contest realms not evident in strictly economic discourse, such as good, evil, morality, and witchcraft. Perhaps it makes explicit some of the unspoken assumptions of neoliberal economic discourse. Perhaps neoliberal economics shares the logic of Protestant NGOs. Perhaps neoliberal economic discourse is not so secular after all. The faith in faith-based development gives voice to the morality of development: Christian business is good development; doing well can be morally dangerous.

The political economy of humanitarian aid is a relational and politically volatile economy. Protestant NGOs mediate this economy, working with and at times doing the welfare work of nation states, donors, and communities. The parties involved in international Christian development see the process from different perspectives, and their views are not always complementary or harmonious. Humanitarian aid affects people materially and spiritually, whether they are donors, beneficiaries, or desperate and disempowered government officials. The Christianity of Christian development is a disciplinary force, and it is a liberatory force that links people like Albert (Chapter 3) with a global, humanitarian Christian family. For Zimbabwean religious NGO workers, Christianity is a taken-for-granted part of life—a sphere of hope and possibility that has, for the last 100 years, been symbolically associated in southern Africa with both missionaries and economic opportunity. The Christianity of Christian development is not an anomaly in the Zimbabwean context. To "do development," to encourage economic change, without acknowledging the spiritual is a more alarming proposition. In the anthropology of development in Zimbabwe, the spiritual is part of the economic. Whether Christian development is "good" or not is not the question at issue here. Rather, one might ask: how does development make things good or not? How does development create moral categories that connect those who help the needy with those who are in need? These relationships, links in the relational economy of humanitarian aid, are expressions of hopes and dreams, and sometimes despair. They are the efforts, products, and contributions of some to change the lives of others, and they are the desires of some to have their lives changed.

Whose lives are changed? As I have sought to demonstrate, the act of receiving is also filled with agency. The dialectic of giving and receiving in the relational economy of humanitarian aid does not produce a synthesis, a coherent whole or a conclusion. As long as there is Christian development, there are those who are in need and those who aim to assist, to respond to the need. Whether needs are produced or met (Chapter 5), relationships live on in this dialectic between sponsors and the children they sponsor, rural communities and NGO workers, United States employees and African employees of NGOs. The ground of transformation charted by these relationships continues long after NGOs have left project sites, and after NGO employees have left their jobs. These relationships are ethereal, and perhaps based on faith: the faith that tomorrow will be different from today, that the poor will no longer be poor, that some will be "saved."

The responsibility of social welfare has shifted historically in Zimbabwe from the charitable acts of colonial missionaries to the state-encouraged entitlement of a newly independent nation. In the late 1990s and under the rubric of neoliberal programs of economic development, social welfare once again became a charitable act, this time of internationally funded NGOs. On the global stage, NGOs act as agents of the political and funding initiatives of wealthy nations. Development, as the charitable act of an international civil society, reifies categories of "beneficiaries," "civil society," and "the state." There is a social tragedy in this process. Efforts to assist the poor through institutionalized forms of assistance tend to efface the politics that categorize those in "need"; how the poor become poor is no longer questioned. In Zimbabwe and in the international context that situates Zimbabwe as a less-developed nation, charitable giving supports the status quo by mitigating extreme forms of social differentiation (cf. Simmel 1994 [1908]). Even so, Christian NGOs, through the language of faith, provide a discursive space to negotiate the morality and injustices of poverty.

Through the work of Christian development, one can see that religion in Zimbabwe is highly political. It is neither a mirror image of the politics of the state, nor simply a reaction to its injustices. Religion is a form of power that is bundled up with politics, which seeps in during moments of structural vulnerability (which may include the phenomenon of weakened African states), and provides explanations of people's lived experiences in moral terms. Categories of good and evil, religion and politics, the individual and the social are locked in an embrace in Christian development. Their separation into discrete realms, bodies of anthropological literature, and intellectual concerns, is a product of our "episteme" (Foucault 1973) that is not relevant in Zimbabwe. The separation of religion and economics in the neoliberal discourse of development is a durable, albeit indirect effect of the Protestant Reformation. This separation fuels the liberal discourse many assume to be secular. As long as discourses about Africa are about development, with its successes and failures, they will also be about good and evil and the moral politics of religious ideas. In the United States as well as in Zimbabwe, many people attribute their economic success to the work of God. In Zimbabwe, the people with whom I discussed the concerns of development did not view religion and politics, religion and development, religion and economics as discrete and dichotomous realms. Rather, they, and I too, saw them as existing in constant relation and continuing living interface in which Christianity is part of development.

APPENDIX 1

Interviews, Groups, Discussions, and Events

Single-person interviews and group discussions are noted as such. Interviews with individuals are listed by organization and by the individual's position within the organization. Events include workshops, training sessions, and fundraising events.

CHRISTIAN CARE

Christian Care, Harare Regional Office

Administrative Secretary, Harare, July 4, 1997.

Agritex and Ministry of Agriculture Meeting (group discussion), Hurungwe, March 19, 1997.

Field Officer, Mashonaland West, Harare, November 19, 1996.

Field Officer, Mashonaland East, Harare, April 14, 1997.

Field Officer, Mashonaland East, West and Central, Harare, April 16, 1997.

Field Worker and Consultant, Harare, June 28, 1997.

Hurungwe Food Production and Storage Community Development Projects (group interviews), Hurungwe, March 19, 1997.

Kariba Fishing Cooperative Community Meeting (annual meeting), Kariba, March 18, 1997.

Mudzi Supplementary Feeding Program (group interviews), Mashonaland East, February 19, 1997.

Musengezi Resettlement Scheme and Community Development Project Community Meeting (group discussion), Hurungwe, August 19, 1997.

Recipient of Aid, Harare, December 9, 1996.

Regional Committee Chairman and Director of Zimbabwe Ecumenical Church Loan Fund (ZECLOF), Harare, July 31, 1997.

Regional Committee Meeting (group discussion), Harare, July 10, 1997.

Regional Committee Member and Pastor, United Church of Christ Mbare Parish, Harare, August 5, 1997.

Regional Director, Harare, August 25, 1995.

Regional Director, Harare, January 21, 1997.

Regional Director, Harare, April 29, 1997.

Regional Office Bookkeeper, Harare, July 4, 1997.

Receptionist, Harare, December 9, 1996.

Tauya Cooperative, Seke Communal Lands, April 22, 1997.

Tauya Cooperative, Seke Communal Lands, August 19, 1997.

Thirtieth Anniversary Celebrations (fundraising event), Seke Communal Lands, Seke, October 7, 1997.

Christian Care Zimbabwe National Office

Deputy Director, Harare, November 25, 1996.

Deputy National Executive Officer, Harare, August 26, 1995.

National Chairman, National Council, Harare, Zimbabwe (also Board Member, Local Governing Board, World Vision Zimbabwe), July 29, 1997.

National Council Member and Director of YWCA Zimbabwe, Harare, August 5, 1997.

National Executive Officer, Harare, January 29, 1997.

National Executive Officer, Harare, July 4, 1997.

Research and Planning Department (group interview), Harare, August 25, 1997.

Treasurer, National Council, Harare, August 14, 1997.

Zimbabwe Council of Churches

Director, Church and Development Department, Harare, July 1, 1997.

Director, Church and Society, Harare, April 11, 1997.

Projects Officer, Church and Development, Harare, April 28, 1997.

Secretary General, Harare, April 23, 1997.

WORLD VISION INTERNATIONAL

World Vision International Office, Monrovia, California, U.S.A.

Administrative Manager (a), MARC Publications, July 8, 1994.

Administrative Manager (b), MARC Publications, July 22, 1994.

Administrative Secretary, Library, July 13, 1994.

Co-Director, Urban Advance, June 3, 1994.

Communications Specialist, July 13, 1994.

Director of Holistic Development Research, May 6, 1994.

Director of Mission and Evangelism, July 20, 1994.

Director, Pastors Conferences, July 13, 1994.

Director, Unreached Peoples Program, July 20, 1994.

Evaluation Associate, July 13, 1994.

Evaluation Specialist, July 6, 1994.
Finance Director, August 1, 1994.
Human Resources Director, Africa Region, June 3, 1994.
Manager, Central Records, July 29, 1994.
Senior Administrative Assistant, MARC Publications, July 20, 1994.

World Vision International Africa Regional Office (in Zimbabwe)

Consultant to World Vision, and Director of Leaders International, Harare, September 19, 1997.
Director, Planning and Evaluation (former Director, World Vision South Africa), Harare, September 1, 1995.
Human Resources Director for Africa, Harare, September 1, 1995.
Program Director, Southern Africa Region, Harare, February 17, 1997.
Sponsorship and Human Resources Consultant, and Information Management Systems Manager for Southern Africa Region (group interview), Harare, August 21, 1997.

World Vision International Relief and Development, U.S.A.

Director, Gender and Development for Africa Region, Washington, DC, July 20, 1998.
Government Relations Associate, Washington, DC, July 21, 1998.
Program Development Manager, Gifts-in-Kind Program, Monrovia, California, July 20, 1994.

World Vision United States, Monrovia, California, U.S.A.

Donor Specialist, Child Sponsorship, July 8, 1994.
Director of Sponsorship Ministry and Funding, July 22, 1994.
Managing Editor, *World Vision* Magazine, July 29, 1994.

World Vision International Zimbabwe

Assistant to the Director, Harare, March 10, 1997.
Assistant to the Director, Harare, April 3, 1997.
Associate Director/Coordinator for Local Fundraising and Sustainability for Programs, Harare, March 11, 1997.
Associate Director Finance and Administration, Harare, March 11, 1997.
Board Member, World Vision International Partnership, Harare, August 9, 1997.
Bookkeeper, Hwino Community Development Project, Hwino Community, Hurungwe, July 15, 1997.
Bookkeeper and Project Committee Chair (group interview), Mabee Community Development Project, Mabee Community, September 9, 1997.
Chitepo Community Meeting (group discussion and interview), Chitepo Community Development Project, Chitepo Community, Chipinge, September 10, 1997.

Chirariro Building Committee (group interview), World Vision Community Development Project, Chirariro Community, Hurungwe, July 16, 1997.

Chirariro Evangelism Committee (group interview), Chirariro Community Development Project, Chirariro Community, Hurungwe, July 16, 1997.

Christian Witness Committee (group discussion), Harare, November 20, 1996.

Christian Witness Committee (group discussion), Harare, February 13, 1997.

Christian Witness Committee (group discussion), Harare, July 3, 1997.

Christian Witness Coordinator, Harare, March 24, 1997.

Christian Witness Coordinator, Harare, May 2, 1997.

Communications and Public Relations Manager, Harare, April 24, 1997.

Correspondence Analyst, Harare, April 24, 1997.

Day of Prayer Celebrations, Harare, October 1, 1997.

Director, Technical Support Services, Harare, March 14, 1997.

Director, Urban Advance, Harare, July 22, 1997.

Dzivaresekwa Candlemaking Group, Urban Advance, Dzivaresekwa, July 22, 1997.

Dzivaresekwa Dressmaking Group (group interview), Urban Advance, Dzivaresekwa, July 22, 1997.

Dzivaresekwa Shoemaking Group (group interview), Urban Advance, Dzivaresekwa, July 22, 1997.

Dzivaresekwa Soapmaking Group (group interview), Urban Advance, Dzivaresekwa, July 22, 1997.

Garabwa Community Meeting (group discussion and interview), Garabwa Community Development Project, Garabwa Community, Chipinge, September 9, 1997.

Kasonde Dressmaking Graduation Ceremony, Kasonde Community Development Project, Kasonde Community, Hurungwe, July 17, 1997.

Librarian/Communications Assistant, World Vision Resource Center, Harare, April 4, 1997.

Mabee Community Meeting (group discussion and interview), Mabee Community Development Project, Mabee Community, Chipinge, September 9. 1997.

Mabee Evangelism Committee (group interview), Mabee Community Development Project, Mabee Community, Chipinge, September 9. 1997.

Manager, Sponsor Relations Services, Harare, March 24, 1997.

Madzimai Kubatana Cooperative (group interview), Epworth, August 7, 1997.

Maparaidze Community Meeting (group discussion and interview), Maparaidze Community Development Project, Maparaidze Community, Chipinge, September 10, 1997.

National Director, World Vision Zimbabwe, Harare, September 1, 1995.

National Director, World Vision Zimbabwe, Harare, April 15, 1997.

National Director, Zimbabwe Assemblies of God Africa (ZAOGA) Dressmaking School, World Vision Community Development Project, Kasonde Community, Hurungwe, July 17, 1997.

Natural Resource Management and Environmental Rehabilitation Coordinator, Harare, August 4, 1997.

Public Relations and Marketing Coordinator, Harare, March 10, 1997.
Project Coordinator (Field Officer) for Masvingo Province, Harare, March 14, 1997.
Project Coordinator (Field Officer) for Mashonaland West Province, Harare, March 14, 1997.
Project Officer, Urban Advance Program, Dzivaresekwa, July 22, 1997.
Regional Manager for Mashonaland East, Central, West and Manicaland, Harare, March 14, 1997.
Research Officer, Harare, July 18, 1997.
Sponsor (American) and US Army Chaplain, Harare, August 27, 1997.
Sponsor (Canadian), Harare, August 26, 1997.
Sponsor (Zimbabwean), Harare, August 14, 1997.
Sponsor Relations Specialist, Harare, June 12, 1997.
Sponsor Relations Supervisor, Harare, June 27, 1997.
Sponsored Child, Harare, August 7, 1997.
Secretary, Harare, March 10, 1997.
Twenty-four Hour Famine (fundraising event), Harare, April 5, 1997.

OTHER NGOS IN ZIMBABWE

CARE International, Zimbabwe

Assistant Director, Harare, November 15, 1996.
Director, Harare, August 24, 1995.
Director, Harare, December 12, 1996.
Masvingo Community Development Project (field visit), Masvingo, September 3, 1995.
Monitoring and Program Development Coordinator, Harare, February 20, 1997.
Field Officer, Harare, September 5, 1995.
Field Officer, Harare, January 25, 1997.

Lutheran World Federation, Zimbabwe

Advocacy and Training Coordinator, Harare, March 17, 1997.
Board Member, Mount Pleasant, February 12, 1997.
Deputy Director, Harare, August 28, 1995.
Director, Harare, September 5, 1995.
Director, Harare, January 22, 1997.

Mennonite Economic Development Associates, Zimbabwe

Accounting and Administration Officer, South Africa Region, Harare, February 22, 1997.
Director, Harare, December 4, 1996.
Regional Manager, Southern Africa, Harare, September 5, 1995.

Save the Children UK in Zimbabwe

Director, Harare, August 23, 1995.

Program Director, Harare, December 5, 1996.

Theoretical PRA Training Session, Harare, February 24-25, 1997.

Practical PRA Training Session, Chiota, February 26, 1997.

Other Organizations

Acting Director, National Association of Non-Governmental Organizations (NANGO), Harare, November 13, 1996.

Bishop, United Church of Christ (former Secretary General, ZCC), Harare, July 2, 1997.

Deputy Director, Opportunity International Zimbabwe, Harare, April 17, 1997.

Dialogue on Witchcraft in Zimbabwe (workshop), Ecumenical Documentation and Information Center for Eastern and Southern Africa, Harare, September 5, 1997.

Director, Catholic Commission for Justice and Peace in Zimbabwe, Harare, January 26, 1997.

Director, Ecumenical Documentation and Information Services for Eastern and Southern Africa (EDICESA), Harare, July 10, 1997.

Director, Ecumenical Support Services, Harare, April 13, 1997.

Director, Hear the Word Ministries, Harare, July 29, 1997.

Director, MWENGO, Harare, April 7, 1997.

Director, Opportunity International Zimbabwe, Harare, August 31, 1995.

Director, World Concern, Seattle, Washington, August 24, 1994.

Economist, Robertson Economic Information Services, Harare, April 14, 1997.

Missionary and Evangelist, Christian Church of Christ, Harare, April 9, 1997.

Program Officer, Human Resources Development, World Bank, Harare, February 21, 1997.

Research Assistant/Shona Tutor, Harare, March 15, 1997.

Regional Director, Africa and the Caribbean, Opportunity International, Harare, January 24, 1997.

Training Officer, Housing People of Zimbabwe, Harare, April 16, 1997.

APPENDIX 2

Zimbabwe Council of Churches

The following churches in 1997 were considered stakeholders in the operations of Christian Care as the development arm of ZCC.

MEMBER DENOMINATIONS

African Methodist Church
African Methodist Episcopal
Anglican Diocese of Harare
Anglican Diocese of Central Zimbabwe
Anglican Diocese of Matabeleland
Anglican Diocese of Manicaland
Christian Marching Church
Church of Christ in Zimbabwe
Church of Central Africa Presbyterian in Zimbabwe
Dutch Reformed Church in Zimbabwe
Evangelical Lutheran Church in Zimbabwe
Independent African Church
Methodist Church in Zimbabwe
United Church of Christ in Zimbabwe
Reformed Church in Zimbabwe
Salvation Army
Presbyterian Church of Southern Africa
United Congregational Church (SA)
United Methodist Church
Ziwezano Church

OBSERVERS

Zimbabwe Assemblies of God Africa
Roman Catholic Church

ASSOCIATE MEMBERS

Bible Society in Zimbabwe
Fambidzano Yamakerekere Avatema
Student Christian Movement in Zimbabwe
Young Women Christian Association
Young Men Christian Association
Zimbabwe Womens Bureau
Ecumenical Arts Association
United Theological College
International Bible Society

ZCC DEPARTMENTS

General Secretariat
Church and Development
Ecumenical University Chaplaincy
Church in Society
Ecumenical Human Resources and Leadership Development

ZCC SERVICE DIVISION

Christian Care
ZECLOF (Zimbabwe Ecumenical Church Loan Fund)

Notes

NOTES TO INTRODUCTION

1. Geertz's definition has been critiqued for being implicitly Christian (see Asad 1993), which is something he did not intend. The implicit Christianity of Geertz's definition of religion does not limit its relevance. He defined religion as "a system of symbols which acts to establish powerful, pervasive, and long-lasting moods and motivations in men by formulating conceptions of a general order of existence and clothing these conceptions with such an aura of factuality that the moods and motivations seem uniquely realistic" (1973:90).

2. Religious-economic law is by no means limited to the Judeo-Christian tradition. Islam offers an elaborate moral cosmology for the uses of interest, usury, and the giving of charity—for example through the religious tax, *zakat*, which structures both the economics of households and cities (Baeck 1991). Islamic law is also concerned with the protection of the rights of individuals regarding private property, education, and human dignity, and theories of monetary exchange in which Allah is the unvarying standard by which all transactions are measured. This is particularly relevant to understandings of interpretation in economic activity, as Maurer (2001) demonstrates in cases of interest or *riba* in practices of Islamic banking.

3. Weber, in his heuristic typology of religions that abnegate the material world in favor of salvation, distinguishes between asceticism, in which salvation is achieved through action in this world (specifically, the avoidance of sensual and material pleasure), and mysticism, which portends salvation through contemplation of and possession by God. Although both "types" are otherworldly-focused, asceticism stresses the mastery of worldly desires, while mysticism diminishes the importance of the material world. Ascetics are God's tools; mystics are God's vessels.

4. To explain this a bit further: rationalization for Weber is a source of religious contradiction and the catalyst for religious questions. It provokes religious creativity, where such seemingly irrational worldly phenomena as evil or suffering must be explained.

5. For evangelism more generally, see Hefner (1993), Schneider and Lindenbaum (1987), and van der Veer (1996); for psychological approaches to conversion see Horton (1993).

NOTES TO CHAPTER 1

1. In terms of research, this category is extensive and has received much attention. For the relationship of the church to the colonial state in Zimbabwe, see Hallencreutz (1988).

2. ZANU-PF (Zimbabwe African National Union-Patriotic Front) was the government in power at the time of this research.

3. To rethink the colonial encounter model in the context of southern Africa, one must keep in mind that natives evangelized in the vernacular (Beach 1973, 1980; Landau 1995), and recall that the region had a history of trade relations with foreigners, including missionaries, before the arrival of the British South Africa Company. Landau (1995) explores how African interpretations of Christianity through the work of native catechists, de-centered the cultural influence of European missionaries. He stresses that the impact of Christianity in nineteenth-century southern Africa included theological innovation and the use of Christianity for political assertion, especially for women, who were active members of early mission churches.

4. Parallel efforts were being carried out by the Catholic Council of Rhodesia and Catholic missions (Hallencreutz 1988a; McLaughlin 1996). The Catholic Council criticized the Constitution in 1969, and protested the Land Tenure Act and educational reforms of the same period. The work of the Catholic Council during this time surely informed CCR's critical stance. The Catholic Commission for Justice and Peace (CCJP) became the official body through which Roman Catholic authorities could critically assess government policies. In 1978, the Catholics proposed a plea for reconciliation, one year before ZCC, although ZCC's plea in 1979 was more demanding toward changing political conditions (Auret 1992; Hallencreutz 1988b).

5. The Welfare Act of 1966. The Statue Law of Rhodesia, printed by the Government Printer, Salisbury, and published in 1967.

6. Ibid.

7. During the struggle for national liberation in Zimbabwe (1965-1980) it was not missionary Christianity but traditional religion that fueled the revolution (Lan 1985; cf. Donham 1999). The role of spirit mediums in the Zimbabwean struggle for independence manifested a cycle of political and structural transformation that began with chiefs and ended with a newly liberated Zimbabwean state. The spirit mediums (*mhondoro*), the ancestral guardians of well-being, were active in the 1890s resistance to the colonial state as well as the 1970s revolution by the *mhondoro* (also royal lineage ances-

tors of territorial cults). They offered legitimacy to the guerillas, who adopted autochthonous identities as royal descendants. Chiefly power, displaced at the time of colonial indirect rule, was transferred to the *mhondoro* and claimed by the guerillas, who observed stringent ritual prohibitions that enforced their status. The guerillas, with their supernatural identities, set up village committees to facilitate organizing in the countryside. After independence, power was ironically transferred to the new state structure that regulated mediums and created district councils (see also Ranger 1985). Christianity was a site of tension during the liberation struggle. As a companion to the work of Lan and Ranger discussed above, Bourdillon and Gundani (1988; also McLaughlin in the case of the Catholic church 1996) found in the case of a rural area in central Zimbabwe that because the guerillas were overtly anti-Christian, and Christianity was associated with the white regime, black Christians experienced a crisis during the war. Many people became "traditionalists" during this time, giving up their Christian practices. However, some refrained from attending church services out of fear, buried their Bibles, and returned to Christianity only after the war was over. The authors emphasize that rural Zimbabweans buried and did not burn their Bibles, and assert that black Christians had material advantages over traditionalists before the war. They were more prosperous; they had received education and material advantages from the missionaries. For black Christians during the liberation struggle, "it was difficult to embrace the political cause, as they wished to do, without also embracing the religious system that had become so closely associated with the political cause, but which they had rejected" (Bourdillon and Gundani 1988:154). This religious and political tension appeared in compromises between peasants and guerillas: guerillas were dependent upon peasants for food and in turn they allowed some peasants to practice Christianity.

8. "Needy" here means both the poor and those who had not been born again—those who were needy of body and needy of soul.

9. In 1942, the National Association of Evangelicals (NAE) was formed.

10. Most of the founders of Fuller seminary were friends of Billy Graham, "one other luminary whose orbit was always close to Fuller" (Marsden 1987b). Carl Henry, the editor of Christianity Today, was one of Billy Graham's lieutenants and Billy Graham became a trustee of Fuller Seminary.

11. World Vision began as a humanitarian organization to aid children in Asia. See Chapter 1 for its history. The child sponsorship program began formally in 1953.

12. Gifts in Kind (GIK) include items such as food, medical supplies, or books, donated by the U.S. government or corporations.

13. "Affirmed by the 1992 World Vision Triennial Council Meeting in Guatemala." The Triennial Council is a meeting held by the board of directors governing the international partnership.

14. This history was given to me by several people in the organization. I received both a full version (a thirteen page, year-by-year summary of World Vision's progress) as well as a two-page brief history.

15. Christian Care Annual Report 1st October 1995—30th September 1996.

16. In 2000-2001 the land was being taken without compensation, often violently.

17. Information in this section was compiled from annual reports from the following NGOs: CARE International in Zimbabwe, World Vision Zimbabwe, Save The Children Zimbabwe, Lutheran World Federation Zimbabwe, Christian Care, Opportunity International in Zimbabwe, Catholic Development Commission, Mennonite Economic Development Associates.

18. Cf. Clifford's (1986) writing on the partiality of ethnography.

19. The majority (67%) of NGOs in Zimbabwe in 1992 had offices in Harare. The National Association of Non-Governmental Organizations' directory of NGOs in Zimbabwe 1992 listed a total of 297 NGO offices distributed geographically as follows: Eastern Region 19, Midlands Region 26, Northern Region 200, Southern Region 13, Western Region 39. These organizations included small community-based organizations (CBOs) as well as larger, transnational organizations. These numbers may have decreased significantly after the violence following the 2000 elections in Zimbabwe and subsequent donor flight from the country.

20. This director was a white Zimbabwean. Hear the Word Ministries was formerly called Rhema Church.

NOTES TO CHAPTER 2

1. A body of literature exists, mainly theological, on what is called Christian development (Bradshaw 1993; Elliston 1989; Lingenfelter 1992; Verstraelen et al. 1995; Yamamori et al. 1996).

2. From a huge literature see: *Mission Handbook* (Siewert and Valdez 1997), updated annually; also the journal *International Bulletin of Missionary Research*, which updates the statistics from Barrett's *Encyclopedia* annually.

3. In Barrett (2001), category titles are "unevangelized who get evangelized," "newly evangelized/formerly unevangelized," and "direct converts" (see Global Diagram 3: "The dynamics of global religious change: annual gains and losses in population, Christians, Non-Christians, evangelized and unevangelized persons, analyzed by Worlds A, B, and C in AD 2000" (Barrett 2001:8). Also in this edition see Global Diagram 1: "Today's global human need: poverty, slums, disasters, deprivation, rights abuses, illness, disease, addiction" for its correlation to need (Barrett 2001:6). In this author's opinion, although exact demographic designations, numbers of Christians for example, deserve questioning, the categories themselves are relevant. Notably absent from these demographics are the contexts in which people decide to become Christian, including colonial histories and political and material relations of power often associated with identifying as Christian.

4. Obviously, many areas of Africa that have already been "evangelized" are economically "underdeveloped." This is a testament to the inefficacies of development as it is currently understood, and perhaps of development itself (for critiques of development see Amin 1976, Rahnema and Bawtree 1997, Rodney 1974, Sachs 1992).

5. The target field of Christian development is mapped out along geographic lines. The urgency of World Vision's evangelistic mission in economic development begins with an outline of the globe divided between Christian and "the least evangelized world." In this polarization, it is not accidental that the latter area is primarily Muslim and/or formerly communist (a landscape ripe for "spreading the news"). The history of development is also tied to efforts to "develop"—i.e. capitalist—nations to eradicate the threat of communism amidst the shift of political allegiances immediately following the Second World War (Cooper and Packard 1997).

6. Noted is the contradiction inherent in the fact that one of the poorest areas of the world, sub-Saharan Africa, is both predominantly Christian and heavily evangelized.

7. Missiology is a term for the academic study of Christian missionary work. Seminaries that offer courses in mission studies sometimes use textbooks with this title as well; for example see Verstraelen (1995).

8. One could make numerous parallels to anthropological approaches of holism that analyze how components of cultures fit together; for example, structural-functional approaches.

9. And an increasing trend in "secular" development (Chambers 1983, 1997b).

10. This was a common theme in my interviews, and was especially prominent in the California offices of WV International.

11. The ecumenical atmosphere was, however, not without conflict. I was told of an instance in which Protestant employees in the California offices of WV International in 1994 were trying to convert Catholic employees. In fact, at one point this reached such extremes that the Catholic employees ate lunch in their cars to avoid being harassed.

NOTES TO CHAPTER 3

1. The extent to which this process is truly "egalitarian" and "democratic" is dealt with in more detail in Chapter 5. Such development processes can be compared to other forms of "participatory" rural development critiqued by a corpus of scholarship on the dynamics of local power relations and stratification in development along the fissures of gender, age, and class.

2. World Vision (1997c).

3. This institutional structure has evolved over time. At the time I conducted my research in the California office in 1994-1995, for example, it was centered more around a hub office called the International Office. Since my initial research, this office has lost much of its control and function and there has been a movement to decentralize the organization and to strengthen the national offices and donor offices respectively.

4. The report states: 43,894,251 people in Africa; 14,067,226 in Asia/Pacific; 1,734,279 in Latin America/Caribbean and 1,758,151 in all other countries. More than 1.1 million children are sponsored worldwide by World Vision by donor countries

including Australia, Austria, Canada, Finland, Germany, Hong Kong, Ireland, Japan, Korea, Netherlands, New Zealand, Singapore, South Africa, Switzerland, Taiwan, the United Kingdom, the United States. WV Zimbabwe is sponsored by donor offices in Australia, Canada, Germany, Hong Kong, Korea, Netherlands, New Zealand, Taiwan, the United Kingdom, and the United States.

5. Interview with child sponsorship specialist, WV Zimbabwe, Harare, 1997. There are also secular NGOs that use the child-sponsorship model, such as Save the Children and Plan International.

6. Focused group discussion with the "Christian Witness Committee" of WV Zimbabwe, Harare, July 3, 1997.

7. Comments from the national director of WV Zimbabwe. Focused group discussion with the Christian Witness Committee of WV Zimbabwe, Harare, July 3, 1997. WV Zimbabwe receives about 12–14 sponsors who come to visit their children each year. During one month, while I was in Zimbabwe, there were three visits scheduled. These visits are often seasonal due to transport limitations during the rainy season.

8. Many of the sponsors were not wealthy in the context of their own national economies; most sponsors were pensioners or "middle class."

9. This name is a pseudonym. Interview with Canadian child sponsor, Harare, August 26, 1997.

10. An ADP, Area Development Project, covers a larger area than a Community Development Project (CDP), Chiloko ADP, World Vision project, Mount Darwin, Zimbabwe.

11. For example, one World Vision staff member asked Peter to help him find funds to go to Australia.

12. He cancelled his credit card after it was stolen.

13. Admittedly, while my analysis concentrates on the work of World Vision as an NGO that facilitates relationships between sponsors and sponsored children, it is an analysis skewed toward the NGO. A promising area of research (but one that is beyond the scope of my study) would be to analyze the experiences of sponsored children at rural development projects. Reynolds (1985) has argued persuasively for a shift in focus to emphasize what children in the Third World do, think and feel. She cautions against approaches to "childhood" that take it as a whole or a level, and proposes one that is many-layered and involves the life decisions and participation of children themselves. Reynolds (1985, 1996; Burman and Reynolds 1986) considers the lives of children central to her ethnography, and presents a compelling argument for the agency of children within kinship structures.

14. Interview with child sponsorship correspondence analyst, Harare, April 24, 1997.

15. This was a common name in Zimbabwe; I met several people who had this name.

16. Narration from the film *The 38th Parallel* (1950) by Bob Pierce, founder of World Vision. Viewed at WV International office, Monrovia, CA, August 1, 1994.

17. This story of Bob Pierce was an institutional "origin myth" that was repeated in numerous interviews in the United States and Zimbabwe, as well as in materials from the World Vision Information and Communications Department (1994). See also Irvine (1996) for the history as told by one director.

18. For a wonderful description of the language of conversion and the concept of being "born-again," see Harding (2000), especially Chapter 1, "Speaking is Believing."

19. Interview with the director of World Vision's "Unreached Peoples" Program, WV International, Monrovia, CA, July 20, 1994.

20. Focused group discussion with the Christian Witness Committee of WV Zimbabwe, Harare, July 3, 1997.

21. As in Ferguson (1999), the terms "witchcraft" and "jealousy" were used in tandem by my informants in Zimbabwe. "Envy" was not used as much by my inform-ants; people used "jealousy" more often when speaking in English and *"kuchiva"* when speaking in Shona. My use of the term jealousy is analogous to colloquial uses of envy (the desire for what someone else has) instead of to the way jealousy is used in American English (as intolerance of unfaithfulness, especially relating to romantic devotion). The dominant quality of jealousy in this chapter refers to desire resulting in harm to others.

22. There is an interesting emerging literature on jealousy and witchcraft in Africa as distinctly modern phenomena (see Comaroff and Comaroff 1999a; England 1996; Geschiere 1997). On witchcraft in southern Africa there is extensive literature containing its own debates—far too broad to address here. Of relevance to this argu-ment, specifically on the relation of witchcraft to power, see Ashforth (1996); on witch-craft in Zimbabwe with the Shona see Bourdillon (1976).

23. Interview with sponsor relations specialist, WV Zimbabwe, Harare, March 24, 1997.

24. This name is a pseudonym. Interview with former sponsored child, Harare, August 7, 1997.

25. Interview with former international sponsorship coordinator for WV International and World Vision Australia, and consultant for WV Zimbabwe. Interview, World Vision Southern Africa Office, Harare, August 21, 1997.

26. World Vision operates throughout Zimbabwe in complex linguistic (Shona, Ndebele, Tonga, as well as specific dialects) and lineage contexts. While my research concentrates on Shona-speaking regions in the northern and central parts of Zimbabwe, Peter's narrative is drawn from the Ndebele-speaking south. Albert was Shona-speak-ing. While it is beyond the scope of this chapter to elaborate on specific kinship struc-tures, some classic texts (Bourdillon 1976; Gelfand 1973) lay a foundation for analysis, still others elaborate on the *mhondoro* (spirit medium) cults that transcend kinship and assert claims to land (Lan 1985; Schoffeleers 1978). Few works document the flux that kinship structures undergo, linking rural/urban settings in cycles of economy and work in contemporary Zimbabwe. For a related analysis, see Ferguson (1994, 1997).

27. Interview with Communications and Public Relations Manager, WV Zimbabwe, Harare, August 24, 1997.

28. See Cronemeyer's compelling historical exegesis on the history of "helping" and international development (1992).

29. A Zimbabwean woman in her early 30s. All of the full-time staff of WV Zimbabwe that I interviewed were black and Zimbabwean, except for one American who was on a three-year contract. His position was Natural Resource Management and Environmental Rehabilitation Coordinator. There were two consultants I interviewed who had held positions in WV Australia and WV USA, but they were not hired as full-time staff of WV Zimbabwe.

30. Aside from the project coordinator, the three other staff members had been elected from the local community. At the front of the room were the chair of the Local Management Committee of the development project, the World Vision field officer with whom I had traveled to the project from Harare, the project clerk, the project bookkeeper, and myself.

31. Community meeting, World Vision Hwino Community Development Project, July 15, 1997.

32. The meeting was attended by members of the rural community that housed the development project. In attendance were the headman, the VIDCO chairman, the headmaster, the School Committee, the chairman of the World Vision Project Committee, the Evangelism Committee, the Women in Development Committee, the project bookkeeper, and the project clerk, along with parents of sponsored children. Some committee members also had children that were being sponsored by World Vision and whose school fees were being paid by the sponsorship.

33. World Vision sets up committees at each Community Development Project (CDP). Elected by the community, these committees oversee the development efforts alongside World Vision staff members that live in the community and those that visit monthly to monitor the project, like the project coordinator.

34. One could also interpret her response as an implicit statement that the father could not be trusted with the money, or that donors who want to assist children do not want to assist "families."

35. A local community member hired by World Vision.

NOTES TO CHAPTER 4

1. "Civil society" is a term much analyzed and critiqued. Here, I am relying on the definition used in much political science literature and theory. Cohen (1992:ix) defines civil society as "a sphere of social interaction between economy and state, composed above all of the intimate sphere (especially the family), the sphere of associations (especially voluntary associations), social movements, and forms of public communication." This is quite a broad sphere indeed, and seems to refer to anything but the nation state. Later (page x), the authors continue, "Civil society refers to the structures of socialization, association, and organized forms of communication of the life-world to the extent that these are institutionalized or are in the process of being institutionalized." See Ferguson and Gupta (2002) for the limits of this concept for ethnographic inquiry.

Gramsci (1991; also see Keane 1988) conceptualized "civil society" via Marx with the socialist goal of ending class- and ultimately state/civil society divisions. Gramscian civil society builds on Marx's idea of civil society in relation to ideology (1975[1843]), characterized by the hegemonic interests of the bourgeoisie. In contrast, Gramsci's civil society, and the inherent potential for resistance that lies within such a category, exists in the realm of culture and cultural institutions (Hall 1986, 1988; for Gramsci's theory put in to practice see Comaroff and Comaroff 1991, 1997). This point is important, for the purposes of this study, as churches and faith-based NGOs fall with-in the realm of cultural institutions. Using the model of trench warfare and a "war of position," Gramsci understands that cultural production involves class struggle. For Gramsci, struggles over ideas and ideals articulate hegemonic and counterhegemonic struggles.

2. Cf. the decline of Zambia (Ferguson 1999).

3. Huge literature: Bayart (1993); Comaroff and Comaroff (1999b); Dorman (2002); Ferguson (forthcoming); Harbeson, Rothchild, and Chazan (1994); Hyden and Bratton (1992); Keane (1988); Mamdani (1996); Marcussen (1996); Maxwell (2000); MWENGO (1993); Ndegwa (1994, 1996); Rich (1997); Sachikonye (1995a); Taylor (1990); Turner and Hulme (1997); Williams (1993); Williams and Young (1994); Woods (1992).

4. Dorman (2002); Gifford (1994); Gundani (1988); Hallencreutz (1988a, 1988b); Hallencreutz and Moyo (1988); Maxwell (1995, 1998, 2000).

5. Alexander and McGregor (2000); Makumbe (1996, 1998); Moore (1999); Munro (1998); Robins (1994); Rutherford (2000); Worby (1998).

6. Bond (1998); Hanlon (2000); Potts (1998); Sachikonye (1995b).

7. For a related argument on the idea of civil society see the introduction in Comaroff and Comaroff (1999b).

8. Mrs. Olivia Muchena was on the International Board of WV International, and was on the National Board of WV Zimbabwe. She was also an MP and the Deputy Minister of Agriculture for the Government of Zimbabwe.

9. World Vision Day of Prayer, Harare, October 1, 1997.

10. Herbst notes that shortly after independence, the civil service was increased from 40,000 to 80,000. The larger civil service was an attempt by the new government to move Africans into the state (Herbst 1990:31).

11. Others, of course, were the majority of Zimbabweans who experienced economic survival becoming increasingly difficult (Potts 1998).

12. Cf. Gupta's description of the Indian state in (Ferguson and Gupta 2002).

13. This process, although interesting, is beyond the scope of this chapter. Scholars studying rural development from the vantage of local communities focus on how local power structures of largely elder men are replicated and reinforced in sup-posedly democratic and participatory processes of community development. In terms of defining the "community," that is being developed, see Chapter 5.

14. WV Zimbabwe project, Mabee.

15. Interview with Christian Care national executive committee member, Harare, August 14, 1997.

16. NGOs involved in the PVO Campaign were Ecumenical Support Services and the Zimbabwe Council of Churches. Other NGOs that spoke out in protest against the legislation included senior staff from the Lutheran World Federation, the Catholic Commission for Justice and Peace, and EDICESA. For an account of the PVO Campaign, see Rich (1997).

17. Internal document dated January 4, 1991.

18. Makumbe (1996, 1998); Raftopoulos (1991).

19. WV Zimbabwe projects, Maparaidze and Chirariro.

20. Christian Care project, Hurungwe. Field Notes: March 19. 1997.

21. WV Zimbabwe project, Kasonde.

22. Translation by Christian Care field officer. I also heard this song sung at World Vision projects.

NOTES TO CHAPTER 5

1. The extent to which this is successful is a debate unto itself (Goebel 1998; Mosse 1995; Rahnema 1992; Vivian 1994).

2. For details on the use of participation in state-oriented development discourse in Zimbabwe see Makumbe (1996).

3. A relevant comparison can be made to "responsibility-based management" (Rose 1993, 1996).

4. Interview with the assistant to the national director. WV Zimbabwe, April 3, 1997.

5. Cf. "the anti-politics machine" (Ferguson 1994).

6. Interview with coordinator for Local Fundraising and Sustainability for Programs, WV Zimbabwe, March 11, 1997.

7. Cf. Jesus as "teacher," and the model of Christian pedagogical relations.

8. He told me he had written his thesis on Derrida.

9. Interview with field officer, WV Zimbabwe, March 14, 1997.

10. Interview with director, Technical Support Services. WV Zimbabwe. March 14, 1997.

11. Community meeting and interview with development committees, WV Zimbabwe, Garabwa Project, September 11, 1997.

12. Community meeting and interview with development committees, WV Zimbabwe, Maparaidze Project, September 10, 1997.

13. Community meeting and interview with development committees, WV Zimbabwe, Chirariro Project, July 16, 1997.

NOTES TO CHAPTER 6

1. For development more broadly, see Cooper (1997:18) and Pigg (1992).

2. Interview with the bookkeeper and project clerk of World Vision project, Hwino.

3. Group discussion with the Christian Witness Committee, WV Zimbabwe, September 25, 1997, Harare.

4. *See* literature on witchcraft and modernity: Comaroff and Comaroff 1993, 1999a); Ellis and Haar (1998); Fisiy and Geschiere (1991); Geschiere (1997); Hodgson (1997); Ranger (1991). There are also critics of the "witchcraft" or "witchcraft as metaphor" for economic ills approach: see Ashforth (1996); England (1996); Rutherford (1999). Ethnographies that have focused on attitudes toward success in the history of rural Africa have inevitably engaged with the theme of witchcraft, especially as it combines with jealousy and spawns tensions between categories of "the community" and "the individual" (extensive literature: Ashforth 1996, 2000; Comaroff and Comaroff 1999a; England 1996; Evans-Pritchard 1958; Fisiy and Geschiere 1991, 1996; Geschiere 1997; Hodgson 1997; Ranger 1991; Rutherford 1999; West 2001).

5. "Modernity" here refers to David Harvey's (1989) exegesis of the project of modernity, and its correlation to Enlightenment thought, modernization theory, and development discourse. Modernism, which began in the late 1800s, was distinguished philosophically by its comprehension of organizing chaos, ephemerality and change. Economically it was eventually identifiable by its Fordist practices. By the mid 1940s, modernism had become a hegemonic belief in linear progress and rationality. More recently, Ferguson's (1999) *Expectations of Modernity: Myths and Meanings of Urban Life on the Zambian Copperbelt* demonstrates how, while modernism and the promises of modernity may be dated narratives, the expectations produced by them (through such organizations as NGOs and programs of development) are alive in Africa today.

6. The term I heard used was *ruchiva*, which is Shona for covetousness, lust, or jealousy.

7. My research assistant worked with me as a Shona tutor and a translator of articles in the vernacular press. He did not accompany me on visits to rural field sites or interviews in the Harare offices of NGOs.

8. Pedagogy is a form of social power.

9. See Fisiy and Geschiere for a discussion of how witchcraft in Africa (their case Cameroon) can occur with either leveling or accumulative intentions (1991).

10. Although this topic was difficult for me to broach, I traveled with Zimbabwean NGO staff familiar with my research interests and with the communities (often having worked with them for many years). They facilitated my asking such socially delicate questions.

11. See Said's *Orientalism* (1978) and Young's *Colonial Desire* (1995) for discussions of desire and colonialism. For example, apartheid would not have been "necessary" if there had not been an impulse to mix.

12. The gardening co-op grew primarily maize and vegetables, although they wanted to plant all types of vegetables: rape, cabbage, *tsunga*, sugar loaf, tomatoes, carrots, onions, cucumber, pumpkins, and paprika.

13. He was the national director of the dressmaking school for all of ZAOGA's 113 centers in Zimbabwe. He explained that it was an extensive operation in Zimbabwe, with 227 instructors for the ZAOGA dressmaking schools in Zimbabwe.

14. This meeting, as well as those that followed, were conducted entirely in Shona. I received translation assistance from World Vision project staff, specifically bookkeepers, project clerks, and drivers. Quotes in translation are the result of this collaboration. In every case, people went to extraordinary lengths to make sure I understood what was being said.

15. I found it quite remarkable that it was as if women did not use their hands already in the myriad of daily rural tasks such as farming and cooking. The skills that were being taught by World Vision were framed as new skills that increased the economic independence of women.

16. David Maxwell (personal communication) pointed out that members of the ZAOGA church believe not only that poverty is evil philosophically, but also that it is the embodiment of evil, the result of an ancestral curse that can only be effaced by hard work and exorcism.

17. He was the director of ZECLOF— the Zimbabwe Ecumenical Church Loan Fund. ECLOF, the Ecumenical Church Loan Fund, was formed in Geneva in 1946. It came to Zimbabwe after the war of liberation through the Zimbabwe Council of Churches. Both ZECLOF and Christian Care are service arms of the Zimbabwe Council of Churches: ZECLOF supplies loans, and Christian Care supplies economic development.

NOTES TO CONCLUSION

1. Hanlon (2000:135) describes foreign aid as a $58 billion a year industry. He estimates that NGOs like World Vision are responsible for $9 billion of the aid industry, noting that NGOs have handled about one-tenth of official aid flows.

2. At the time of this writing, President Bush had just formed a new "Office of Faith-Based and Community Initiatives" that was to redirect much of the United States' funding for social services to faith-based institutions. This initiative was controversial and focused primarily on welfare programs within the United States. For policy-related discussions on this see: Dione (1999); The Brookings Institute (1999a, 1999b); Loury (1999).

Bibliography

Alexander, Jocelyn, and JoAnn McGregor. 2000. Wildlife and Politics: CAMPFIRE in Zimbabwe. *Development and Change* 31 (3):605-627.

Amin, Samir. 1976. *Unequal Development: An Essay on the Social Formations of Peripheral Capitalism*. Translated by B. Pearce. New York and London: Monthly Review Press.

Anderson, Benedict. 1983. *Imagined Communities: Reflections on the Origin and Spread of Nationalism*. London; New York: Verso.

Anderson, Lisa, Hugh Dellios, Mike Dorning, Laurie Goering, Gary Marx, Michael Tackett, David Jackson, Storer H. Rowley, Uli Schmetzer, and John Crewdson. 1998. *The Miracle Merchants* [electronic source]. Duenes, Steve, Mills, Marja 1998 [March 15, 1998]. http://chicagotribune.com/ws/children.

Appadurai, Arjun. 1990. Disjuncture and Difference in the Global Cultural Economy. *Public Culture* 2 (2):1-24.

———. 1996. The Production of Locality. In *Modernity at Large*. Minneapolis: University of Minnesota Press.

Asad, Talal. 1993. *Genealogies of Religion: Discipline and Reasons of Power in Christianity and Islam*. Baltimore and London: The Johns Hopkins University Press.

Ashforth, Adam. 1996. Of Secrecy and the Commonplace: Witchcraft and Power in Soweto. *Social Research* 63 (4):1183-1233.

———. 2000. *Madumo: A Man Bewitched*. Chicago: University of Chicago Press.

Auret, Diana. 1990. *A Decade of Development. Zimbabwe 1980-1990*. Gweru: Mambo Press.

———. 1992. *Reaching for Justice: The Catholic Commission for Justice and Peace 1972-1992*. Harare: Mambo Press.

Baeck, Louis. 1991. The Economic Thought of Classical Islam. *Diogenes* 154:99-115.

Balleis, Peter S.J. 1992. *ESAP and Theology*. Vol. No.1, *Silveira House Social Series*. Gweru: Mambo Press.

Banana, Canaan. 1982. *Theology of Promise: The Dynamics of Self-Reliance*. Harare: The College Press (Pvt.) Ltd.

Barrett, David. 1982. *World Christian Encyclopedia: A Comparative Study of Churches and Religions in the Modern World AD 1900-2000*. Nairobi; New York: Oxford University Press.

Barrett, David B., George Thomas Kurian, and Todd M. Johnson. 2001. *World Christian Encyclopedia: A Comparative Survey of Churches and Religions in the Modern World*. 2nd ed. Oxford; New York: Oxford University Press.

Bates, Robert. 1981. *Markets and States in Colonial Africa*. Berkeley, Los Angeles and London: University of California Press.

Bayart, Jean-Francois. 1993. *The State in Africa: The Politics of the Belly*. New York: Longman.

Beach, David. 1973. The Initial Impact of Christianity on the Shona: The Protestants and the Southern Shona. In *Christianity South of the Zambezi Volume 1*, edited by J. A. Dachs. Salisbury: Mambo Press.

————. 1980. *The Shona and Zimbabwe 900-1850: An Outline of Shona History*. London: Heinemann.

Beckman, Bjorn. 1993. The Liberation of Civil Society: Neo-Liberal Ideology and Political Theory. *Review of African Political Economy* No .58:20-33.

Bediako, Kwame. 1995. *Christianity in Africa: The Renewal of a Non-Western Religion*. Edinburgh: Edinburgh University Press.

Behar, Ruth. 1996. *The Vulnerable Observer: Anthropology That Breaks Your Heart*. Boston, MA: Beacon Press.

Beigbeder, Yves. 1991. *The Role and Status of International Humanitarian Volunteers and Organizations: The Right and Duty to Humanitarian Assistance*. Dordrecht, Boston and London: Martinus Nijhoff Publishers.

Bell, G.K.A. 1979. *The Kingship of Christ: The Story of the World Council of Churches*. Westport, CT: Greenwood Press.

Biko, Stephen. 2000[1978]. *I Write What I Like*. Edited by A. Stubbs C.R. London: Bowerdean Press.

Bock, Paul. 1974. *In Search of a Responsible World Society: The Social Teachings of the World Council of Churches*. Philadelphia: The Westminster Press.

Bond, Patrick. 1991. Geopolitics, International Finance and National Capital Accumulation—Zimbabwe in the 1980s and 1990s. *Tijdschrift voor economische en sociale geografie* 82 (5):325-337.

————. 1998. *Uneven Zimbabwe: A Study of Finance, Development, and Underdevelopment*. Trenton, NJ: Africa World Press.

Bonsen, Roland, Hans Marsks, and Jelle Miedema, eds. 1990. *The Ambiguity of Rapprochement: Reflections of Anthropologists on Their Controversial Relationship with Missionaries*. Nijmegen: The Netherlands: Focaal Foundation.

Bourdillon, Michael. 1976. *The Shona Peoples: An Ethnography of the Contemporary Shona, with Special Reference to Their Religion.* Gwelo, Rhodesia: Mambo Press.

Bourdillon, Michael, and Paul Gundani. 1988. Rural Christians and the Zimbabwe Liberation War: A Case Study by M. Bourdillon and P. Gundani. In *Church and State in Zimbabwe,* edited by C. F. Hallencreutz and A. M. Moyo. Harare: Mambo Press.

Bradshaw, Bruce. 1993. *Bridging the Gap: Evangelism, Development and Shalom.* Monrovia, CA: MARC Publishers.

Brand, C. M. 1977. African Nationalists and the Missionaries in Rhodesia. In *Christianity South of the Zambezi Vol. 2,* edited by M. F. C. Bourdillon. Gwelo: Mambo Press.

Brandt, Donald. 1995. The Poor and the Lost: A Holistic View of Poverty. *Missiology* 13 (3):260-266.

Bratton, Michael. 1989a. Beyond the State: Civil Society and Associational Life in Africa. *World Politics* 41 (3):407-430.

——. 1989b. The Politics of Government-NGO Relations in Africa. *World Development* 17 (4):569-587.

Brookings Institute. 1999a. *Congregations, the Government and Social Justice: Community Development* [electronic document]. The Brookings Institute [January 31, 2001]. http://www.brook.edu/dybdocroot/com.

——. 1999b. *Sacred Places, Civic Purposes: Congregations, the Government, and Social Justice* [electronic source]. The Brookings Institute [January 31, 2001]. http://www.brook.edu/dybdocroot/gs/.

Burman, Sandra, and Pamela Reynolds. 1986. *Growing up in a Divided Society: The Contexts of Childhood in South Africa.* Johannesburg: Ravan Press.

Chambers, Robert. 1983. *Rural Development: Putting the Last First.* London, Lagos and New York: Longman.

——. 1994a. The Origins and Practice of Participatory Rural Appraisal. *World Development* 22 (7):953-969.

——. 1994b. Participatory Rural Appraisal (PRA): Analysis of Experience. *World Development* 22 (9):1253-1268.

——. 1994c. Participatory Rural Appraisal (PRA): Challenges, Potentials and Paradigm. *World Development* 22 (10):1437-1454.

——. 1997a. Editorial: Responsible Well-Being—a Personal Agenda for Development. *World Development* 25 (11):1743-1754.

——. 1997b. *Whose Reality Counts: Putting the Last First.* London, UK: Intermediate Technology Publications.

Chatterjee, Partha. 1990. A Response to Taylor's "Modes of Civil Society". *Public Culture* 3 (1):119-132.

Chazan, Naomi. 1994. Engaging the State: Associational Life in Sub-Saharan Africa. In *State Power and Social Forces: Domination and Transformation in the Third*

World, edited by J. S. Midgal, A. Kohli and V. Shue. Cambridge, England: Cambridge University Press.

Chepkwony Ongaro, Agnes. 1991. The Role of the Church in the Development Market—The Case of Zimbabwe. In *Religion and Politics in Southern Africa*, edited by C. F. Hallencreutz and M. Palmberg. Uppsala: The Scandinavian Institute of African Studies.

Christian Care Annual Report 1995-1996. Harare: Christian Care Ecumenical Services Zimbabwe.

Clark, Ann Marie. 1995. Non-Governmental Organizations and Their Influence on International Society. *Journal of International Affairs* 48 (2):507-525.

Clark, John. 1991. *Democratizing Development*. Hartford, Connecticut: Kumarian Press.

Clifford, James, and George E. Marcus. 1986. *Writing Culture: The Poetics and Politics of Ethnography*. Berkeley: University of California Press.

Cohen, Jean L., and Andrew Arato. 1992. *Civil Society and Political Theory*. Cambridge, MA: MIT Press.

Comaroff, Jean. 1985. *Body of Power, Spirit of Resistance: The Culture and History of a South African People*. Chicago: University of Chicago Press.

———. 1991. Missionaries and Mechanical Clocks: An Essay on Religion and History in South Africa. *The Journal of Religion*:1-17.

Comaroff, Jean, and John Comaroff. 1999a. Occult Economies and the Violence of Abstraction: Notes from the South African Postcolony. *American Ethnologist* 26 (2):279-303.

Comaroff, Jean, and John L. Comaroff. 1991. *Of Revelation and Revolution: Christianity, Colonialism and Consciousness in South Africa. Vol. 1*. Chicago: University of Chicago Press.

———. 1993. *Modernity and Its Malcontents: Ritual Power in Postcolonial Africa*. Chicago: University of Chicago Press.

Comaroff, John L. 1989. Images of Empire, Contests of Conscience: Models of Colonial Domination in South Africa. *American Ethnologist* 16 (4):661-764.

Comaroff, John L., and Jean Comaroff. 1997. *Of Revelation and Revolution: The Dialectics of Modernity on a South African Frontier. Vol. 2*. Chicago: University of Chicago Press.

———. 1999b. *Civil Society and the Political Imagination in Africa: Critical Perspectives*. Chicago: University of Chicago Press.

Cooper, Frederick, and Randall Packard. 1997. Introduction. In *International Development and the Social Sciences: Essays on the History and Politics of Knowledge*, edited by F. Cooper and R. Packard. Berkeley: University of California Press.

Cooper, Frederick, and Ann Stoler. 1989. Introduction: Tensions of Empire Colonial Control and Visions of Rule. *American Ethnologist* 16 (4):609-684.

Cowen, M. P., and R. W. Shenton. 1996. *Doctrines of Development*. New York: Routledge.

Crewe, Emma, and Elizabeth Harrison. 1998. *Whose Development? An Ethnography of Aid.* New York: Zed Books.

Dale, D. 1992. *Duramazwi: A Basic Shona-English Dictionary.* Harare: Mambo Press.

Davidson, Basil. 1974. *Can Africa Survive?* Boston and Toronto: Atlantic Monthly Press.

Diamond, Larry. 1994. Toward Democratic Consolidation. *Journal of Democracy* 5 (3).

Dione, E.J., and John Jr. DiIulio. 1999. *What's God Got to Do with the American Experiment?* [electronic document]. The Brookings Institute [January 31, 1999]. http://www.brook.edu/dybdcroot/com.

Donham, Donald L. 1999. *Marxist Modern: An Ethnographic History of the Ethiopian Revolution.* Berkeley: University of California Press: Oxford England: J. Currey.

Dorman, Sara Rich. 2002. Rocking the Boat?: Church-NGOs and Democratization in Zimbabwe. *African Affairs* 101:75-92.

Duff, Edward S.J. 1956. *The Social Thought of the World Council of Churches.* New York: Association Press.

Dumont, Rene. 1969. *False Start in Africa.* Translated by P. N. Ott. New York and Washington: Fredrick A. Praeger.

Ellis, Stephen, and Gerrie ter Haar. 1998. Religion and Politics in Sub-Saharan Africa. *Journal of Modern African Studies* 36:175-201.

Elliston, Edgar J. 1989. *Christian Relief and Development: Developing Workers for Effective Ministry.* Dallas and London: Word Publishing.

Englund, Harri. 1996. Witchcraft, Modernity and the Person: The Morality of Accumulation in Central Malawi. *Critique of Anthropology* 16 (3):257-279.

Escobar, Arturo. 1995. *Encountering Development: The Making and Unmaking of the Third World.* New Jersey: Princeton University Press.

Evans-Pritchard, E. E. 1958. *Witchcraft, Oracles and Magic among the Azande.* Oxford: The Clarendon Press.

Eyoh, Dickson. 1996. From Economic Crisis to Political Liberalization: Pitfalls of the New Political Sociology for Africa. *African Studies Review* 39 (3):43-80.

Farrington, John, Anthony Bebbington, Kate Wellard, and David J. Lewis. 1993. *Reluctant Partners: Non Governmental Organizations, the State and Sustainable Agricultural Development.* London and New York: Routledge.

Ferguson, James. 1994. *The Anti-Politics Machine.* Minneapolis: University of Minnesota Press.

——. 1995. From African Socialism to Scientific Capitalism: Reflections on the Legitimation Crisis in IMF-Ruled Africa. In *Debating Development Discourse,* edited by D. B. Moore and C. J. Schmitz. New York: St. Martin's.

——. 1997. The Country and the City on the Copperbelt. In *Culture Power Place: Explorations in Critical Anthropology,* edited by A. Gupta and J. Ferguson. Durham: Duke University Press.

——. 1999. *Expectations of Modernity: Myths and Meanings of Urban Life on the Zambian Copperbelt.* Berkeley: University of California Press.

———. Forthcoming. Of Ministry and Membership: Africans and the "New World Society."

Ferguson, James, and Akhil Gupta. 2002. Spatializing States: Toward an Ethnography of Neoliberal Governmentality. *American Ethnologist* 29(4): 981–1002.

Fields, Karen. 1985. *Revival and Rebellion in Colonial Central Africa.* Princeton: Princeton University Press.

Fisher, William F. 1997. Doing Good? The Politics and Antipolitics of NGO Practices. In *Annual Review of Anthropology Volume 26*, edited by W. Durham. Palo Alto: Annual Reviews Inc.

Fisiy, Cyprian F., and Peter Geschiere. 1991. Sorcery, Witchcraft and Accumulation: Regional Variations in South and West Cameroon. *Critique of Anthropology* 11 (3):251–278.

———. 1996. Witchcraft, Violence and Identity: Different Trajectories in Postcolonial Cameroon. In *Postcolonial Identities in Africa*, edited by R. Werbner and T. Ranger. London: Zed Books.

Foster, Robert J. 1991. Making National Cultures in the Global Ecumene. *Annual Review of Anthropology* 20:235–260.

Foucault, Michel. 1973. *The Order of Things: An Archaeology of the Human Sciences.* New York: Vintage Books.

Gal, Susan. 1989. Language and Political Economy. *Annual Review of Anthropology* 18:345–367.

Geertz, Clifford. 1973. Religion as a Cultural System. In *The Interpretation of Cultures.* New York: Basic Books.

Gelman, Richard. 1960. *Let My Heart Be Broken... With the Things That Break the Heart of God.* New York: McGraw-Hill.

Gelfand, Michael. 1973. *The Genuine Shona: Survival Values of an African Culture.* Gwerru: Mambo Press.

Geschiere, Peter. 1997. *The Modernity of Witchcraft: Politics and the Occult in Postcolonial Africa.* Charlottesville, VA: University Press of Virginia.

Gifford, Paul. 1990. Prosperity: A New and Foreign Element in African Christianity. *Religion* 20:373–388.

———. 1992. American Evangelicalism in Zimbabwe. In *Christianity and Hegemony: Religion and Politics on the Frontiers of Social Change*, edited by J. N. Pieterse. New York and Oxford: Berg.

———. 1994. Some Recent Developments in African Christianity. *African Affairs* 93:513–534.

———. 1995. *The Christian Churches and the Democratisation of Africa.* New York: E.J. Brill.

———. 1998. *African Christianity: Its Public Role.* Bloomington: Indiana University Press.

Goebel, Allison. 1998. Process, Perception and Power: Notes from 'Participatory' Research in a Zimbabwean Resettlement Area. *Development and Change* 29 (2):277–305.

Gonzalez, Justo L. 1990. *Faith and Wealth: A History of Early Christian Ideas on the Origin, Significance, and Use of Money*. New York: Harper and Row.

Government of Zimbabwe. 1997. Statistical Yearbook 1997. Harare: Central Statistical Office.

Gramsci, Antonio. 1991. *Selections from the Prison Notebooks of Antonio Gramsci*. Translated by Q. Hoare and G. N. Smith. New York: International Publishers.

Greenhouse, Carol J., Barbara Yngvesson, and David M. Engel. 1994. *Law and Community in Three American Towns*. Ithaca: Cornell University Press.

Gronemeyer, Marianne. 1992. Helping. In *The Development Dictionary*, edited by W. Sachs. London: Zed Books.

Gundani, Paul. 1988. The Catholic Church and National Development in Independent Zimbabwe. In *Church and State in Zimbabwe*, edited by C. F. Hallencreutz and A. M. Moyo. Harare: Mambo Press.

Gupta, Akhil. 1998. *Postcolonial Developments: Agriculture in the Making of Modern India*. Durham: Duke University Press.

Gupta, Akhil, and James Ferguson. 1997a. Beyond "Culture": Space, Identity, and the Politics of Difference. In *Culture Power Place: Explorations in Critical Anthropology*, edited by A. Gupta and J. Ferguson. Durham: Duke University Press.

———. 1997b. Culture, Power, Place: Ethnography at the End of an Era. In *Culture Power Place: Explorations in Critical Anthropology*, edited by A. Gupta and J. Ferguson. Durham: Duke University Press.

———, eds. 1997c. *Anthropological Locations: Boundaries and Grounds of a Field Science*. Berkeley: University of California Press.

Guyer, Jane. 1994. The Spatial Dimensions of Civil Society in Africa: An Anthropologist Looks at Nigeria. In *Civil Society and the State in Africa*, edited by J. W. Harbeson, D. Rothchild and N. Chazan. London: Lynne Rienner.

Gyimah-Boadi, E. 1996. Civil Society in Africa. *Journal of Democracy* 7 (2):118-132.

Hall, Stuart. 1986. Gramsci's Relevance for the Study of Race and Ethnicity. *Journal of Communication Inquiry* 10 (2):5-27.

———. 1988. Gramsci and Us. In *The Hard Road to Renewal: Thatcherism and the Crisis of the Left*. London: Verso.

Hallencreutz, Carl. 1988a. A Council in Crossfire: ZCC 1964-1980. In *Church and State in Zimbabwe*, edited by C. F. Hallencreutz and A. M. Moyo. Gweru: Mambo Press.

———. 1988b. Ecumenical Challenges in Independent Zimbabwe: ZCC 1980-1985. In *Church and State in Zimbabwe*, edited by C. F. Hallencreutz and A. M. Moyo. Gweru: Mambo Press.

Hallencreutz, Carl F., and Ambrose M. Moyo. 1988. *Church and State in Zimbabwe*. Gweru: Mambo Press.

Hancock, Graham. 1989. *Lords of Poverty: The Power, Prestige and Corruption of the International Aid Business*. New York: Atlantic Monthly Press.

Hanlon, Joseph. 2000. An 'Ambitious and Extensive Political Agenda': The Role of NGOs and the Aid Industry. In *Global Institutions and Local Empowerment: Competing Theoretical Perspectives*, edited by K. Stiles. New York: St. Martins.

Hannan, M. 1996. *Standard Shona Dictionary*. Harare: College Press Publishers (Pvt) Ltd.

Hannerz, Ulf. 1987. The World in Creolization. *Africa* 57 (4):546-559.

———. 1996. *Transnational Connections: Culture, People, Places*. New York: Routledge.

Harbeson, John W., Donald Rothchild, and Naomi Chazan. 1994. *Civil Society and the State in Africa*. London: Lynne Rienner.

Harding, Susan. 2000. *The Book of Jerry Falwell: Fundamentalist Language and Politics*. Princeton, NJ: Princeton University Press.

Harvey, David. 1989. *The Condition of Postmodernity: An Enquiry into the Origins of Cultural Change*. Cambridge, MA: Basil Blackwell.

Hefner, Robert W. 1993. *Conversion to Christianity: Historical and Anthropological Perspectives on a Great Transformation*. Berkeley: University of California Press.

Herbst, Jeffrey. 1990. *State Politics in Zimbabwe*. Harare: University of Zimbabwe.

Hiebert, Paul G. 1994. *Anthropological Reflections on Missiological Issues*. Grand Rapids, MI: Baker Books.

Hill, Polly. 1986. *Development Economics on Trial*. Cambridge: Cambridge University Press.

Hodgson, Dorothy. 1997. Embodying the Contradictions of Modernity: Gender and Spirit Possession among Maasai in Tanzania. In *Gendered Encounters: Challenging Cultural Boundaries and Social Hierarchies in Africa*, edited by Grosz-Ngate and O. H. Kokole. New York: Routledge.

Horton, Robin. 1993. African Traditional Religion and Western Science. In *Patterns of Thought in Africa and the West: Essays on Magic, Religion and Science*. Cambridge: Cambridge University Press.

Hunter, Monica. 1961. *Reaction to Conquest: Effects of Contact with Europeans on the Pondo of South Africa*. London: Oxford University Press.

Hyden, Goran. 1980. *Beyond Ujamaa in Tanzania*. London, Iban and Nairobi: Heinemann.

Hyden, Goran, and Michael Bratton, eds. 1992. *Governance and Politics in Africa*. Boulder, CO: Lynne Reinner.

Irvine, Graeme S. 1996. *Best Things in the Worst Times: An Insider's View of World Vision*. Wilsonville, OR: BookPartners Inc.

Jenkins, Karen. 1994. The Christian Church as an NGO in Africa: Supporting Post-Independence Era State Legitimacy or Promoting Change? In *The Changing Politics of Non-Governmental Organizations and African States*, edited by E. Sandberg. Westport, CT: Praeger.

Keane, John, ed. 1988. *Civil Society and the State: New European Perspectives*. New York: Verso.

Keck, Margaret E., and Kathryn Sikkink. 1998. *Activists Beyond Borders: Advocacy Networks in International Politics.* Ithaca: Cornell University Press.

Kelsall, Tim, and Claire Mercer. 2000. Empowering the People? World Vision and 'Transformatory Development' in Northern Tanzania. Paper read at Review of African Political Economy Millennium Conference and Leeds ASU: Africa—Capturing the Future, University of Leeds, April 28-30.

Kiernan, J. P. 1982. The "Problem of Evil" in the Context of Ancestral Interventions in the Affairs of the Living in Africa. *Man* 17:287-301.

Kilby, Christopher. 2000. Sovereignty and NGOs. In *Global Institutions and Local Empowerment: Competing Theoretical Perspectives*, edited by K. Stiles. New York: St. Martins.

Lan, David. 1985. *Guns and Rain: Guerrillas and Spirit Mediums in Zimbabwe.* Berkeley: University of California Press.

Landau, Paul Stuart. 1995. *The Realm of the Word: Language, Gender and Christianity in a Southern African Kingdom.* Portsmouth, NH: Heinemann.

Leftwich, Adrian. 1994. Governance, the State and the Politics of Development. *Development and Change* 25:363-386.

Leyshon, Andrew, and Nigel Thrift. 1997. *Money Space: Geographies of Monetary Transformation.* London and New York: Routledge.

Linder, Robert D. 1975. The Resurgence of Evangelical Social Concern (1925-75). In *The Evangelicals*, edited by D. F. Wells and J. D. Woodbridge. New York: Abingdon Press.

Lingenfelter, Sherwood. 1992. *Transforming Culture: A Challenge for Christian Mission.* Grand Rapids, MI: Baker Book House.

Long, Norman. 1968. *Social Change and the Individual: A Study of the Social and Religious Responses to Innovation in a Zambian Rural Community.* Manchester: Institute for Social Research.

Loury, Glenn. 1999. A Considered Opinion [electronic source]. The Brookings Institute [January 31, 2001]. http://brookings.edu/press/review/spring99/considered.pdf.

Makumbe, John Mw. 1996. *Participatory Development: The Case of Zimbabwe.* Harare: University of Zimbabwe.

———. 1998. *Democracy and Development in Zimbabwe: Constraints of Decentralisation.* Harare: SAPES Books.

Malkki, Liisa H. 1995. *Purity and Exile: Violence, Memory and National Cosmology among Hutu Refugees in Tanzania.* Chicago: University of Chicago Press.

———. 1996. Speechless Emissaries: Refugees, Humanitarianism, and Dehistoricization. *Cultural Anthropology* 11 (3):377-404.

———. 1997. Children, Futures, and the Domestication of Hope. Paper presented at the University of California Humanities Research Institute, group convened by Susan Harding, "Histories of the Future." University of California, Irvine.

Mamdani, Mahmood. 1996. *Citizen and Subject: Contemporary Africa and the Legacy of Late Colonialism.* Princeton, NJ.

Mararike, Claude G. 1995. *Grassroots Leadership: The Process of Rural Development in Zimbabwe*. Harare: University of Zimbabwe.

Marcus, George E. 1998. *Ethnography through Thick and Thin*. Princeton, NJ: Princeton University Press.

Marcussen, Henrick Secher. 1996. NGOs, the State and Civil Society. *Review of African Political Economy* 69:405-423.

Maren, Michael. 1997. *The Road to Hell: The Ravaging Effects of Foreign Aid and International Charity*. New York: The Free Press.

Marsden, George M. 1975. From Fundamentalism to Evangelicalism: A Historical Analysis. In *The Evangelicals*, edited by D. F. Wells and J. D. Woodbridge. New York: Abingdon Press.

——. 1987a. Evangelical and Fundamental Christianity. In *The Encyclopedia of Religion Vol. 5*, edited by M. Elaide. New York: MacMillan.

——. 1987b. *Reforming Fundamentalism: Fuller Seminary and the New Evangelicalism*. Grand Rapids, MI: William B. Eerdmans Publishing.

——. 1991. *Understanding Fundamentalism and Evangelicalism*. Grand Rapids, MI: Williams B. Eerdmans Publishing.

Marty, Martin E. 1975. Tensions within Contemporary Evangelicalism: A Critical Appraisal. In *The Evangelicals*, edited by D. F. Wells and J. D. Woodbridge. New York: Abingdon Press.

Marx, Karl. 1975 [1843]. On the Jewish Question. In *Early Writings*. New York: Vintage.

Maurer, Bill. 2001. Engineering an Islamic Future: Speculations on Islamic Financial Alternatives. *Anthropology Today* 17 (1):8-11.

Mauss, Marcel. 1990 [1950]. *The Gift*. New York and London: W.W. Norton.

Maxwell, David. 1995. The Church and Democratisation in Africa: The Case of Zimbabwe. In *The Christian Churches and the Democratisation of Africa*, edited by P. Gifford. Leiden, New York and Koln: E.J. Brill.

——. 1998. Delivered from the Spirit of Poverty?: Pentecostalism, Prosperity and Modernity in Zimbabwe. *Journal of Religion in Africa* 28 (3):350-373.

——. 1999. *Christians and Chiefs in Zimbabwe: A Social History of the Hwesa People*. Westport, CT. and Edinburgh: Praeger International African Library.

——. 2000. 'Catch the Cockerel before Dawn': Pentecostalism and Politics in Postcolonial Zimbabwe. *Africa* 70 (2):249-277.

McLaughlin, Janice. 1996. *On the Frontline: Catholic Missions in Zimbabwe's Liberation War*. Harare: Baobab Books.

McLean, Stuart D. 1996. Evangelism. In *Dictionary of Ethics, Theology and Society*, edited by P. B. Clarke and A. Linzey. New York: Routledge.

Miller, Darrow L. 1989. The Development Ethic: Hope for a Culture of Poverty. In *Christian Relief and Development: Developing Workers for Effective Ministry*, edited by E. J. Elliston. Dallas, London, Sydney and Singapore: Word Publishing.

Mitchell, J. C. 1956. *The Kalela Dance*. Manchester: Manchester University Press.

Moore, David. 1995. Development Discourse as Hegemony: Towards an Ideological History 1945-1995. In *Debating Development Discourse*, edited by D. Moore and G. J. Schmitz. New York: St. Martin's Press.

Moore, David, and Gerald J. Schmitz. 1995. *Debating Development Discourse*. New York: St. Martin's Press.

Moore, Donald. 1999. The Crucible of Cultural Politics: Reworking "Development" in Zimbabwe's Eastern Highlands. *American Ethnologist* 26 (3):654-689.

Mosse, David. 1995. Authority, Gender and Knowledge: Theoretical Reflections on Participatory Rural Appraisal. *Economic and Political Weekly* 30 (11):569-578.

Moyo, Ambrose M. 1987. Religion and Politics in Zimbabwe. In *Religion, Development, and African Identity*, edited by K. H. Petersen. Uppsala: Scandinavian Institute of African Studies.

Moyo, Sam. 1991. *NGO Advocacy in Zimbabwe: Systematising and Old Function or Inventing a New Role?* Vol. No. 1, *IDS Working Papers*. Harare: ZERO Publications.

Mudimbe, V. Y. 1997. *Tales of Faith: Religion as Political Performance in Central Africa.* London: The Athlone Press.

Munro, William A. 1998. *The Moral Economy of the State: Conservation, Community Development, and State Making in Zimbabwe.* Monographs in International Studies Africa Series No. 68. Athens, OH: Ohio University Center for International Studies.

MWENGO, AACC and. 1993. Civil Society, the State, and African Development in the 1990s. Paper read at Receding Role of the State in African Development and Emerging Role of NGOs, at Arusha, Tanzania 2nd-6th August.

Ndegwa, Stephen N. 1994. Civil Society and Political Change in Africa: The Case of Non-Governmental Organizations in Kenya. *International Journal of Comparative Sociology* 35 (1-2):19-36.

———. 1996. *The Two Faces of Civil Society: NGOs and Politics in Africa.* Hartford, CT: Kumarian Press.

Nisbet, Robert. 1980. *History of the Idea of Progress.* New York: Basic Books.

Noll, Mark A., David W. Bebbington, and George A. Rawlyk. 1994. *Evangelicalism: Comparative Studies of Popular Protestantism in North America, the British Isles, and Beyond, 1700-1990.* New York: Oxford University Press.

O'Gorman, Frances. 1992. *Charity and Change: From Band-Aid to Beacon.* Australia: World Vision Australia.

O'Malley, Pat, and Darren Palmer. 1996. Post-Keynesian Policing. *Economy and Society* 25 (2):137-155.

Palmer, Robin, and Neil Parson, eds. 1977. *The Roots of Rural Poverty in Central and Southern Africa.* Vol. 25, *Perspectives on Southern Africa.* Berkeley: University of California Press.

Phiri, Isabel Apawo, Kenneth R. Ross, and James L. Cox, eds. 1996. *The Role of Christianity in Development, Peace and Reconstruction.* Nairobi: All Africa Conference of Churches.

Pieterse, Jan Nederveen. 1992. *Christianity and Hegemony: Religion and Politics on the Frontiers of Social Change*. New York and Oxford: Berg.

Pigg, Stacy Leigh. 1992. Inventing Social Categories through Place: Social Representations and Development in Nepal. *Comparative Studies in Society and History* 34:491-513.

Pobee, John S. 1992. *Skenosis: Christian Faith in an African Context*. Gweru, Zimbabwe: Mambo Press.

Poewe, Karla. 1989. *Religion, Kinship, and Economy in Luapula, Zambia*. African Studies Volume 9. Lewiston, NY: The Edwin Mellen Press.

Potts, Deborah. 1995. Shall We Go Home? Increasing Urban Poverty in African Cities and Migration Processes. *Geographical Journal*, Nov. 245.

———. 1998. 'Basics Are Now a Luxury': Perceptions of Structural Adjustment's Impact on Rural and Urban Areas in Zimbabwe. *Environment and Urbanization* 10 (1):55-75.

———. 2000. Urban Unemployment and Migrants in Africa: Evidence from Harare 1985-1994. *Development and Change* 31 (4):879-910.

Raftopoulos, Brian. 1991. *Beyond the House of Hunger: The Struggle for Democratic Development in Zimbabwe*. Harare: Zimbabwe Institute of Development Studies.

Rahnema, Majid. 1992. Participation. In *The Development Dictionary*, edited by W. Sachs. London, UK: Zed Books.

Rahnema, Majid, and Victoria Bawtree. 1997. *The Post-Development Reader*. London: Zed Books.

Ranger, Terence O. 1962. *State and Church in Southern Rhodesia 1919-1939*. Local Series No. 4, Historical Association of Rhodesia and Nyasaland. Salisbury, Southern Rhodesia: Historical Association of Rhodesia and Nyasaland.

———. 1967. *Revolt in Southern Rhodesia 1896-97*. Evanston: Northwestern University Press.

———. 1985. *Peasant Consciousness and Guerrilla War in Zimbabwe*. Berkeley: University of California Press.

———. 1989. Missionaries, Migrants and the Manyika: The Invention of Ethnicity in Zimbabwe. In *The Creation of Tribalism in Southern Africa*, edited by L. Vail. Berkeley: University of California Press.

———. 1991. Religion and Witchcraft in Everyday Life in Contemporary Zimbabwe. In *Cultural Struggle and Development in Southern Africa*, edited by P. Kaarsholm. Portsmouth, N.H.: Heinemann.

Rea, W. F. 1962. *The Missionary Factor in Southern Rhodesia*. Historical Association of Rhodesia and Nyasaland. Local Series No. 7. Salisbury.

Reynolds, Pamela. 1985. Children in Zimbabwe: Rights and Power in Relation to Work. *Anthropology Today*, June. 16-20.

———. 1996. *Traditional Healers and Childhood in Zimbabwe*. Athens, OH: Ohio University Press.

Rich, Sara. 1997. The State of NGOs in Zimbabwe: Honeymoon Over? *Southern Africa Report* 12 (3):17-20.

Riddell, Roger C., and Mark Robinson. 1995. *Non-Governmental Organizations and Rural Poverty Alleviation.* Oxford: Clarendon Press.

Riles, Annelise. 2000. *The Network Inside Out.* Ann Arbor: University of Michigan Press.

Robins, Steven L. 1994. Contesting the Social Geometry of State Power: A Case Study of Land-Use Planning in Matabeleland, Zimbabwe. *Social Dynamics* 20 (2):91-118.

———. 1998. Breaking out of the Straitjacket of Tradition: The Politics and Rhetoric of 'Development' in Zimbabwe. *World Development* 26 (9):1677-1694.

Rodney, Walter. 1974. *How Europe Underdeveloped Africa.* Washington, D.C.: Howard University Press.

Rose, Nikolas. 1993. Government, Authority and Expertise in Advanced Liberalism. *Economy and Society* 22 (3):283-299.

———. 1996. The Death of the Social? Re-Figuring the Territory of Government. *Economy and Society* 25 (3):327-356.

Rouse, Roger. 1991. Mexican Migration and the Social Space of Postmodernism. *Diaspora* 1 (1):8-23.

———. 1995. Thinking through Transnationalism: Notes on the Cultural Politics of Class Relations in the Contemporary United States. *Public Culture* 7:353-402.

Rutherford, Blair. 1999. To Find an African Witch: Anthropology, Modernity, and Witch-Finding in North-West Zimbabwe. *Critique of Anthropology* 19 (1):105-125.

———. 2000. Learning About Power: Development and Marginality in an Adult Literacy Center for Farm Workers in Zimbabwe. *American Ethnologist* 27 (4):839-854.

Sachikonye, Lloyd M. 1995a. Democracy, Civil Society and Social Movements: An Analytical Framework. In *Democracy, Civil Society and the State: Social Movements in Southern Africa,* edited by L. Sachikonye. Harare: SAPES Books.

———. 1995b. From 'Equity' and 'Participation' to Structural Adjustment: State and Social Forces in Zimbabwe. In *Debating Development Discourse,* edited by D. B. Moore and G. J. Schmitz. New York: St. Martin's.

Sachs, Wolfgang. 1992. *The Development Dictionary: A Guide to Knowledge as Power.* London: Zed Books.

Sandeen, Ernest R. 1970. *The Roots of Fundamentalism: British and American Millenarianism, 1800-1930.* Chicago: University of Chicago Press.

Sanneh, Lamin. 1989. *Translating the Message: The Missionary Impact on Culture.* Maryknoll, NY: Orbis.

Sbert, Jose Maria. 1992. Progress. In *The Development Dictionary: A Guide to Knowledge as Power,* edited by W. Sachs. London: Zed Books.

Schneider, Jane, and Shirley Lindenbaum. 1987. Special Issue: Frontiers of Christian
    Evangelism. *American Ethnologist* 14 (1).

Schoffeleers, J. M. 1978. *Guardians of the Land: Essays on Central African Territorial
    Cults.* Gwelo: Mambo Press.

Siewert, John A., and Edna G. Valdez. 1997. *Mission Handbook 1998-2000.* Monrovia,
    CA: MARC Publications.

Simmel, Georg. 1990 [1907]. *The Philosophy of Money.* Translated by T. Bottomore and
    D. Frisby. Edited by D. Frisby. London and New York: Routledge.

——. 1994 [1908]. The Poor. In *On Individuality and Social Forms,* edited by D. N.
    Levine. Chicago: University of Chicago Press.

Smelser, Neil J. 1995. Economic Rationality as a Religious System. In *Rethinking
    Materialism: Perspectives on the Spiritual Dimension of Economic Behavior,*
    edited by R. Wuthnow. Grand Rapids, Michigan: William B. Eerdmans.

Spiegel, Andrew. 1989. Towards an Understanding of Tradition: Uses of Tradition(al) in
    Apartheid South Africa. *Critique of Anthropology* vol. ix, no. 1.

Stephens, Sharon. 1995. *Children and the Politics of Culture.* Princeton, NJ: Princeton
    University Press.

Stipe, Claude E. 1980. Anthropologists Versus Missionaries: The Influence of
    Presuppositions. *Current Anthropology* 21 (2):165-179.

Stone, Jon R. 1997. *On the Boundaries of American Evangelicalism: The Postwar
    Evangelical Coalition.* New York: St. Martin's Press.

Sundkler, Bengt. 1960. *The Christian Ministry in Africa.* London: SCM Press Ltd.

——. 1961. *Bantu Prophets.* London: Oxford University Press.

Taylor, Charles. 1990. Modes of Civil Society. *Public Culture* 3 (1):95-118.

Tendler, Judith. 1975. *Inside Foreign Aid.* Baltimore and London: The Johns Hopkins
    University Press.

Thornton, R. J., and M. Ramphele. 1989. Community: Concept and Practice in South
    Africa. *Critique of Anthropology* 9 (1):75-87.

Turner, Mark, and David Hulme. 1997. *Governance, Administration and Development:
    Making the State Work.* Hartford, CT: Kumarian Press.

Vail, Leroy, ed. 1991. *The Creation of Tribalism in Southern Africa.* Berkeley:
    University of California Press.

Vakil, Anna C. 1997. Confronting the Classification Problem: Toward a Taxonomy of
    NGOs. *World Development* 25 (12):2057-2070.

van der Geest, Sjaak. 1990. Anthropologists and Missionaries: Brothers under the Skin.
    Man 25 (4):588-601.

van der Veer, Peter. 1996. *Conversion to Modernities: The Globalization of Christianity.*
    New York: Routledge.

Van Ufford, Philip Quarles, and Matthew Schoffeleers. 1988. Towards a
    Rapprochement of Anthropology and Development Studies. In *Religion and
    Development: Towards an Integrated Approach,* edited by P. Q. Van Ufford and
    M. Schoffeleers. Amsterdam: Free University Press.

Verhelst, Thierry G. 1990. *No Life without Roots: Culture and Development*. Translated by B. Cumming. London and New Jersey: Zed Books Ltd.

Vermaat, J. A. Emerson. 1989. *The World Council of Churches and Politics 1975-1986.* Vol. No. 6. Focus on Issues. New York: Freedom House.

Verstraelen, Frans J., A. Camps, L. A. Hoedemaker, and M. R. Spindler. 1995. *Missiology: An Ecumenical Introduction*. Grand Rapids, MI: William B. Erdmans.

Vivian, Jessica. 1994. NGOs and Sustainable Development in Zimbabwe: No Magic Bullets. *Development and Change* 25:167-193.

Walzer, Michael, ed. 1995. *Toward a Global Civil Society*. Providence, RI: Berghahn Books.

Weber, Max. 1946 [1915]. Religious Rejections of the World and Their Directions. In *From Max Weber: Essays in Sociology*, edited by H. H. Gerth and C. W. Mills. New York: Oxford University Press.

——. 1958 [1920]. *The Protestant Ethic and the Spirit of Capitalism*. Translated by Talcot Parsons. New York: Charles Scribners Sons.

——. 1993 [1922]. *The Sociology of Religion*. Boston: Beacon Press.

Weisgrau, Maxine K. 1997. *Interpreting Development: Local Histories, Local Strategies.* New York: University Press of America.

Wellard, Kate, and James G. Copestake. 1993. *Non-Governmental Organizations and the State in Africa: Rethinking Sustainable Agricultural Development.* New York: Routledge.

Weller, John, and Jane Linden. 1984. *Mainstream Christianity to 1980 in Malawi, Zambia and Zimbabwe*. Gweru: Mambo Press.

Wells, David F., and John D. Woodbridge. 1975. *The Evangelicals: What They Believe, Who They Are, Where They Are Changing*. New York: Abingdon Press.

West, Harry. 2001. Sorcery of Construction and Socialist Modernization: Ways of Understanding Power in Postcolonial Mozambique. *American Ethnologist* 28 (1):119-150.

Williams, David. 1993. Liberalism and Development Discourse. *Africa* 63 (3):419-429.

Williams, David, and Tom Young. 1994. Governance, the World Bank and Liberal Theory. *Political Studies* XLII:84-100.

Williams, Raymond. 1973. *The Country and the City*. New York: Oxford University Press.

——. 1983. Community. In *Keywords*. New York: Oxford University Press.

Woods, Dwayne. 1992. Civil Society in Europe and Africa: Limiting State Power through a Public Sphere. *African Studies Review* 35 (2):77-100.

Worby, Eric. 1998. Inscribing the State at the "Edge of Beyond:" Danger and Development in Northwestern Zimbabwe. *Political and Legal Anthropology Review* 21 (2):55-70.

World Bank. World Development Indicators Database, April 2001. *Zimbabwe Data Profile.* The World Bank Group 2001 [June 7, 2001]. http://devdata.world-

bank.org/external/CPProfile.asp?SelectedCountry=ZWE&CCODE=ZWE&C
NAME=Zimbabwe&PTYPE=CP.

World Council of Churches. A Half-Century of Service. 2000. *World Council of Churches: A Half-Century of Service*. World Council of Churches [July 21, 2001], http://www.wcc-coe.org/wcc/who/service-e.html.

World Factbook. CIA. 2000. *Country Listing: Zimbabwe* [electronic source]. Central Intelligence Agency [June 7, 2001], http://www.odci.gov/cia/publications/fact-book/geos/zi.html.

World Vision, Communications Service. 1994. *World Vision History*. Monrovia, California: World Vision International.

World Vision, International. 1997a. *World Vision Annual Report*. Monrovia, California.

World Vision, U.S. 1997b. *The Benefits of the First Sponsorship Program* [electronic document]. World Vision, U.S. [February 23, 1999]. http://web2.worldvision.org/852564580064A76D/0/BA0BF334E8E957882 565BF00738192Open.

———. 1997c. *Community Development Efforts: World Vision Policy Paper on Child Sponsorship* [electronic document]. World Vision U.S. [February 23, 1999]. http://web2.worldvision.org/852564580064A76D/0/C076BCE746D43D3E882 565BF00738195Open.

———. 1997d. *Creating a Ministry of Presence: World Vision Policy Papers* [electronic]. World Vision U.S. [February 23, 1999]. http://web2.worldvision.org/852564580064A76D/0/0814EB763C7FE857882 565BF00738199Open.

World Vision Zimbabwe Annual Report. 1994. Harare: World Vision Zimbabwe.

Yamamori, Tetsunao, Bryant L. Myers, Kwame Bediako, and Larry Reed, eds. 1996. *Serving with the Poor in Africa*. Monrovia, CA: MARC Publications a division of World Vision International.

Zelizer, Viviana. 1985. *Pricing the Priceless Child: The Changing Social Value of Children*. New York: Basic Books.

Zvobgo, Chengetai J. M. 1996. *A History of Christian Missions in Zimbabwe 1890-1939*. Gweru: Mambo Press.

Index

accountability, financial, 40, 69, 79, 102,
    113–14
advocacy, political, 12, 29, 99, 103, 109
Alexander, Jocelyn, 106, 189n5
almsgiving, 3, 107
ancestral spirits (*vadzimu*), 90, 147
Anderson, Benedict, 125
Appadurai, Arjun, 72, 125
Asad, Talal, 5, 181n1
Ashforth, Adam, 146, 147, 150, 187n22,
    191n4
Auret, Diana, 3, 182n4

Banana, Canaan, 15
Barrett, David B., 46, 184n2–3
Bediako, Kwame, 68, 88
Bible
    economic justice and, 3
    evangelicals and, 17–20
    Hear the Word and, 31–34
    in development, use of, 49, 52, 55,
        57, 60, 64, 78–80, 85, 132, 138,
        148, 154–5, 160
    liberation struggle and, 182–83n7
Biko, Stephen, 125
Bond, Patrick, 24, 97, 189n5
Bourdillon, Michael, 146, 183n7, 187n22,
    187n26
Brandt, Donald, 47

Bratton, Michael, 98–99, 100, 122, 189n3
British South Africa Company, 11–12,
    182n3

Calvinism, 3–4, 17, 19
Catholic Commission for Justice and
    Peace (CCJP), 16, 103, 105,
    182n4
Chambers, Robert, 3, 47, 122–23, 131,
    137, 185n9
charity, 3, 10, 14, 90–92, 107, 116–17,
    133–34, 137, 139
Chatterjee, Partha, 101–2
Chazan, Naomi, 101, 189n3
Chepkwony Ongaro, Agnes, 16
child sponsorship
    belonging and, 88–92, 94
    correspondence of, 77–80, 86
    donors and, 69–70, 81–82
    families and, 81–82, 85–88, 90–93
    local sustainability of, 68, 88–92
    mechanics of, 67–95
    political economy of, 67–73
Christian business, 156, 160, 162–67,
    170
Christian Care
    history of, 22–24
    See also church; NGOs

Christian Council of Rhodesia (CCR), 13
Christian development, 9, 11, 37–41, 46–54, 119–120, 184n1, 185n5
Christian witnessing, 53, 55, 62–65. *See also* conversion
church
  Christian Care and, 104–5
  NGOs and, 102–6
  state and, 9–17
  World Vision and, 105
civil society, 98–102, 114, 116, 123, 171, 188–89n1, 189n7. *See also* NGOs
civilizing mission, 4–5, 11, 145
Clifford, James, 184n18
Cold War, 14–16, 21, 28, 106
colonialism, 11–12
Comaroff, Jean, 4, 11, 55
Comaroff, John L., 12
Comaroff, Jean and John L., 4, 11, 39, 59, 146, 152, 167, 187n22, 189n1, 189n3, 189n7, 191n4
community
  as sacred, 125–29
  concept of, 119–21
conversion
  development and, 47, 50, 52
  ethnography and, 27, 30–36, 41–44
  power and, 58–59, 65
Cooper, Frederick, 11, 185n5, 190n1
Cooperative for Assistance and Relief Everywhere (CARE), 108, 130–32
development
  as religious act, 130–32
  critiques of, 3, 184n4
  democratization and, 98
  faith and, 1–8, 50–51, 54, 58–65, 82, 162–66
  from within, 132–37
  transformation and, 129, 133
  types of projects, 25–27
  See also morality

Donham, Donald, 3, 182n7
Durkheim, Emile, 31
economic justice, 3, 16, 29, 105
economic rationality, 2–3
Ecumenical Support Services (ESS), 105, 190n16
ecumenism, 22–24
empowerment
  conversion and, 55
  participation and, 125, 129, 136–37
  women and, 55
Englund, Harri, 187n22, 191n4
ethnography, institutional, 27–44
evangelical theology, 17, 94
evangelicalism, 17–22
evangelism
  colonial, 182n3
  development and, 26, 46–58, 80–83, 104–5, 148–49, 154–55
  structural adjustment and, 16–17
  World Vision and, 17–22
Evans-Pritchard, E. E., 146, 150, 191n4
  evil spirits, 146–55
faith. *See* development
Ferguson, James, 3, 40, 42, 46, 72, 98, 101, 106, 114, 120, 141, 187n21, 187n26, 188n1–3, 190n5, 191n5
Fields, Karen, 11–12
Fisher, William, 99
Fisiy, Cyprian F., 169, 191n4, 191n9
foreign aid
  bypassing the state, 16, 106
  journalistic critiques of, 99
Foster, Robert, 73
Foucault, Michel, 38, 172
free markets, 2, 97, 108
Fuller, Charles, 19–20
Fuller theological seminary, 19–20, 183n10
  fundamentalism, 19–20
Geertz, Clifford, 2, 5, 181n1

Gehman, Richard, 20, 81
Geschiere, Peter, 169, 191n4, 191n9
Gifford, Paul, 15–16, 31, 189n4
gift notifications, 78–79, 83
giving, 88–91, 116
globalization, 17, 67–73, 170–171
good governance, 16, 98, 100
gospel of prosperity, 30–36
governmentality, 10–11, 102, 139
Gramsci, Antonio, 189n1
Gronemeyer, Marianne, 188n28
Gundani, Paul, 15, 48, 183n7, 189n4
Gupta, Akhil, 40, 98, 101, 114, 120, 125, 137, 188n1, 189n12
Guyer, Jane, 98

Hall, Stuart, 189n1
Hallencreutz, Carl, 13, 15, 182n2, 182n4, 189n4
Hanlon, Joseph, 16, 97, 99, 116, 189n5, 192n1
Hannerz, Ulf, 73
Harding, Susan, 19, 35, 187n18
Harvey, David, 71, 191n5
Hear the Word Church, 30–36, 184n20
Herbst, Jeffrey, 189n10
Hefner, Robert, 182n5
helping, 69, 73–75, 82, 90–91, 165
Henry, Carl, 20, 183n10
HIV/AIDS, 24, 25, 90–92, 121, 154
holism, 48–50
humanitarianism, 67–73, 94

indirect rule, 12, 182–3n7
individual, concept of
   child sponsorship and, 83, 87
   evangelicalism and, 17, 22
   participation and, 119
   relation to Christian God and, 5
   witchcraft and, 167, 191n4
International Monetary Fund (IMF), 7, 16, 105, 108, 131, 155
Irvine, Graeme, 20, 71, 81, 187n17

jealousy, 83–88, 142, 146, 154, 160–61, 187n21–22, 191n6. See also witchcraft
Jenkins, Karen, 15, 16

Kingdom of God, 22, 23, 97, 106–8, 112
kinship, child sponsorship and, 85–88, 90–94. See also child sponsorship

Lan, David, 12, 125, 182n7, 187n26
Landau, Paul Stuart, 182n3
liberation struggle, 10, 12–14, 104–5, 182n7
lifestyle evangelism, 50–54
Long, Norman, 3, 156
loyalty
   of NGOs, 113, 117
   of ethnographer, 117
   politics of, 40
Lutheran World Federation (LWF), 120, 190n16

Makumbe, John, 190n2
Malkki, Liisa H., 71–72, 73, 83
Marcus, George, 35, 184n18
Marsden, George, 17–18, 183n10
Marty, Martin, 17, 18
Marx, Karl, 3, 189n1
Maurer, Bill, 181n2
Mauss, Marcel, 107
Maxwell, David, 13, 15, 16, 55, 163, 189n3–4, 192n16
McLaughlin, Janice, 15, 182n4, 183n7
Mennonite Economic Development Association (MEDA), 165
mhondoro (spirit medium), 182n7, 187n26
missiology, 47–48, 88, 187n7
missionaries:
   Christian Care and, 23
   colonial, 4, 106, 156, 167
   NGOs as, 9–17, 46–54, 102, 169–172
   World Vision and, 20, 80–83

Moore, David, 3
Moore, Donald, 189n5
morality
    child sponsorship and, 70–73
    development and, 1–2, 5–8, 48–50,
        111, 169–172
    economics and, 2–3, 166
    ethnography and, 30–41
    participation and, 119, 125–29
    Kingdom of God and, 107–8
    success and, 141–61
Mosse, David, 124, 190n1
Moyo, Ambrose, 15, 189n4
Moyo, Sam, 99
Mudimbe, V.Y., 35
Mugabe, Robert Gabriel, 15, 98, 108,
        112–13
Munro, William, 10, 12, 189n5
muti, 142, 151, 156, 165
Mwari, 147
MWENGO, 16, 189n3

National Association of Non–govern-
        mental Organizations
        (NANGO), 184n19
Ndegwa, Stephen N., 99, 100, 103, 109,
        189n3
need
    determining, 124–29, 137–39
    spiritual and material, 46–50, 183n8
neoliberal economics, 100, 106, 108–9,
        170, 172
new evangelicalism, 17–21
Nisbet, Robert, 5
non–governmental organization (NGOs)
    churches and, 12–17, 103–6
    civil society and, 98–102
    demographics of, 184n19
    secular versus religious, 105,
        170–72
    the state and, 12, 15, 98–102, 101,
        105, 108, 115

Opportunity International, 43, 184n17

participation, critiques of, 121, 124–25
participatory rural appraisal (PRA),
        120–28, 131–32
Pierce, Bob, 60, 80–81, 186n16
Pieterse, Jan Nederveen, 16, 49
Pigg, Stacy Leigh, 120, 190n1
Pobee, John S., 68, 88
Poewe, Karla, 3
potential, individual and community,
        129, 132–37
Potts, Deborah, 24, 120, 189n5, 189n11
prayer, in NGO offices, 58–65
Private Voluntary Organizations (PVO)
        Act, 103–6, 190n16
progress, Protestant ideas and, 1–5
Protestant ethic, 3–4, 163, 166, 167

Raftopoulos, Brian, 190n2
Rahnema, Majid, 3, 121, 184n4, 190n1
Ramphele, M., 125
Ranger, Terence 11, 106, 183n7, 191n4
religious socialism, 15
revivalism (American), 18
Reynolds, Pamela, 186n13
Rhodes, Cecil, 12
Riles, Annelise, 3, 23, 40, 98
Rouse, Roger, 69, 72, 125
Rutherford, Blair, 147, 189n5, 191n4

salvation
    charity and, 116
    development as, 50–51
    ideas of, 3–4
Sachikonye, Lloyd M., 101, 189n3,
        189n5
Sachs, Wolfgang, 3, 184n4
Sanneh, Lamin, 68, 88
Sbert, Jose Maria, 5
Schoffeleers, J. M., 47, 187n26
Simmel, Georg, 73–83, 116, 172
Smith, Adam, 2
Smith, Ian, 12–14
social gospel, 22–24
Spiegel, Andrew, 125
spiritual insecurity, 147, 150

sponsor visits, 73–77
stakeholders, 113–14
Stephens, Sharon, 71
Stoler, Ann, 11
structural adjustment policies, 15–17,
        24, 98, 110, 155
Sundkler, Bengt, 11
theology
        economics and, 3
        of development, 15, 58,
        of sponsorship, 80–83
Thornton, R.J., 125
transnational families
        child sponsorship and, 81–82
        Christian faith and, 58–63
        loss and, 70–71

Unilateral Declaration of Independence
        (UDI), 12

van der Geest, Sjaak, 47–48
van der Veer, Peter, 182n5
varoyi (witches), 145–55
Verstraelen, Frans, 47, 185n7
Vivian, Jessica, 190n1
vulnerability:
        spiritual, 30–36
        structural, 41–44

Weisgrau, Maxine, 99, 100, 125
Weber, Max 3–4, 51, 163, 165, 167,
        181n3, 182n4
Welfare Act, 13–14, 103, 182n5
West, Harry, 191n4

witchcraft
        child sponsorship and, 83–85
        dangers of, 145–55
        fears of in development, 151–52
        modernity and, 191n4–5
        See also jealousy
Witchcraft Suppression Act, 147
Worby, Eric, 10, 106, 189n5
World Bank, 7, 16, 105, 108, 131, 155
World Council of Churches (WCC), 13,
        22–24, 27
World Vision. history of: 21–22, 80–81.
        See also church, NGOs

ZECLOF, 166, 192n17
Zelizer, Viviana, 71
Zimbabwe African National Union
        Patriotic Front (ZANU–PF),
        10, 14–15, 101, 105–13, 163
Zimbabwe Assembly of God in Africa
        (ZAOGA), 162–64, 192n13,
        192n16
Zimbabwe Council of Churches (ZCC),
        13, 14–15, 29, 46, 104–6, 107
Zimbabwe economy, 24–27, 102
Zvogbo, Chengetai, 11
zvishiri, 146–55
zvidhoma, 84–85, 146–55
zvikwambo 142–45